Study Guide

for use with

Principles of Microeconomics

Second Edition

Robert H. Frank
Cornell University

Ben S. Bernanke
Princeton University

Prepared by
Jack Mogab
Southwest Texas State University

Bruce McClung
Southwest Texas State University

 Irwin

Boston   Burr Ridge, IL   Dubuque, IA   Madison, WI   New York   San Francisco   St. Louis
Bangkok   Bogotá   Caracas   Kuala Lumpur   Lisbon   London   Madrid   Mexico City
Milan   Montreal   New Delhi   Santiago   Seoul   Singapore   Sydney   Taipei   Toronto

Study Guide for use with
PRINCIPLES OF MICROECONOMICS
Robert H. Frank and Ben S. Bernanke

Published by McGraw-Hill/Irwin, an imprint of The McGraw-Hill Companies, Inc., 1221 Avenue of the Americas, New York, NY 10020. Copyright © 2004 by The McGraw-Hill Companies, Inc. All rights reserved. No part of this publication may be reproduced or distributed in any form or by any means, or stored in a database or retrieval system, without the prior written consent of The McGraw-Hill Companies, Inc., including, but not limited to, in any network or other electronic storage or transmission, or broadcast for distance learning.

2 3 4 5 6 7 8 9 0 QPD/QPD 0 9 8 7 6 5 4 3

ISBN 0-07-282600-2

The McGraw-Hill Companies

To the Student

Welcome to the study of economics. We believe you will find the subject thoroughly intriguing. As you become an "economic naturalist" you will gain a clearer understanding of many important issues that currently may be perplexing to you. For example, what determines the cost of a car, or the salary you will earn when you graduate? Why does the economy experience booms and busts? How does the banking system create money? Why are federal deficits and surpluses so controversial?

These and many other topics are addressed in *Principles of Economics, Principles of Microeconomics,* and *Principles of Macroeconomics,* 2nd Editions by Robert H. Frank and Ben S. Bernanke, for which these Study Guides have been written. The Study Guide chapters parallel the chapters in the corresponding textbook, and each contains the following eight sections designed to assist your learning and to enhance your understanding of economics:

1. **Pretest.** This will test what you really know about the basic concepts and principles in the chapter and what you need to review before continuing on with more in-depth testing.
2. **Key Point Review.** The Learning Objectives for the chapter are listed to identify important concepts to master. The chapter's main ideas are summarized, and new terms are defined. **Hints** and **Notes** are provided to alert you to "tricks, clues and short-cuts".
3. **Self-Test: Key Terms**. All new terms are listed. Check your knowledge of key definitions by matching the term in the right-hand column with the appropriate definitions in the left-hand column.
4. **Self-Test: Multiple-Choice Questions.** Strengthen your grasp of the chapter material by choosing the correct answer from the alternatives for each question. Your ability to answer multiple-choice questions should serve as a good indicator of success on exams. You may wish to study for exams by reviewing these questions.
5. **Self-Test: Short Answer/Problems.** Here you will discover how the tools of economics can be applied to explore and clarify important issues. Problems are developed step by step. You are asked to analyze graphs and tables, to perform basic computations, and to select the best answers to a variety of fill-in statements.
6. **Economic Naturalist Applications.** Become an economic naturalist by applying the tools of economics to discuss these real-world issues with your classmates.
7. **Go To The Web.** This section will serve as a bridge between the Study Guide and the web-based E-Learning materials at http://www.mhhe.com/economics/frankbernanke2.
8. **Solutions**. Solutions, with explanations for the more complex and difficult items in the self-tests, are provided for the key-term, and multiple-choice questions, as well as for the short answer/problems.

The following suggestions will help make your study of economics successful:

Class Preparation or Must I Turn Off the TV?
It is essential that you prepare assignments BEFORE attending class so that you can understand the lecture and ask questions. Your instructor typically will not present all the materials in the text, but rather will concentrate on explaining the more complex ideas and applications.In preparing for class, first read the "Key Point Review" to identify the learning objectives for the chapter. Next, go to the chapter in the text. Read the "Summary," "Core Principles," and the "Key Terms" at the **end** of the chapter. Then, read the introductory

section that will provide an overview of the topics to be covered in the chapter. The number of topics will range from 4 to 7. Read and study one topic at a time, i.e., begin at the bold, upper-case red color heading and read until you get to the "Recap" box. Look for the paragraphs in the chapter that define and explain the concepts, principles, and laws related to that topic. These concepts, principles, and laws are listed at the end of each chapter as "Key Terms." As you read, mark these "terms" (as many as 3 to 5 per topic). You will notice that each topic can be presented in three modes--verbal, numerical (tables), and visual (graphs). This variety of presentation is important since economics is communicated through all three modes, and the test questions will reflect all three. After you have completed reading a topic, take a few minutes to read the Recap box. Verify that (1) you know (i.e. remember) the topic and important terms; (2) you understand (i.e. comprehend) that material; (3) you can relate the terms to one another when appropriate; and (4) you can relate the topic to the other topics in the chapter. Complete all the assigned topics in the above manner and write down any questions you have for the instructor.

Class Attendance or Why Not Go To the Rec Center?

Frankly, economics is such a demanding course that you will need all the help you can get. A great deal of that help comes from your instructor's lectures. The instructor's style and presentation will show you not only what the instructor considers to be important, but also how s/he approaches this subject. Getting notes from a friend will not give you this information. If you have followed the above suggestions in preparing for class, you will have some knowledge and understanding of the assigned topics. In class, the trick is to carefully combine four classroom skills - listening, taking notes, answering questions, and responding to questions. Listen with your mind. Be selective in what you write down. If you try to write everything that the instructor says, you will not have time to learn anything. For example, do not write a definition that has been given in the text. Listen for examples that differ from those in the text, special emphasis on a relationship between topics, and frequently repeated principles. Asking questions is the responsibility of the student. If you don't know enough to ask questions, you haven't done your job. If you have difficulty formulating questions during class, you should spend some time before class developing a list of questions you need to have answered. On the other side of the coin, you should also respond to the instructor's questions. You should not be shy about answering questions in class. An incorrect answer given in class is a free shot, while the same wrong answer on the test is very costly. The most effective way to use class time is to develop your ability to comprehend and apply economics concepts.

After Class or Do I Have To Do This Again?

Even if you have meticulously prepared for class and performed those four classroom behaviors, you still have a couple of things to do before you will be at the mastery level of the material. First, your class notes should be sketchy. You need to rewrite these notes in a more complete way before they get cold. Next, return to the Study Guide. Complete the three Self-Tests without referring to the text, and check your answers with the Solutions at the end of the Study Guide chapter. If your answers are correct, go onto the Economic Naturalist and the Go To The Web sections. If your answers to some of the questions are incorrect, go back and review the text and your class notes for those topics. Then return to the Study Guide Self-Tests to complete the questions you answered incorrectly (to further test your mastery of the material, go to the Electronic Learning Session in the Student Center at the Frank/Bernanke web site: http://www.mhhe.com/economics/ frankbernanke2). If you still do not understand the answers to the questions, either ask questions in the next class or go see your instructor for help.

If You Want To Learn It, Teach It.
To further test your comprehension of a topic, try explaining it in your own words to a classmate. Illustrate the idea with an example. If you can explain it clearly and give a good example, you have mastered the concept and its time to move on to the next chapter.

A Final Word
If the strategy outlined above seems like a lot of work, it is. You cannot achieve success in economics without hard work. It is estimated that the average student should spend 2-3 hours of quality study time for every hour spent in class.

Acknowledgments
It is a pleasure to acknowledge the assistance and support of Irwin McGraw-Hill in the preparation of this Study Guide. Particular thanks go to our capable and patient editors Tom Thompson and Paul Shensa.

Bruce McClung
Jack Mogab
June 2003

Contents

Chapter 1
Thinking Like An Economist

I. Pretest: What Do You Really Know?

Circle the letter that corresponds to the best answer. (Answers appear immediately after the final question).

1. Economics is conventionally divided into two subjects called
   A. marginal benefit and marginal cost.
   B. reservation price and opportunity cost.
   C. microeconomics and macroeconomics.
   D. rational economics and irrational economics.
   E. economic surplus and economic deficit.

2. When someone makes a choice, the value of the next best alternative not selected defines
   A. marginal costs.
   B. opportunity costs.
   C. opportunity benefits.
   D. average costs.
   E. economic surplus.

3. In deciding the number of students to allow to enroll in the economics classes, the Chairperson of the Economics Department is making a(n) _____ decision.
   A. microeconomic
   B. macroeconomic
   C. economic surplus
   D. marginal
   E. imperfect

4. When economists say there is no such thing as a free lunch, they mean that
   A. we must pay money for everything we get.
   B. it is against the law to accept goods or services without paying for them.
   C. the more lunch a person eats the more weight the person will gain.
   D. each day we decide to eat lunch is another day we must pay out money.
   E. every choice we make involves a tradeoff.

5. The concept of scarcity applies equally to Bill Gates and a homeless person because
    A. they have the same legal rights protected by the U.S. constitution.
    B. they have the same access to the markets for goods and services.
    C. there are only 24 hours in the day for both of them.
    D. they are both consumers.
    E. both must breathe air in order to live.

6. Sunk costs are _____ when deciding between alternatives.
    A. irrelevant
    B. highly important
    C. important
    D. slightly important
    E. the only factor to consider

7. Which of the following is *not* a synonym for "marginal" in economics?
    A. Extra
    B. Additional
    C. One more
    D. Change
    E. Average

8. Which of the following topics is most likely to be studied in microeconomics?
    A. Tax policies
    B. The rate of inflation
    C. National output
    D. The auto market
    E. The unemployment rate

9. People who have well-defined goals and try to fulfill those goals as best they can are known as
    A. rational.
    B. macroeconomists.
    C. microeconomists.
    D. maximizers.
    E. opportunists.

10. Which of the following is true of economic models and how they are used to study behavior?
    A. Economists believe people literally behave according to the model.
    B. Economic models capture every detail of a given situation not matter how small.
    C. Economists rely exclusively on verbal descriptions of their models.
    D. Economic models explain everyone's behavior.
    E. Economic models are simplifications of a given situation with the important details included.

Solutions and Feedback to Pretest
For each question you answered incorrectly, we strongly recommend taking the time to review the appropriate material before continuing. In the table below, the relevant textbook pages are listed for each question as well as the pertinent Learning Objective from the following Key Point Review.

Correct Answer	Textbook Page Numbers	Learning Objective
1. C	p 15	5
2. B	pp. 6 - 7	2
3. A	p. 15	5
4. E	p. 4	1
5. C	p. 5	1
6. A	pp. 10 - 11	4
7. E	p. 11	4
8. D	p. 15	5
9. A	p. 5	2
10. E	p. 7	3

II. Key Point Review
This chapter presents the essence of economics as a field of study and as a way of thinking about the world around you.

Learning Objective 1: Define the field of study known as economics. Explain the logical relationship between the Scarcity Principle and the Cost-Benefit Principle. Understand the universality of the two principles.
Economics is the study of how people make choices under conditions of scarcity and how the results of those choices affect society. The **Scarcity Principle** (aka the **No-Free-Lunch Principle**) indicates that all the resources available to the individual are finite but the needs and wants of the individual are infinite. Satisfying all, or even most, of the requirements and desires of people is an impossibility. Thus, an individual is forced to make choices because more of one item means less of some other. How then does an individual make the choices that scarcity demands of him or her? Economists presume the individual employs the **Cost-Benefit Principle** when making choices. The principle suggests people will take an action, if and only if, the extra benefits from the action are greater than or equal to the extra costs of the action. Importantly, the two fundamental principles apply to all people, all societies, all countries, and to the entire history of mankind.

Learning Objective 2: Discuss the meaning of a rational person in an economic context. How do the concepts of economic surplus and opportunity cost relate to rational behavior?
A **rational person** has well-defined goals and endeavors to fulfill them as best as he or she can. The Cost-Benefit Principle is a tool that assists individuals in making rational choices. The difference between the benefits of taking an action and the costs of the action defines **economic surplus**. Rational behavior then means taking the actions for which the economic surplus is positive and refusing those for which it is negative. The **opportunity cost** of a choice or

decision is the value of the next-best alternative that must be sacrificed. To practice rational behavior, the opportunity cost of the alternatives being considered must be recognized and counted, even if they do not involve explicit monetary payments.

Learning Objective 3: Defend the economist's use of models to explain behavior.
Economists use abstract models to describe and predict behavior. The Cost-Benefit Principle is an example of a behavioral model: it indicates how an idealized rational person can maximize his or her economic surplus when choosing among alternatives. All fields of study that describe or predict behavior, from Physics to Sociology, use models. A model is a simplified version of reality. Superior models capture the most important elements of reality and ignore minor relationships and the inconsequential details. A model that included every facet of a particular behavior wouldn't be a model; it would be reality. If reality could be understood, then a model would not have been needed initially. A frequent but misguided criticism directed at the field of economics condemns the use of models to describe and predict behavior. The critics point out that people do not explicitly calculate the net benefits of going to a movie or a basketball game when deciding how to spend a Friday night. Of course this is correct, but it misses the point. People behave *as if* they do the calculations using their experiences and trial and error to approximate the value of benefits and costs. Of course mistakes are made and people fail to choose rationally. But believing people are constantly using their "calculators" to assess whether to have Chinese take-out or pizza delivered is **not** necessary to using the Cost-Benefits Principle as a description of how people make choices.

> **Hint:** In order to successfully understand economics and perform well on exams, you must think in terms of the ideas presented in the textbook and lectures. Do not give in to the temptation to create your own model. In a physics class it is unlikely you would question the existence or behavior of gravity. Even though you have made many economic decisions already, it does not mean you fully understand all the underlying concepts any more than being held down to the planet means you fully understand the physicist's model of gravity.

Learning Objective 4: List and differentiate among the four decision-making pitfalls. Give contrasting examples of the Not All Costs and Benefits Matter Equally Principle.
The usefulness of the Cost-Benefit Principle, either at an intuitive level or for an explicit calculation, depends on the proper assessment of the costs and benefits of the choices. While everyone may have a natural tendency to weigh costs and benefits, a natural tendency to accurately measure costs and benefits may not exist and certainly can be improved upon.

Measuring costs and benefits as proportions rather than as absolute values defines the first decision-making pitfall. As the examples in the textbook emphasize, if it worthwhile to take an action that saves you $10, then it is worthwhile when the list price of the item is $1,000 (a 1% savings) or $20 (a 50% savings). Net benefits (economic surplus) are measured in dollars, not percentages. The extent of the relative savings has no bearing on the decision to take the action; only the extent of the absolute savings should be considered.

Another common oversight is ignoring opportunity costs. Choosing a particular alternative means an infinite number of alternative will not be chosen. To accurately gauge the net benefits of a decision, one must recognize the alternatives and value them honestly. If spending a beautiful, sunny Wednesday afternoon at the lake means you take an unpaid day off from work, then the forgone earnings must be included in the assessment of costs. The reason class attendance is nearly 100% on the day of an exam but noticeably less on lecture days stems from the difference in opportunity costs of not attending class.

Note: Frequently, to introduce the concept and importance of opportunity costs, economists use time and the resulting forgone earnings as example. Do not be mislead by our tendencies. All choices have an opportunity cost. Buying a car means not buying other consumer goods, the most valuable of which measures the opportunity cost.

The third pitfall in evaluating costs and benefits stems from including costs that are irrelevant. Costs that cannot be recovered define the idea of **sunk costs**. For example, suppose you purchased a nonrefundable, nontransferable front row ticket to see your favorite pop star. Suppose further that your economics professor announces at the last minute a test on the day after the concert. Whether you go to the concert depends on your valuation of the costs and benefits. However, it is entirely incorrect to include the cost of your ticket in the decision. The ticket has been paid for and cannot be sold, given away, or refunded; it is a sunk cost. The temptation to count the ticket price is strong but will lead to an overstated estimate of costs.

The fourth common pitfall in quantifying the consequence of choosing a particular alternative stems from a failure to distinguish between average and marginal measures. The change in the total costs of an activity resulting from a one-unit change in the level of the activity defines **marginal costs**. The resulting change in total benefits of an activity when a one-unit change in the level of activity occurs identifies **marginal benefits**. The Cost-Benefit Principle indicates that as long as the marginal benefits are greater than the marginal costs, the level of the activity should be increased. The other type of measurement variables are the average measures. **Average benefits** are the total benefits of n units of the activity divided by n. The total costs of n units of the activity divided by n define the **average costs**. Measuring average costs and benefits is much easier than marginal costs and benefits, which contributes to the frequent reliance on averages to guide decision making. The convenience of average measures does not, unfortunately, change the inappropriateness of using average measures to make marginal decisions. If the average benefits of a given level of activity exceed the average costs of the same level of activity, increasing the activity is not necessarily the maximizing choice. Comparison of average benefits to average costs offers no guidance on whether to lessen or expand the level of the activity to reach maximization.

Note: The mathematically inclined reader may realize that comparing the marginal benefits to the marginal costs is an application of the first derivative test from calculus. Seeking to maximize the net benefits (total benefits minus total costs) of an activity results in choosing the level of activity where the marginal benefits equal the marginal costs.

The four cautions listed above can be combined into an overall principle. The **Not All Costs and Benefits Matter Equally Principle** simply suggests that some costs and benefits (e.g., opportunity costs; marginal costs and benefits) matter in the decision of which alternative to pick while other costs and benefits (e.g., sunk costs; average costs and benefits) are irrelevant or misleading.

Learning Objective 5: Distinguish between Macroeconomics and Microeconomics.
Economics divides into two major sub-fields. **Microeconomics**, concentrates on the choices individuals make under scarcity and the implications for prices and quantities in individual markets. The impact of a war with Iraq on the price of gasoline would constitute a microeconomic topic. **Macroeconomics** studies the performance of economies at the national level and the effect of governmental policies on the national economy's output. The resulting change in gross domestic product from President Bush's tax reform proposal is a proper macroeconomic question.

Learning Objective 6: Recognize the abundance of opportunities to apply economic reasoning—to practice "Economic Naturalism."
Economic naturalism refers to the application of the basic tents of economics to understand and explain everyday behaviors. The textbook gives several examples of common phenomena that can be easily understood by applying the Cost-Benefit Principle. Setting the specific examples aside, the main point is to encourage you to use what you are learning to understand behavior that has seemed perplexing or inconsistent. You may find actions or choices made by you or others that once confused or baffled can now be easily comprehended. Of particular importance, the behavior of the political process is more clearly grasped within the simple framework of the Cost-Benefit Principle.

Learning Objective 7 (Appendix): Understand how to translate a verbal statement into an equation. Clearly define the following: equation, variable, dependent variable, independent variable, and constant (parameter).
Economic models are frequently expressed in mathematical terms. A mathematical model possesses a greater degree of precision than a model expressed in verbal terms. But model development always begins with verbal statements and then proceeds to a mathematical version of the statements. An **equation** is a mathematical expression of the relationship between two or more variables. **Variables** are items thought to be related and that can take on different numerical values. By convention, the variable (or variables) that is thought to determine the magnitude of some other variable is placed on the right-hand side of the equation; the variable being determined is placed on the left-hand side. The right-hand side variables are called **independent variables** and the left-hand side variables are called the **dependent variables**. Often a **constant** (or **parameter**) is included on the right-hand side of the equation with a value that is fixed. The statement "I think my GPA will improve this semester because I got a laptop for Christmas" can be translated into an equation like GPA = f(new laptop). GPA is the dependent variable and the laptop is the independent variable. The laptop presumably improves your productivity in some fashion, which in turn improves your test scores and therefore your GPA. Obviously, GPA does not "cause" a laptop but a laptop may "cause" a higher GPA. Use

the term cause with reservation; to say X "causes" Y is a difficult proposition to prove. More accurately, say X "strongly influences" or X has a "significant effect" on Y.

Learning Objective 8 (Appendix): Starting with an equation, illustrate the equation with a graph. Define the following: vertical intercept, slope, rise, and run.
For an equation of the form $Y = a + b*X$, Y is the dependent variable and X is the independent variable. The **vertical intercept** is the value of Y when X is zero; it is the value of "a" in the equation above. The **slope** of the equation, signified by "b" in the equation above, is the ratio of the change in Y when some change in X occurs. The change in Y is termed **rise** and the change in X is called **run**. These terms come from the orientation of the graph: X is on the horizontal axis (hence run) while Y is placed on the vertical axis (hence rise). Slope is often defined as rise over run. To plot an equation, first determine the vertical intercept's value and put a point on the vertical axis at this value (remember X = 0). Then calculate a value of Y when X is not equal to 0 (pick easy X values like 1 or 10). To accomplish this, take the value of X you picked, multiply it by "b" and then add "a" to arrive at the value of Y. For linear relationships (straight lines), two pairs of coordinates are enough to completely describe the equation. Thus, after marking the vertical intercept and calculating the value of Y, you can run a line through the two points. You have now illustrated the equation in the form of a graph.

Learning Objective 9 (Appendix): Starting with a graph, determine the underlying equation.
If this was a repair manual for a car, it would say installation is the reverse of disassembly. Look at the graph and note where it crosses or intersects the vertical axis. This is the vertical intercept "a." Now calculate the slope. Depending on the scale (the units X and Y are measured in) of the graph, pick two X values and note the resulting Y values in the graph. Say the values of X are 10 and 15 and the corresponding values for Y are 30 and 20. Slope is calculated as (20-30)/(15-10) = (-10)/(5) = -2. The rise of the graph is -10 when the run is 5. A negative relationship exists between X and Y, i.e., as X gets larger, Y gets smaller. Now simply take your results for "a" and "b" and write it out in equation form (as in the preceding learning objective).

Learning Objective 10 (Appendix): Demonstrate how a change in (1) the vertical intercept and (2) the slope affect the graph of the equation.
Continuing with the $Y = a + b*X$ example, a change in the vertical intercept means a change in how large Y is when X = 0. When "a" changes, the position of the line in the graph changes. The change in position can be called a "shift" in the curve. It shifts up if the value of "a" gets larger and it shifts down if the value of "a" decreases. Note that the slope of the equation is the same as before and therefore the new line *must* be parallel to the original line. When the slope changes, the shape of the line in the graph changes. The line pivots through the unchanging vertical intercept. The new line will be steeper if the absolute value of the slope is greater than it was before; the line will be flatter if the absolute value of the slope is smaller than it was before. Recall that the flattest line is a horizontal line with a slope of zero and the steepest line is a vertical line with a slope of infinity.

Learning Objective 11 (Appendix): Beginning with a table of data, know how to construct the graph of a relationship and how to determine the underlying equation.
When working with tabular data, first figure out which is the dependent variable (Y) and which is the independent variable (X). Next, place the dependent variable on the vertical axis of your graph and the independent variable on the horizontal axis. Plot some of the data points by locating the value of the dependent variable and the associated value of the independent variable. Now use the techniques outlined above to either graph the function or determine the underlying equation.

III. Self-Test

Key Terms
Match the term in the right-hand column with the appropriate definitions in the left-hand column by placing the letter of the term in the blank in front of its definition. (Answers are given at the end of the chapter.)

1. ____ The study of how individuals make choices under conditions of scarcity and the resulting effects.

a. average benefits

2. ____ A person with well-defined goals who tries to achieve them.

b. average costs

3. ____ The subfield of economics that concentrates on the performance of the national economy and the effects of governmental policies.

c. economics

4. ____ The value of the next-best alternative not selected.

d. economic surplus

5. ____ The difference between the benefits of taking an action and the costs of taking the action.

e. marginal benefits

6. ____ The extra benefits experienced as a result of a one-unit increase in the amount of an activity chosen.

f. marginal costs

7. ____ The total costs of *n* units of activity divided by *n*.

g. macroeconomics

8. ____ The subfield of economics that concentrates on the behavior of individual markets.

h. microeconomics

9. ____ The extra costs experienced as a result of a one-unit increase in the amount of an activity chosen.

i. opportunity cost

10. ____ Costs that cannot be recovered regardless of the alternative chosen.

j. rational person

11. ____ The total benefits of *n* units of activity divided by *n*.
Appendix

k. sunk costs

12. ____ A value in an equation that is fixed.

l. constant

13. ____ The variable or variables that cause or determine the relationship in an equation.

m. dependent variable

14. ____ A measure of how much the dependent variable changes for some given change in the independent variable.

n. equation

15. ____ The variable that is caused or is being determined in an equation.

o. independent variable

16. ____ A mathematical statement of the relationship between two or more variables.

p. parameter

17. ____ Items thought to be related that can take on different

q. rise

numerical values.

18. ___ When calculating slope, the change in the dependent variable.   r. run

19. ___ The value of the dependent variable when the value of the   s. slope
independent variable is zero.

20. ___ When calculating slope, the change in the independent   t. variables
variable.

u. vertical intercept

Multiple-Choice Questions
Circle the letter that corresponds to the best answer. (Answers are given at the end of the chapter.)

1. The scarcity principle indicates that
   A. no matter how much one has, it is never enough.
   B. compared to 100 years ago, individuals have less time today.
   C. with limited resources, having more of "this" means having less of "that."
   D. because tradeoffs must be made, resources are therefore scarce.
   E. the wealthier a person is, the fewer the number of tradeoffs he or she must make.

2. Benny has one hour before bedtime and he can either watch TV or listen to his new Korn CD. He chooses to listen to the CD. The scarcity principle's influence on Benny is seen in
   A. the decision to listen to music.
   B. the decision not to watch TV.
   C. the fixed amount of time before bed.
   D. the decision to choose between TV and music.
   E. Benny's taste in music.

3. Choosing to study for an exam until the extra benefit (improved score) equals the extra cost (mental fatigue) is
   A. not rational.
   B. an application of the cost-benefit principle.
   C. an application of the scarcity principle.
   D. the relevant opportunity cost.
   E. less desirable than studying for the entire evening.

4. The scarcity principle indicates that _____ and the cost-benefit principle indicates _____.
   A. choices must be made; how to make the choices
   B. choices must be made; the choices will be good
   C. choices must be made; just one of many possible ways to make the choices
   D. choices must be made; the choices will be poor
   E. choices must be made; the costs can never outweigh the benefits of the choices

5. Amy is thinking about going to the movies tonight to see Nutty Professor 2. A ticket costs $7 and she will have to cancel her dog-sitting job that pays $30. The cost of seeing the movie is
   A. $7.
   B. $30.
   C. $37.
   D. $37 minus the benefit of seeing the movie.
   E. indeterminate.

6. The use of economic models, like the cost-benefit principle, means economists believe that
   A. this is how people explicitly chose between alternatives.
   B. this is a reasonable abstraction of how people chose between alternatives.
   C. those who explicitly make decisions this way are smarter.
   D. with enough education, all people will start to explicitly make decisions this way.
   E. this is the way the world ought to explicitly make decisions.

7. Tony notes that an electronics store is offering a flat $20 off all prices in the store. Tony reasons that if he wants to buy something with a price of $50 that it is a good offer, but if he wants to buy something with a price of $500 it is not a good offer. This is an example of
   A. inconsistent reasoning; saving $20 is saving $20.
   B. the proper application of the cost-benefit principle.
   C. rational choice because in the first case he saves $40% and in the second case he saves 4%.
   D. marginal cost equals marginal benefit thinking.
   E. opportunity costs.

8. That individuals make inconsistent choices and that inconsistencies have a strong pattern is, in the view of the textbook,
   A. evidence of the severe limitations of economic models.
   B. an indication of widespread irrationality.
   C. support for the study of economics to improve decision making.
   D. of limited importance.
   E. a well-kept secret that should remain that way.

9. Sunk cost are different from other concepts of cost in that they
   A. can be either variable or fixed.
   B. cannot be lessened by choosing any particular course of action.
   C. influence the decision of which activity to do or not do.
   D. rise as the level of the activity rises.
   E. must be included for an accurate cost-benefit analysis.

10. Which of the following statements would *not* be part of microeconomics?
    A. What college major to select.
    B. How to make the largest profit.
    C. Whether to study or watch TV tonight.
    D. How an early freeze in California will affect the price of fruit.
    E. If the federal budget should always be balanced.

11. When making a decision, the important costs to identify and consider are the _____ costs and the _____ costs.
    A. opportunity; marginal
    B. opportunity; fixed
    C. sunk; marginal
    D. marginal; average
    E. marginal; fixed

12. Janie can either mow the lawn or wash clothes, earning her a benefit of $30 or $45, respectively. Janie will therefore choose to _____because the economic surplus is _____.
    A. mow; greater
    B. wash; greater
    C. mow; smaller
    D. wash; smaller
    E. mow; the same as for washing

13. Any time one purchases a ticket in advance of an event, if the ticket is non-refundable and non-transferable then on the day of the event, the ticket is
    A. part of the cost of going.
    B. a variable cost.
    C. part of the cost of going if it was expensive.
    D. a sunk cost and should play no role in the decision to go or not.
    E. a fixed cost but not a sunk cost.

14. The average cost of 20 units of an activity is the
    A. total cost of 20 units of the activity divided by 20.
    B. 20 units divided by the total cost of 20 units of the activity.
    C. extra cost of 20 units of the activity divided by 20.
    D. reciprocal of the total cost of 20 units of the activity.
    E. change in total cost of the activity.

15. Class attendance on exam days is nearly 100% but on lecture days it is less. The likely explanation for this would be that
    A. the opportunity cost of not attending on exam day is much higher than usual.
    B. it's random chance.
    C. the episode of Jerry Springer was a rerun.
    D. students thought today's class was a review.
    E. the opportunity cost of attending on exam day is much higher than usual.

16. To avoid the mistake of ignoring opportunity costs, the textbook recommends framing questions in the form,
    A. Should I do A?
    B. Should I do B?
    C. Why should I do A?
    D. Should I do A or B?
    E. Should I do A or B or C or... Z?

17. On the first day of the semester, David finds he has one hour of time in the evening to allocate. He can do one of two things. He can watch TV for one hour or he can open his economics textbook and read for an hour. Assume that the benefit of watching TV is 30 and the benefit or reading about economics is 20. The cost of watching TV is _____ and the cost of reading his economics textbook is _____.
   A. 20; 30
   B. 0; 0
   C. 30; 20
   D. 20; 0
   E. indeterminate; indeterminate

18. Continuing with the information in question 17, if David applies the cost-benefit principle accurately, he will
   A. read his economics textbook.
   B. watch TV.
   C. watch TV but fret that he should be reading.
   D. read his economics textbook but resent missing TV.
   E. flip a coin because the net benefits are the same.

19. Continuing with the information in question 17, suppose that instead of the first day of the semester, it is the night before David's first exam in economics. One could reasonably predict that
   A. the benefit of watching TV will rise.
   B. the benefit of reading about economics will fall.
   C. the cost of watching TV will rise.
   D. the cost of reading economics will rise.
   E. he will continue to make the same choice.

20. In general, to make optimal decisions one needs information on the
   A. average benefits and marginal costs.
   B. marginal benefits and marginal costs.
   C. marginal benefits and average costs.
   D. average benefits and average costs.
   E. benefits and costs, which can be either average or marginal.

Short Answer Problems
(Answers and solutions are given at the end of the chapter.)

1. Enid has two exams tomorrow: one in economics and one in marketing. She has a total of 4 hours available for studying. The table below shows the test scores she will make with different amounts of studying time. For example, if she spends 1 hour studying economics she makes a 77 on the economics test and makes a 79 on the marketing test, having spent 3 hours (4-1) studying for it.

	Hours Spent Studying Economics				
	0	1	2	3	4
Economics Score	65	77	86	89	91
Finance Score	80	79	77	70	50

A. The scarce resource Enid is allocating is (time/intelligence) _____. The opportunity cost of an extra hour studying economics is the (improvement in economics score/reduction in marketing score) _____.

B. Calculate the marginal benefit of spending 1, 2, 3, and 4 hours studying economics: the 1st hour ____; the 2nd _____; the 3rd ____; and the 4th ____.

C. Calculate the marginal cost of spending 1, 2, 3, and 4 hours studying economics: the 1st hour ____; the 2nd _____; the 3rd ____; and the 4th ____.

D. If Enid is rational, she should spend _____ hours studying economics and _____ hours studying marketing.

E. Calculate the total points from both tests when 0 to 4 hours are spent studying economics: 0 hours ____; 1 hour ____; 2 hours _____; 3 hours _____; and 4 hours _____. Does the answer to "D" agree with the answer here (yes/no) _____.

2. Ontel engineers proposed developing a 5 Gigahertz microprocessor in early 2003 at a cost of $50 million for a working prototype. By mid 2004, the $50 million had been spent with no prototype. The engineers request an additional $10 million to finish the project. For convenience, assume (1) the marginal cost of producing the chip once it is developed is zero and (2) with the additional funding, the probability of producing a prototype is 1.

A. In January, 2003 the sunk costs of this project were _____ and in July 2004, the sunk costs of the project are _____.

B. Assume Ontel estimates it will earn revenues of $40 million on a 5 Gigahertz chip. If the extra funding is not approved, then Ontel will lose ($50 million/$10 million) _____. If the extra $10 million is granted, Ontel will lose ($60 million/$20 million) _____. Therefore, the extra $10 million (should/should not) _____ be granted.

3. The following table contains information about the costs and benefits of engaging in different amounts of an activity. Presume the cost data reflects both monetary and opportunity costs.

Units of Activity	Costs	Benefits	Average Costs	Average Benefits	Marginal Costs	Marginal Benefits
0	$0	$0	0	0	n/a	n/a
1	30	100				
2	35	150				
3	50	180				
4	70	200				
5	120	205				

A. Calculate the average costs and benefits for the different levels of activity. Likewise, calculate the marginal costs and benefits.

B. The level of activity consistent with the Cost-Benefit Principle occurs at (4/5) _____ units. The (4/5) _____ units would represent excess activity because the (marginal costs/average costs) _____ are greater than the (marginal benefits/average benefits) _____.

C. The difference between the benefits and the costs is the same for units (3 and 4/2 and 3) _____. Why then is there only one maximum point? Explain. _____
_____

IV. Economic Naturalist Application

A frequent complaint of the wealthy is that, while they can purchase virtually any item they want, the one item they can't purchase more of is time. How then are the wealthy identical to the lower classes with respect to time? Is their a difference in their opportunity cost of time compared with the lower classes? Suppose some wealthy person decides to retire. Will he still lament his lack of time? Why?

V. Go to the Web: Graphing Exercises Using Interactive Graphs
For practice using interactive graphs, please go to the Electronic Learning Session in the Student Center at the Frank/Bernanke web site: http://www.mhhe.com/economics/frankbernanke2.

VI. Self -Test Solutions

Key Terms
1. c
2. j
3. g
4. i
5. d
6. e
7. b
8. h

9. f
10. k
11. a
Appendix
12. l, p
13. o
14. s
15. m
16. n
17. t
18. q
19. u
20. r

Multiple-Choice Questions
1. C
2. C
3. B
4. A
5. C
6. B
7. A
8. C
9. B
10. E
11. A
12. A
13. D
14. A
15. A
16. D
17. A
18. B
19. C
20. B

Short Answer Problems
1.
A. time; reduction in marketing score
B. 12; 9; 3; 2.
C. 1; 2; 7; 20.
D. 2; 2.
E. 148; 156; 163; 159; 141. yes.
2.
A. 0; $50 million.
B. $50 million. $20 million. should.

3.

Units of Activity	Costs	Benefits	Average Costs	Average Benefits	Marginal Costs	Marginal Benefits
0	$0	$0	0	0	n/a	n/a
1	30	100	$30.0	$100	$30	100
2	35	150	17.5	75	5	50
3	50	180	16.7	60	15	30
4	70	200	17.5	50	20	20
5	120	205	24.0	41	50	5

A. See table.

B. 4. 5; marginal costs; marginal benefits.

C. 3 and 4. The difference is *maximized* at 4 units; if one stops at 3 units, the maximum net benefits will not be realized.

Chapter 2
Comparative Advantage:
The Basis for Exchange

I. Pretest: What Do You Really Know?

Circle the letter that corresponds to the best answer. (Answers are given at the end of the chapter.)

1. If Leslie can produce two pairs of pants in an hour while Eva can make one pair an hour, then
   A. Leslie has a comparative advantage.
   B. Eva has an absolute advantage.
   C. Leslie has an absolute advantage.
   D. Eva has a comparative advantage.
   E. Leslie has a comparative disadvantage.

2. Application of the Principle of Comparative Advantage leads to
   A. greater specialization of labor and other factors of production.
   B. lesser specialization of labor.
   C. societies where everyone can do a little of everything.
   D. lower total output.
   E. misallocation of resources.

3. The greatest gains from specialization result when
   A. the differences in producers' opportunity costs are small.
   B. producers have neither an absolute nor a comparative advantage in the production of the goods and services that they specialize in producing.
   C. producers have an absolute but not a comparative advantage in the production of the goods and services that they specialize in producing.
   D. producers have an absolute and a comparative advantage in the production of the goods and services that they specialize in producing.
   E. the differences in producers' absolute advantages are greatest.

4. An outward shift in a production possibilities curve can be caused by
   A. scarcity.
   B. improved technology.
   C. increasing opportunity cost.
   D. absolute advantage.
   E. low-hanging fruit.

5. Increased specialization in the production of goods
   A. always increases net benefits.
   B. never increases net benefits.
   C. has benefits, but no costs.
   D. has costs, but no benefits.
   E. has costs and benefits.

6. If a given production combination is known to be attainable, then it must be
   A. on the production possibilities curve.
   B. beyond the production possibilities curve.
   C. an efficient point.
   D. an inefficient point.
   E. either an inefficient or efficient point.

7. Which of the following can be a source of comparative advantage for a nation?
   A. natural resources
   B. entrepreneurship
   C. speaking the English language
   D. standards of production quality
   E. all of the above

8. If a country experiences increasing opportunity costs, its production possibilities curve will
   A. be a straight line.
   B. bow outward.
   C. bow inward.
   D. shift out from the origin.
   E. shift in toward the origin.

9. According to the Low-Hanging-Fruit Principle, in expanding production of a good, you should first employ those resources
   A. where you have comparative advantage.
   B. where you have absolute advantage.
   C. with the highest opportunity cost.
   D. with the lowest opportunity cost.
   E. that have the lowest price.

10. Which of the following is the basis for an argument against free trade?
   A. the Principle of Comparative Advantage
   B. the change in the total value of goods and services resulting from trade
   C. the distribution of the benefits from trade
   D. the Principle of Increasing Opportunity Costs
   E. all of the above

Solutions and Feedback to Pretest
For each question that you answered incorrectly, it is strongly recommended that you review the appropriate text pages and Key Point Review Learning Objective indicated in the following table.

Correct Answers	Text Page Numbers	Learning Objective
1. C	pp. 34 - 38	1
2. B	pp. 34 - 38	1
3. D	pp. 44 - 45	2
4. B	pp. 47 - 49	7
5. E	pp. 49 - 50	3
6. E	pp. 39 - 42	4
7. E	pp. 38 - 39	1
8. B	pp. 45 - 47	5
9. D	pp. 46 - 47	6
10. C	p. 51	8

II. Key Point Review

This chapter shows that comparative advantage is the reason that economic systems based on specialization and the exchange of goods and services are generally far more productive than those based on less specialization. To see more precisely how specialization enhances the productive capacity of an economy based on specialization, the production possibilities curve is introduced.

Objective 1: Define comparative and absolute advantage and discuss the sources of comparative advantage.
Economies can be based on specialization and the exchange of goods and services or on generalization and self-sufficiency in the production of goods and services. Economic systems that are based on specialization and exchange are generally far more productive than those lacking specialization. The benefits of specialization derive from what economists call comparative advantage. A person has a **comparative advantage** over another if that person's opportunity cost of performing a task is lower than another person's opportunity cost. This concept is so fundamental to economics that the authors have identified it as a core idea of the course. The Principle of Comparative Advantage asserts that everyone does best when each person (or each country) concentrates on the activities for which his or her opportunity cost is lowest. The sources of comparative advantage come from inborn talent, education, training, and experience on the individual level, and from differences in natural resources, society and culture

at the national level. Comparative advantage is distinguished from absolute advantage. A person has an **absolute advantage** over another if he or she takes fewer hours to perform a task than the other person. One need not have an absolute advantage in the production of a good in order to have a comparative advantage.

> **Note:** It cannot be emphasized strongly enough that the principle of comparative advantage is a *relative* concept – one that makes sense only when the productivities of two or more producers (or countries) are being compared.

Objective 2: Discuss the conditions that result in the greatest benefits from specialization.

The benefits from specialization and exchange are greatest when people (or nations) have an absolute *and* comparative advantage in the production of the goods and services that they specialize in producing. In addition, when the differences in opportunity cost are more pronounced the benefits from specialization are greater. Despite the prodigious gains that can result from specialization, many countries have not benefited significantly from specialization because of low population density or laws or customs that limit people's freedom to transact freely with one another.

Objective 3: Identify the benefits and costs of specialization.

In addition to the gains achieved through preexisting differences, specialization deepens individuals' skills through practice and experience. It also eliminates the switching and start-up costs of moving back and forth among numerous tasks, thus providing further economic benefits. Despite the significant gains that derive from specialization, specialization can be taken to0 far, resulting in mind-numbing, repetitive work.

> **Note:** While, in theory, excessive specialization can be detrimental, it is safe to say that we can provide for our material needs in the shortest time if we concentrate at least a significant proportion of our efforts on those tasks for which we have a comparative advantage. The result will be more free time to do whatever other activities we may desire.

Objective 4: Define production possibilities curve, and identify attainable, unattainable, efficient, and inefficient points on a production possibilities curve.
The production possibilities curve can be used to demonstrate the benefits of producing in accordance with comparative advantage. The **production possibilities curve** is a graph that describes the maximum amount of one good that can be produced for every possible level of production of the other good. Points that lie on the production possibilities curve are both **efficient points** and **attainable points**, while points that lie below the curve are only **attainable points**. Points that lie outside the production possibilities curve represent combinations of goods that cannot be produced using the currently available resources and are **unattainable points**. Any combination of goods, for which currently available resources enable an increase in the production of one good without a reduction in the production of the other good, represents **inefficient points**.

Objective 5: Explain why the production possibilities curve is downward sloping.
The production possibilities curve is downward sloping, reflecting the principle of scarcity (the idea that, because our resources are limited, producing more of one good generally means producing less of another good). The slope of the production possibilities curve represents the opportunity cost of producing additional units of one good, measured in terms of the amount of production of the other good that is foregone.

> **Note:** The opportunity cost of producing one good in terms of another good is equal to the absolute value of the slope of a production possibilities curve for the two goods. When computing the opportunity cost of one good in terms of another, we must pay close attention to the form in which the productivity information is presented.

Objective 6: Explain the Principle of Increasing Opportunity Cost (aka "The Low-Hanging-Fruit Principle").
The same logic that leads individuals in an economy to specialize and exchange goods also leads nations to specialize and trade among themselves. An individual's production possibilities curve is linear (a straight line), but the production possibilities curve for two or more people is bowed outward because of individual differences in opportunity costs. The production possibilities curve for a multi-person economy is bowed outward because all resources are not equally suited to the production of all goods. When the production possibilities curve is bowed outward, the slope increases as you move along the curve, indicating that the opportunity cost increases as additional units of a good are produced. This **principle of increasing opportunity cost** (also called "the low-hanging-fruit principle") states that, in expanding the production of any good, you should first employ those resources with the lowest opportunity cost, and only afterward turn to resources with higher opportunity costs.

Objective 7: Discuss the factors that shift the economy's production possibilities curve.
An outward shift in the production possibilities curve represents an increase in the production of all goods (typically referred to as economic growth). Economic growth can result from an increase in the quantity of productive resources and, more importantly, from improvements in knowledge and technology.

Objective 8: Discuss why some people oppose free trade agreements.
The patterns of international trade today largely reflect the benefits shown in the production possibilities analysis. Despite the aggregate gains that derive from specialization and international trade, not everyone benefits, and this has often led to strong opposition to free trade agreements.

III. Self-Test

Key Terms
Place the letter of the term in the right-hand column in the appropriate blank of the definitions in the left-hand column. (Answers are given at the end of the chapter.)

1. _____ Having a lower opportunity cost of performing a task than another person.

2. _____ Any combination of goods that cannot be produced using currently available resources.

3. _____ A graph showing the various combinations of goods and services that an individual or economy can produce.

4. _____ Any combination of goods for which currently available resources do not allow an increase in the production of one without a reduction in the production of the other.

5. _____ Taking fewer hours to perform a task than another person.

6. _____ Any combination of goods for which currently available resources enable an increase in the production of one without a reduction in the production of the other.

7. _____ Any combination of goods that can be produced using currently available resources.

a. absolute advantage

b. attainable point

c. comparative advantage

d. efficient point

e. inefficient point

f. production possibilities curve

g. unattainable point

Multiple-Choice Questions
Circle the letter that corresponds to the best answer. (Answers are given at the end of the chapter.)

1. Jane can produce 50 pizzas or 100 hamburgers per day, while Sam can produce 30 pizzas or 90 hamburgers per day. Jane has an
   A. absolute advantage in the production of pizzas, but not hamburgers, and has a comparative advantage in the production of pizzas.
   B. absolute advantage in the production of hamburgers, but not pizzas, and has a comparative advantage in the production of hamburgers.

C. absolute advantage in the production of hamburgers and pizzas, as well as a comparative advantage in the production of hamburgers.

D. absolute advantage in the production of hamburgers and pizzas, as well as a comparative advantage in the production of pizzas.

E. absolute advantage in the production of hamburgers and pizzas, as well as a comparative advantage in the production of hamburgers and pizzas.

2. When an individual concentrates on performing the tasks and producing the goods for which he or she has the lowest opportunity cost, he or she is producing in accordance with the principle of
   A. increasing opportunity cost.
   B. decreasing opportunity cost.
   C. comparative advantage.
   D. scarcity
   E. low-hanging fruit.

3. At the individual level, comparative advantage results from
   A. differences in natural resources.
   B. cultural differences.
   C. language differences.
   D. the amount of resources available.
   E. differences in education or training.

4. Production possibilities curves are downward sloping, reflecting the principle of
   A. scarcity.
   B. comparative advantage.
   C. increasing opportunity cost.
   D. absolute advantage.
   E. low hanging fruit.

5. Maria can produce 100 pounds of tomatoes or 25 pounds of squash in her garden each summer, while Tonya can produce 50 pounds of tomatoes or 25 pounds of squash. The absolute values of the slope of Maria's and Tonya's production possibilities curves, respectively, are
   A. ¼ and ½ .
   B. ½ and ¼ .
   C. 4 and 2.
   D. 2 and 4.
   E. 100 and 50.

6. A country's production possibilities curve is concave to the origin (i.e., bowed outward) because
   A. of the principle of scarcity.
   B. the production of a good is expanded by first employing those resources with an absolute advantage.

C. the production of a good is expanded by first employing those resources with the lowest opportunity cost.

D. there is a tradeoff that requires a decrease in the production of one good in order to increase the production of another good.

E. of the principle of absolute advantage.

7. The gains from specialization and exchange are greatest when individuals or nations
   A. have a comparative and absolute advantage in the goods they produce, and the differences in opportunity costs are minimal.
   B. have a comparative and absolute advantage in the goods they produce, and the differences in opportunity costs are large.
   C. have only a comparative advantage in the goods they produce, and the differences in opportunity costs are minimal.
   D. have only an absolute advantage in the goods they produce, and the differences in opportunity costs are large.
   E. have neither a comparative nor absolute advantage in the goods they produce, but the differences in opportunity costs are large.

8. Specialization of labor not only results in the ability to produce a larger amount of goods due to innate differences in people's skills, but also by
   A. rigidly segmenting work.
   B. switching back and forth among numerous tasks.
   C. breaking a task down into mind-numbing repetitive tasks.
   D. deepening skills through practice and experience.
   E. eliminating the need to train and educate the workers to perform different tasks.

9. Professor N. Gregory Mankiw has a comparative advantage in the production of economics textbooks, and a neighbor's child has a comparative advantage in mowing the lawn. Professor Mankiw
   A. should never mow his own lawn.
   B. should only write economics textbooks.
   C. may be better off mowing his lawn if he felt like taking a break from writing textbooks.
   D. will always be better off hiring the neighbor's child to mow his lawn.
   E. may be better off hiring the neighbor's child to write his economics textbooks if his lawn needs mowing.

10. By specializing in accordance with its comparative advantage and trading with other nations, the small nation of Islandia will benefit
    A. less than larger nations.
    B. more than larger nations.
    C. only if its trading partners suffer losses.
    D. more or less, depending on the combination of goods it chooses to consume.
    E. regardless of the combination of goods it chooses to consume.

11. Despite the benefits of specialization and exchange indicated in the theory of comparative advantage, some groups have opposed free trade agreements because
    A. wealthier economies gain, but poor nations lose from free trade.
    B. in order for one nation to gain from trade, another nation must lose.
    C. they don't understand the theory of comparative advantage.
    D. not every individual gains from trade.
    E. contrary to the theory of comparative advantage, evidence suggests that there are few benefits from free trade.

12. Yolanda can produce 2 dresses or 4 shirts in 8 hours of work, while Sandra can produce 3 dresses or 7 shirts in the same amount of time. Yolanda has a(n)
    A. absolute advantage in producing dresses and shirts, and a comparative advantage in producing dresses, while Sandra has a comparative advantage in producing shirts.
    B. comparative advantage in producing shirts, while Sandra has an absolute advantage in producing dresses and shirts, and a comparative advantage in producing dresses.
    C. comparative advantage in producing dresses, while Sandra has an absolute advantage in producing dresses and shirts, and a comparative advantage in producing shirts.
    D. absolute advantage in producing dresses and shirts, and a comparative advantage in producing shirts, while Sandra has a comparative advantage in producing dresses.
    E. absolute advantage and a comparative advantage in producing dresses and shirts.

13. One of the major factors contributing to the United States achieving a global comparative advantage in producing movies, books, and popular music is because
    A. the United States has more capital used in the production of mass media than other nations.
    B. the United States has more entrepreneurs than other nations.
    C. the United States has a better educational system than other nations.
    D. English is the native language of the United States and the *de facto* world language.
    E. the United States has more writers with an innate superiority over writers in other nations.

14. A point on Joseph's production possibilities curve represents 6 music CDs and 2 videos produced in a week. A combination of 4 music CDs and 2 videos is a(n)
    A. efficient and attainable point.
    B. efficient but not attainable point.
    C. attainable and inefficient point.
    D. unattainable point.
    E. unattainable and inefficient point.

15. The slope of an individual's production possibilities curve
    A. decreases as more units of a particular good are produced.
    B. is negative and constant along the entire curve.
    C. is positive and constant along the entire curve.
    D. varies as the amount of output changes.
    E. is the same for all individuals.

16. Point A on a production possibilities curve represents a combination of 10 bicycles and 4 tricycles, and point B represents 6 bicycles and 6 tricycles. The absolute value of the slope of the production possibilities curve between points A and B equals
    A. 2.
    B. 4.
    C. ½.
    D. ¼.
    E. 6.

17. In a two-person economy, Little Joe can trap a maximum of 6 rabbits or catch 10 fish per week, while his father can trap 12 rabbits or catch 15 fish per week. If their family wants to consume 20 fish per week, while maximizing their joint production,
    A. his father should specialize in producing only fish, and Little Joe should produce both fish and rabbits.
    B. Little Joe should specialize in producing only fish, and his father should produce both fish and rabbits.
    C. Little Joe should specialize in producing fish, and his father should produce only rabbits.
    D. Little Joe should specialize in producing rabbits, and his father should produce only fish.
    E. each should produce both fish and rabbits.

18. When individuals or groups specialize in producing those goods for which they have a comparative advantage and exchange those goods with one another,
    A. those with an absolute advantage will gain the most, while those without an absolute advantage will lose.
    B. those with a comparative advantage will gain the most, while those without a comparative advantage will lose.
    C. total production will be greater than it would be without specialization, but would be the greatest if they produced those goods for which they have an absolute advantage.
    D. total production will be less than it would be without specialization.
    E. total production will be the greatest that they can achieve given the available resources.

19. Increased specialization in the production of goods
    A. always increases net benefits.
    B. never increases net benefits.
    C. has benefits, but no costs.
    D. has costs, but no benefits.
    E. has costs and benefits.

20. The opportunity for a small nation to trade with an economic superpower
   A. will increase the consumption possibilities for the small nation and the economic superpower.
   B. will increase the consumption possibilities for the small nation only.
   C. will increase the consumption possibilities for the economic superpower only.
   D. will increase the consumption possibilities for the economic superpower, but will decrease the consumption possibilities for the small nation.
   E. will increase the consumption possibilities for the small nation, but will decrease the consumption possibilities for the economic superpower.

Short Answer Problems
(Answers and solutions are given at the end of the chapter.)

1. Production Possibilities Curve for an Individual
A. If Ian allocates all of his resources, he can write 4 short stories in a month; or he can allocate all his resources to crafting 20 leather belts. Draw his production possibilities curve on the graph below, measuring the production of leather belts on the vertical axis and short stories on the horizontal axis (Be sure to label the axes.)

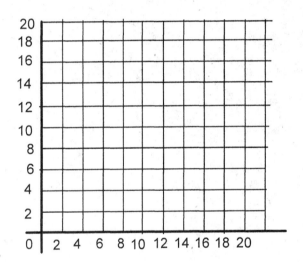

B. Ian is currently allocating all of his resources to producing leather belts. If he decides to reallocate his resources so as to produce 1 short story, he will incur an opportunity cost of

_____.

C. Based on your answer to Question 1B, the absolute value of the slope of Ian's production possibilities curve equals _____ .

D. On the graph above, draw a point representing the combination of 12 leather belts and 4 short stories (label it A). Point A is a(n) _____ point.

E. On the graph above, draw a point representing the combination of 5 leather belts and 3 short stories (label it B). Point B is a(n) _____ and _____ point.

F. On the graph above, draw a point representing the combination of 2 leather belts and 2 short stories (label it C). Point C is a(n) _____ point.

2. Production Possibilities and Comparative Advantage

Sean and Shirley are proprietors of small fabrication plants that design and manufacture integrated chips (ICs) for specialized electronic products. The table below shows their respective productivity for ICs used in cellular phones and video-game machines.

	Time to design and manufacture ICs for cellular phones	Time to design and manufacture ICs for video-game machines
Sean's plant	4 days	4 days
Shirley's plant	1 day	2 days

A. Draw the production possibilities curves for Sean's and Shirley's fabrication plants on the graph below, showing their respective production of ICs for cellular phones and video-game machines in 40 days.

ICs for
Game
Machines

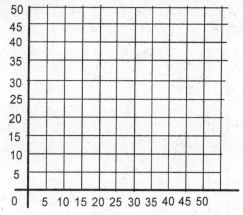

ICs for Cellular Phones

B. Sean's plant has an opportunity cost for producing ICs for cellular phones of _____ and for producing ICs for video-game machines of _____. Shirley's plant has an opportunity cost for producing ICs for cellular phones of _____ and for producing ICs for video-game machines of _____.

C. _____ has an absolute advantage in producing ICs for cellular phones and video-game machines.

D. _____ has a comparative advantage in producing ICs for cellular phones, and _____ has a comparative advantage in producing ICs for video-game machines.

E. In order to maximize the total production of ICs for cellular phones and video-game machines, Sean should specialize in the production of ICs for _____ and Shirley should specialize in the production of ICs for _____.

F. Because the demand for her ICs for cellular phones increased to 45 per month, Shirley buys Sean's fabrication plant. Draw the production possibilities curve showing the combined maximum production of the two fabrication plants.

ICs for
Game
Machines

```
50 ┬─┬─┬─┬─┬─┬─┬─┬─┬─┬─┐
45 ┼─┼─┼─┼─┼─┼─┼─┼─┼─┼─┤
40 ┼─┼─┼─┼─┼─┼─┼─┼─┼─┼─┤
35 ┼─┼─┼─┼─┼─┼─┼─┼─┼─┼─┤
30 ┼─┼─┼─┼─┼─┼─┼─┼─┼─┼─┤
25 ┼─┼─┼─┼─┼─┼─┼─┼─┼─┼─┤
20 ┼─┼─┼─┼─┼─┼─┼─┼─┼─┼─┤
15 ┼─┼─┼─┼─┼─┼─┼─┼─┼─┼─┤
10 ┼─┼─┼─┼─┼─┼─┼─┼─┼─┼─┤
 5 ┼─┼─┼─┼─┼─┼─┼─┼─┼─┼─┤
 0 ┴──────────────────────
    5 10 15 20 25 30 35 40 45 50
```

ICs for Cellular Phones

G. Prior to the merger of the fabrication plants and specialization, the slopes of Shirley's and Sean's PPCs were (constant/decreasing/increasing) _____. After the merger and specialization, the slope of the combined plants PPC (is constant/decreases/increases) _____ after _____ ICs for cellular phones are produced, reflecting the Law of _____ (also called the _____).

H. In order to maximize production of ICs and produce 45 ICs for cellular phones per month, _____ fabrication plant should completely specialize in producing ICs for cellular phones, and _____ fabrication plant should produce ICs for cellular phones and video-game machines.

I. Your answers to Questions 2G and 2H imply that, in order to maximize production of ICs while producing 45 ICs for cellular phones, they must allocate ¾ of the combined production time of the two plants (i.e., 40 days of production in Shirley's fab plus 20 days of production in Sean's fab = 60 days, divided by 80 of combined production days). The remaining ¼ of the combined time would be allocated to producing ICs for video-game machines. If, prior to the buyout, each fabrication plant had allocated ¾ of its time (i.e., 30 days) to producing ICs for cellular phones, Shirley's fabrication plant would have produced _____ ICs and Sean's fabrication plant would have produced _____ ICs. Similarly, if each fabrication plant had allocated ¼ (i.e., 10 days) of its time producing ICs for video-game machines, Shirley's fabrication plant would have produced _____ ICs and Sean's fabrication plant would have produced _____ ICs.

J. Based on your answer to Question 2I, the total number of ICs that would have been produced prior to the merger and specialization would have equaled _____ ICs, but after the merger and specialization the two fabrication plants would produce _____ ICs.

K. Based on your answers to Question 2J, the gains from specialization would equal _____ ICs.

3. Gains from Trade

The following table shows the combinations of strawberries and personal computers (PCs) that can be produced by Centralamericana.

Strawberries (millions of tons)	Personal computers (thousands of PCs)
8	0
6	8
0	12

A. On the graph below, plot Centralamericana's production possibilities curve.

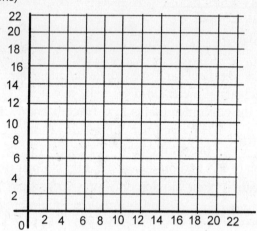

Strawberries (mil. tons)

Personal Computers (1,000s)

B. The economy of Centralamericana is closed (i.e., no trade is allowed) and the country has chosen to produce a combination of 6 million tons of strawberries and 8,000 PCs. Identify this combination on the above graph by labeling it point A.

C. By means of an international treaty, the economy of Centralamericana is opened to international trade. The prevailing exchange rate is 1 million tons of strawberries for 1,000 PCs. On the graph above, draw Centralamericana's new PPC after opening its economy to international trade, assuming it is producing at point A and could exchange as much of its strawberry and PC production as it chooses to at the prevailing exchange rate.

D. What combination of consumption of strawberries and PCs would not result in gains from international trade for Centralamericana? _____ million tons of strawberries and _____ PCs.

E. If Centralamericana started at Point A and chose to sell 4,000 PCs (at the prevailing exchange rate), it would then be able to consume _____ million tons of strawberries and _____ PCs. Label this point B. As a result of trade, it would have increased its consumption of strawberries by _____ million tons compared to what it would have been able to produce without trade.

F. If Centralamericana started at point A and chose to sell 3 million tons of strawberries at the prevailing exchange rate, it would then be able to consume _____ million tons of strawberries and _____ PCs. Label this point C. As a result of trade, it would have increased its consumption of PCs by _____ millions tons compared to what it would have been able to produce without trade.

V. Economic Naturalist Application

Economic Naturalist 2.1,"Where have all the .400 hitters gone?" focuses on the effects of specialization on batting averages. The sport of track and field provides a means of testing whether specialization improves athletes. In Olympic track and field competition, "generalists" compete in the decathlon (a series of ten events), while "specialists" compete in similar individual events. The table below lists the winning time/distance for the events during the 2000 Olympics in Sydney, Australia.

Event	Decathlon Competition	Individual Event Competition
Pole Vault	5.1 m.	5.9 m.
Javelin	69.94 m.	90.17 m.
Discus Throw	49.55 m.	69.30 m.
1500 m.	4:29.48 min.	3:32.07 min.
110 m. Hurdles	13.87 sec.	13.00 sec.
Shot Put	15.91 m.	21.29 m.
Long Jump	7.77 m.	8.55 m.
High Jump	2.21 m.	2.35 m.
400 m.	46.41 sec.	43.84 sec.
100 m.	10.48 sec.	9.87 sec.

Based on the 2000 Olympics results, did specialization in these track and field events improve the competitors' performance? What three events showed the greatest improvement from specialization? Based on the textbook discussion of conditions that lead to the greatest gains from specialization, what can we infer about the decathletes' opportunity cost of training for those three events?

VI. Go to the Web: Graphing Exercises Using Interactive Graphs

Changes in Productivity and Gains from Specialization

How do changes in productivity affect overall production and the gains from specialization in an economy?
Answer:

To review the answer to this question and learn more about the use of economic theory to analyze this issue (and other macroeconomic issues), please go to the Electronic Learning Session in the Student Center at the Frank/Bernanke web site: http://www.mhhe.com/economics/frankbernanke2.

VI. Self-Test Solutions

Key Terms

1. c
2. g
3. f
4. d
5. a
6. e
7. b

Multiple-Choice Questions

1. D Jane can produce more pizzas and hamburgers than Sam and, thus, has an absolute advantage in producing both. Jane's opportunity cost of producing pizzas is 2 hamburgers, while Sam's opportunity cost of producing pizzas is 3 hamburgers. Since Jane's opportunity cost of producing pizzas is less than Sam's, she has a comparative advantage in producing pizzas.
2. C
3. E
4. A
5. C The slope of Maria's PPC equals 100/25 or 4 and Tonya's equals 50/25 or 2.
6. C By exploiting the lowest cost production first the opportunity cost of producing additional units of a good increases and, thus, the slope of PPC increases (i.e., it is bowed outward).
7. B
8. D
9. C We can only be certain that Professor Mankiw will be better off writing his textbooks rather than mowing his lawn, if he is equally happy doing either.
10. D
11. D
12. C Yolanda's opportunity cost of producing dresses is 2 shirts, while Sandra's opportunity cost of producing dresses is 2 ½ shirts. Since Yolanda's opportunity cost of producing dresses is less than Sandra's, she has a comparative advantage in producing dresses. Sandra can produce more dresses and shirts than Yolanda and, thus, has an absolute advantage in producing both. Sandra's opportunity cost of producing a shirt is 3/7 of a dress, while Yolanda's is 1/2 dress; thus, Sandra has a comparative advantage in producing shirts.
13. D

14. C The combination of 4 CDs and 2 videos produced would lie below Joseph's production possibilities curve and, thus, would be attainable, but would also be inefficient.
15. B The individual's PPC is downward sloping (i.e., negative) and a straight line (i.e., constant).
16. A The slope equals the absolute value of $(10 - 6)$ divided by $(4 - 6)$, or 4/2 which equals 2.
17. B Little Joe's opportunity cost of catching a fish is 3/5 rabbit, while his father's is 4/5 fish. Little Joe has a comparative advantage in catching fish and, thus, should specialize in fishing to catch his 10 fish. The father should catch the additional 10 fish and spend his remaining time trapping rabbits.
18. E
19. E
20. A

Short Answer Problems

1.
A.
Leather
Belts

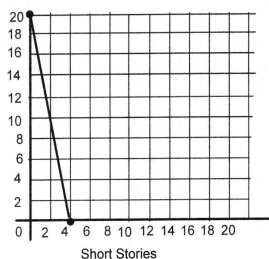

Short Stories

B. 5 leather belts
C. 5

D. unattainable

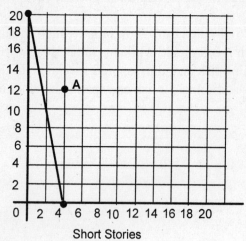

E. attainable; efficient

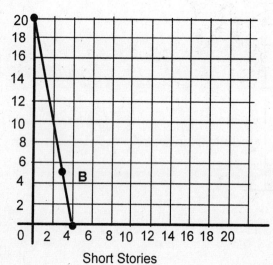

F. inefficient

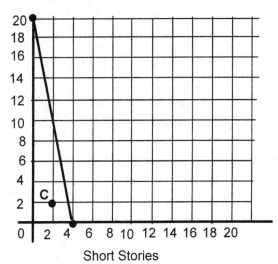

Short Stories

2.

A.

ICs for
Game
Machines

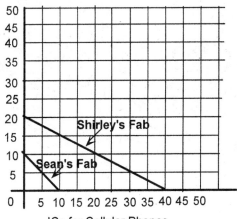

ICs for Cellular Phones

B. 1 IC for video-game machines; 1 IC for cellular phones; 1/2 IC for video-game machines; 2
   ICs for cellular phones

C. Shirley

D. Shirley; Sean

E. video-game machines; cellular phones

F.
ICs for
Game
Machines

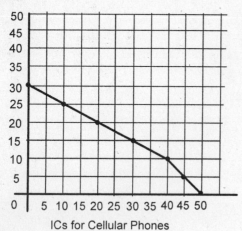

ICs for Cellular Phones

G. constant; increases; 40; increasing opportunity cost; low-hanging fruit ; principle of increasing
   Opportunity cost
H. Shirley's; Sean's
I. 30; 7 ½ ; 5; 2 ½
J. 45; 50
K. 5

3.
A.
Strawberries
(mil. tons)

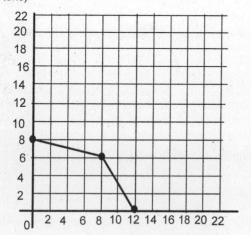

Personal Computers (1,000s)

B.

Strawberries
(mil. tons)

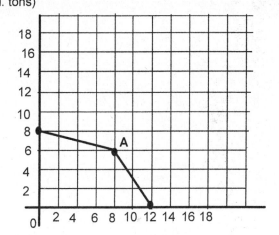

Personal Computers (1,000s)

C.

Strawberries
(mil. tons)

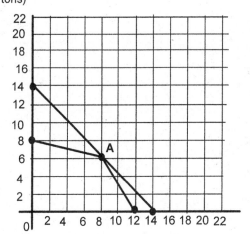

Personal Computers (1,000s)

D. 6; 8,000

E. 10; 4,000; 3

Strawberries
(mil. tons)

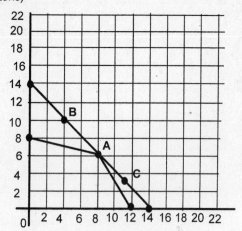

Personal Computers (1,000s)

F. 3; 11,000; 1

Strawberries
(mil. tons)

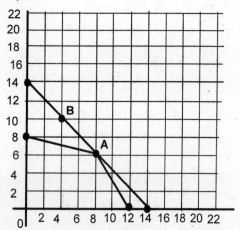

Personal Computers (1,000s)

Chapter 3
Supply and Demand: An Introduction

I. Pretest: What Do You Really Know?

Circle the letter that corresponds to the best answer. (Answers appear immediately after the final question).

1. If the price of tea increases and the demand for sugar decreases, then
   A. tea and sugar are complements.
   B. tea is a normal good and sugar is inferior.
   C. tea and sugar are substitutes.
   D. tea is an inferior goods and sugar is normal.
   E. tea and sugar are unrelated to each other.

2. If the demand for a good increases as consumer incomes rise, the good is termed a(n)
   A. inferior good.
   B. complement good.
   C. normal good.
   D. substitute good.
   E. typical good.

3. Which of the following is not a characteristic of a market in equilibrium?
   A. Quantity demanded equals quantity supplied.
   B. Excess supply is zero.
   C. All consumers are able to purchase as much as they wish.
   D. Excess demand is zero.
   E. The equilibrium price is stable, i.e., there is no pressure for it to change.

4. An increase in the demand for coal with no concurrent change in the supply of coal will result in a _____ equilibrium price and a(n) _____ equilibrium quantity.
   A. higher; lower
   B. lower; lower
   C. higher; unchanged
   D. higher; higher
   E. lower; higher

5. As the price of cookies increases, firms that produce cookies will
   A. increase the supply of cookies.
   B. increase the quantity of cookies supplied.
   C. decrease the supply of cookies.
   D. decrease the quantity of cookies supplied.
   E. leave their production unchanged.

6. Under what circumstance is it not possible for individuals to arrange a transaction that creates additional economic surplus? When
   A. price is above equilibrium.
   B. price is below equilibrium.
   C. price is at equilibrium.
   D. there is a shortage.
   E. there is a surplus.

7. When a market is operating at its point of equilibrium, the
   A. market is inefficient.
   B. output level is socially optimal.
   C. amount of "cash-on-the-table" is positive.
   D. output level is above the socially optimal level.
   E. output level is below the socially optimal level.

8. An increase in price will
   A. decrease demand.
   B. decrease quantity demanded.
   C. increase demand.
   D. increase quantity demanded.
   E. not affect quantity demanded.

9. If the price of a substitute for your product rises, it will _____ for your product.
   A. decrease demand
   B. decrease quantity demanded
   C. increase demand
   D. increase quantity demanded
   E. not affect quantity demanded

10. If an increase in income leads to a decrease in the demand for a good, the good is a(n)
   A. substitute good.
   B. complementary good.
   C. inferior good.
   D. normal good.
   E. superior good.

Solutions and Feedback to Pretest
For each question you answered incorrectly, we strongly recommend taking the time to review the appropriate material before continuing. In the table below, the relevant textbook pages are

listed for each question, as well as the pertinent Learning Objective from the following Key Point Review.

Correct Answer	Textbook Page Numbers	Learning Objective
1. A	pp. 72 - 79	5
2. C	pp. 72 - 74	5
3. C	pp. 64 - 67	4
4. D	pp. 72 - 75	6
5. B	pp. 62 - 63	3
6. C	pp. 81 - 82	7
7. B	p. 82	8
8. B	pp. 61 - 62	2
9. C	pp. 72 - 74	5
10. C	pp. 72 - 74	5

II. Key Point Review

An old joke asks, "How do you make an economist? You teach a parrot to say 'Supply and Demand,' 'Supply and Demand.'" The importance of understanding supply and demand, both for success in the classroom as well as in the business and political environment, cannot be overstated.

Learning Objective 1: Discuss the two alternative institutional arrangements for answering basic economic questions. Define a market.

From the beginning, man has had to answer certain economic questions: "What goods will be produced?"; "How will the goods be produced?" and "Who will receive the goods?" The institutional structure used to supply the answers comes in two flavors. Centralized decision making by an individual or a small group accounts for one alternative. The former Soviet Union and many Eastern European countries practiced central planning for most of the 20th century. The only remaining examples are Cuba, North Korea, and China. The other arrangement is decentralized decision-making by individuals in the context of private markets, commonly referred to as capitalism or free enterprise. No country practices perfect capitalism: government intervention exists in all free market economies. By and large, decisions are left in the hands of individuals. A **market** consists of all the buyers and sellers of a particular good or service.

Learning Objective 2: Understand the precise nature of what the demand curve does and does not illustrate. Define the two effects that give the demand curve its shape and the buyer's reservation price.

The **demand curve** of a good shows the total quantity of that good buyers are willing and able to purchase at each possible price. The nature of the relationship between the price of a good and the quantity is exactly what you know from experience. At higher prices, consumers wish to buy less and, at lower prices, consumers wish to buy more. The reason consumers behave this way stems from two different effects. First, as the price of a good rises, consumers switch to substitute goods. If the campus bookstore raises its prices for textbooks, students will investigate prices at off-campus bookstores or on the Internet. The change in quantity demanded that results from switching to alternative goods is called the **substitution effect**. The other effect is called the **income effect**: when a price changes, the purchasing power of a consumer's income changes. If you were to buy the same number of units of a good after its price had fallen, then you would have some unspent income. Thus, you may use this "savings" to purchase more of the good. Note that both effects move in the same direction. A price decrease causes consumers to (1) buy fewer substitute goods and more of the good itself and (2) buy more of the good itself because of an increase in the purchasing power of a consumer's income. The demand curve is, therefore, downward sloping. A negative, or inverse, relationship exists between price and the quantity demanded.

An easily overlooked feature of the demand curve involves an implication of the price-quantity combinations. Suppose a consumer's demand curve shows that 1 unit of a good is demanded when the price is $3. If the market price (the price in the store) is $3.50, the consumer would pass up the purchase. If the market price is, say, $2.50, the consumer would make the purchase, and possibly buy more than 1 unit. Each price along a buyer's demand curve is the *maximum* price he will pay. The **buyer's reservation price** is the largest dollar amount the buyer would be willing to pay for a good.

Learning Objective 3: Describe what is meant by the supply curve and give a definition of the seller's reservation price.
The **supply curve** of a good is a curve that relates the total quantity of the good producers are willing and able to sell at each possible price. It is based on the assumption that producers will be willing to sell the good as long as the price they receive is sufficient to cover their opportunity costs. Since some people have low opportunity costs, other have moderate opportunity costs, and still others have high opportunity costs, supply curves must slope upward. At low prices, only the low-opportunity-cost individuals will find it worthwhile to produce the good. To acquire more of the good, more individuals must be drawn into production. These are the people with moderate opportunity costs. Only with a higher price will the moderate-opportunity-cost individuals find it beneficial to become producers. To induce the high-opportunity-cost individuals to join the market, an even higher price must be forthcoming. Thus, a positive, or direct relationship exists between price and the quantity supplied. The **seller's reservation price** is the smallest dollar amount for which a seller would be willing to sell an additional unit, usually equal to the seller's marginal costs.

Learning Objective 4: Define equilibrium, the equilibrium price and quantity, and market equilibrium. Discuss the consequences of excess supply and excess demand and describe the process of equilibration in the marketplace.
The idea of **equilibrium**—when the forces within a system cancel each other out, resulting in an unchanging situation—appears in both the physical and social sciences. In economics, the forces are supply and demand and the system is the marketplace. The **equilibrium price** and **equilibrium quantity** of a good are determined at the point where the demand curve intersects the supply curve or where quantity demanded equals quantity supplied. A **market equilibrium** occurs when all buyers and sellers are satisfied with their respective quantities at the market price.

> **Note:** "Satisfied" does not mean that buyers would not like a lower price or that sellers would be displeased with a higher price. It simply means that those buyers willing to pay the equilibrium price can acquire exactly the amount they wish. Likewise, sellers who are willing to accept the equilibrium price can sell the exact amount they

At prices above the equilibrium price, buyers wish to acquire a relatively small amount of a good, but many suppliers can cover their opportunity costs, so a large amount of the good is produced. When quantity supplied exceeds quantity demanded, the market experiences **excess supply** or a surplus. Since suppliers are unable to sell all they have produced, they are dissatisfied with the current market situation. When searching for ways to correct the problem, the most obvious solution is to lower price. Lowering the price will induce some consumers to make purchases that were passed over at the higher price. Similarly, the lower price means some firms will no longer cover their opportunity costs and will leave the market. The net result is for price to be lower and the difference between quantity supplied and quantity demanded to narrow. Firms will continue to reduce price until excess supply is zero. At this point, firms will have reached the equilibrium price and will be satisfied with the market situation.

Conversely, at prices below the equilibrium price, buyers wish to acquire a relatively large amount of the good, but few suppliers can cover their opportunity costs, so only a small amount of the good is produced. When quantity demanded exceeds quantity supplied, the market experiences **excess demand** or a shortage. Since buyers are unable to acquire all they wish at the going price, they are unhappy with the current market situation. Consumers are dissatisfied; some are unable to acquire the good at the going price. These unfulfilled consumers have an incentive to offer a higher price to enlarge the chance that they will receive some of the production. The higher price will drive some of the consumers out of the market while encouraging new suppliers to join the market. The net result is for price to be higher and the difference between quantity demanded and quantity supplied to shrink. Consumers will continue to offer higher prices until excess demand is zero. When this point is reached, the equilibrium price will have been achieved, and consumers will be satisfied with the market situation.

Learning Objective 5: Distinguish between a change in quantity demanded and a change in demand; repeat for a change in quantity supplied and a change in supply. List and analyze the variables responsible for shifting the demand curve; do the same for the supply curve. Two different kinds of change can be illustrated by the demand and supply curves. A **change in quantity demanded** is a movement along a demand curve in response to a change in the price of the good. A **change in demand** occurs when the entire demand curve shifts. Identical concepts exist for the supply curve. A **change in quantity supplied** is a movement along a supply curve in response to a change in the price of the good. A **change in supply** describes a shift of the entire supply curve.

Note: The importance of having a clear understanding of the difference between a "change in quantity demanded" and a "change in demand" cannot be overstated. A change in the price of the good is the only variable that can cause a change in quantity demanded. All other variables that influence demand (income, prices of related goods) result in a change in demand. The same distinction holds for a change in quantity supplied versus a change in supply.

Several variables can induce the demand curve to shift. Prices of related goods affect consumer demand for a particular good. Two different goods, M and N, can be related in one of two ways: substitutes or complements. Being substitutes means that M and N are similar and can be used in place of one another. Dell computers and Compaq computers are substitutes. Formally, two goods are classified as **substitutes** if an increase in the price of one causes an increase in demand (rightward curve shift) for the other. If Dell raises the price of its computers, demand for Compaq computers will shift to the right. Being complements means that M and N are typically used together. VCRs and TVs are complements. Two goods are considered **complements** if an increase in the demand for one causes a decrease in demand (leftward curve shift) for the other. If the price of TVs increases, consumers will purchase fewer TVs and, as a result, demand fewer VCRs regardless of price of VCRs. The buyer's income acts as an independent influence on the amount of a good purchased. A **normal good** is one for which demand increases (curve shifts to the right) when consumer incomes rise. Most, but not all, goods and services follow this pattern. An **inferior good** is one for which demand decreases (curve shifts to the left) when consumer incomes rise.

A different set of variables causes the supply to shift. The first variable is the price of input used in the production of the good. All firms make use of some labor input, so wages are the most common input price. If wages rise, the cost of producing the good will rise. This means that a higher price will be required in order for firms to continue producing as much as they were before the wage increase. Alternatively, at the same price as before the wage increase, fewer units will be supplied. In either case, the previous relationship between price and quantity supplied has been altered; at any price, firms are willing and able to produce less of the good. A decrease in supply has occurred, and the entire supply curve has shifted to the left. The second variable that causes supply to shift is technological change. Technological change reduces the cost of production in some fashion. As a result, firms can receive a lower price and continue to make as much money as they were prior to the technological change. If firms were to receive the same price as they were before the change, they will now produce more. An increase in supply has occurred, and the entire supply curve has shifted to the right.

Learning Objective 6: Use the supply and demand model to examine how various shifts of the supply and demand curves affect the equilibrium price and quantity.

The supply and demand model allows four strong statements to be made about the direction of changes in the equilibrium price and quantity when supply and demand shift. If demand increases (rightward shift) and supply is constant, then the equilibrium price and quantity will rise. If demand decreases (leftward shift) and supply is constant, then the equilibrium price and quantity will fall. On the other hand, if supply increases (rightward shift) and demand is constant, the equilibrium price will fall, and the equilibrium quantity will rise. But if supply decreases (leftward shift) with demand constant, the equilibrium price will rise and the equilibrium quantity will fall. Finally, when both supply and demand shift at the same time, the direction of change will be known for only price or quantity, but not both. For example, if both supply and demand increase (rightward shift), it is certain that the equilibrium quantity will rise. But the new equilibrium price could be higher, lower, or unchanged. Which of the three possibilities for price will come to bear depends on the relative magnitudes of the supply and demand shifts. If the supply increase is very small and the demand increase is quite large, then the new equilibrium price will be higher. As another example, suppose demand decreases and supply increases. The new equilibrium price must be lower, but the new equilibrium quantity could be larger, smaller, or unchanged. It again depends on the relative size of the supply shift compared to the demand shift. A small decrease in demand coupled with a large increase in supply would produce a new equilibrium quantity larger than the original.

Learning Objective 7: Define buyer's surplus, seller's surplus, and total surplus. What is meant by the phrase "cash on the table"?
Assuming all economic transactions are voluntary, trades between buyers and sellers can only occur if both parties realize an economic surplus. The **buyer's surplus** equals the difference between the buyer's reservation price and the price actually paid. Similarly, the difference between the actual price and the seller's reservation price defines the **seller's surplus**. The **total surplus** is the sum of the buyer's and seller's surpluses or the difference between the buyer's reservation price and the seller's reservation price. Whenever a market is in disequilibrium (excess demand or excess supply), it is always possible to identify trades that have not been made for which the total surplus is positive. That is to say, there is "cash on the table," a metaphor for unrealized opportunities.

Learning Objective 8: Define the socially optimal quantity of a good and economic efficiency. Discuss the Efficiency Principle and the Equilibrium Principle.
The quantity of a good that results in the maximum total economic surplus defines the **socially optimal quantity of a good**. If production of a good is less than optimal, then increasing production will increase the economic surplus. Alternatively, if the optimal amount is exceeded by actual production, economic surplus can be increased by lowering production. **Economic efficiency** exists when all goods and services produced by an economy are at their socially optimal levels. The **Efficiency Principle** indicates the economic efficiency is an important social goal, as it ensures the size of the slice of the economic pie available to everyone is as large as possible. In future chapters, circumstances will be analyzed in which the goal of efficiency causes problems requiring market intervention. The **Equilibrium Principle** summarizes a basic idea: A market in equilibrium leaves no unexploited opportunities for individuals, but may not exploit all gains achievable through collective action.

III. Self-Test

<u>Key Terms</u>
Match the term in the right-hand column with the appropriate definition in the left-hand column by placing the letter of the term in the blank in front of its definition. (Answers are given at the end of the chapter.)

1. ____ The amount of a good or service that will be exchanged when quantity demanded equals quantity supplied.
2. ____ When buyers are willing and able to purchase more of a good or service at each and every price.
3. ____ Goods or services for which an increase in the buyer's income causes an increase in demand.
4. ____ A graph that illustrates the total quantity buyers are willing and able to purchase at each and every price.
5. ____ The response by a manufacturing firm when the price of a good changes.
6. ____ The market outcome when the price is below the equilibrium value.
7. ____ The set containing all buyers and sellers of a particular good.
8. ____ A circumstance where all the forces that influence a system are canceled by each other, resulting in a stable situation.
9. ____ A graph that illustrates the total quantity sellers are willing to produce at each and every price.
10. ____ The market outcome when the price is above the equilibrium value.
11. ____ Goods or services for which an increase in the buyer's income causes a decrease in demand.
12. ____ The response of consumers when the price of a good changes.
13. ____ Goods for which a price increase of one leads to a decrease in demand for the other.
14. ____ When sellers change the amount of a good they are willing to produce at each and every price.
15. ____ The market outcome when all buyers and sellers are satisfied with their respective quantities at the market price.
16. ____ Goods for which an increase in the price of one causes an increase in demand for the other.
17. ____ The price that results when quantity demanded equals quantity supplied.
18. ____ The maximum dollar amount the buyer is willing to pay for a good or service.
19. ____ The difference between the buyer's reservation price and the market price.
20. ____ The change in the quantity demanded due to a change in the purchasing power of buyer's income, resulting from a price change.

a. buyer's reservation price
b. buyer's surplus
c. cash on the table
d. change in demand
e. change in quantity demanded
f. change in quantity supplied
g. change in supply
h. complements
i. demand curve
j. efficiency
k. equilibrium
l. equilibrium price
m. equilibrium quantity
n. excess demand
o. excess supply
p. income effect
q. inferior good
r. market
s. market equilibrium
t. normal good

21. ___ The difference between the market price and the seller's reservation price.
22. ___ The change in the quantity demanded due to buyer switching to or away from substitute goods as a result of a price change.
23. ___ The outcome when all markets operate at their socially optimal quantity.

24. ___ The sum of the buyer's surplus and the seller's surplus.
25. ___ The minimum dollar amount the firm is willing to accept to produce another unit.
26. ___ The output level which maximizes the total economic surplus.
27. ___ A metaphor for unexploited opportunities.
28. ___ A maximum legal price for a good or service.

u. price ceiling
v. seller's reservation price

w. seller's surplus
x. socially optimal quantity

y. substitutes
z. substitution effect
aa. supply curve
bb. total surplus

Multiple-Choice Questions
Circle the letter that corresponds to the best answer. (Answers are given at the end of the chapter.)

1. Which of the following is not a characteristic of a market in equilibrium?
    A. Quantity demanded equals quantity supplied.
    B. Excess supply is zero.
    C. All consumers are able to purchase as much as they wish.
    D. Excess demand is zero.
    E. The equilibrium price is stable, i.e., there is no pressure for it to change.

2. If the price of an item falls, then one would expect to see
    A. an increase in demand.
    B. an increase in quantity demanded.
    C. a decrease in quantity supplied.
    D. a decrease in supply.
    E. fewer consumers.

3. Which of the following could never be a feature of an unregulated market in a state of disequilibrium?
    A. Excess supply.
    B. A stable price.
    C. Excess demand.
    D. Changes in the equilibrium quantity.
    E. The bidding up of the price.

4. Assume that government imposes a price control on butter, i.e., the price of butter can not rise above a certain level. The most likely outcome of this policy is
    A. the quality of butter will rise.
    B. farmers and ranchers will increase their holdings of dairy cows.
    C. more individuals will be motivated to enter dairy farming.
    D. the butter market will exhibit chronic excess demand.

E. the butter market will exhibit chronic excess supply.

5. Which of the following is not a determinant of demand for gasoline, i.e., does not cause the demand curve to shift?
   A. The price of gasoline.
   B. The price of diesel.
   C. The price of automobiles.
   D. The quantity of gasoline supplied.
   E. Consumers' incomes.

6. If, when the price of X increases, the demand for Y decreases, one can conclude that
   A. X and Y are complements.
   B. X and Y are substitutes.
   C. X and Y are normal.
   D. X and Y are inferior.
   E. X and Y are superior.

7. Which of the following would cause an increase in quantity supplied?
   A. The price that farmers receive for their crops rises.
   B. The United Auto Workers negotiates a wage increase for its union members.
   C. The price firms pay for liability insurance falls.
   D. New, faster computer processors are introduced.
   E. OPEC limits the production of crude oil.

8. At the beginning of the fall semester, college towns experience large increases in their populations, causing a(n)
   A. increase in the quantity of apartments demanded.
   B. increase in the supply of apartments.
   C. increase in the demand for apartments.
   D. decrease in the quantity of apartments supplied.
   E. decrease in the supply of apartments.

9. Increases in the prices firms pay for inputs causes
   A. a decrease in quantity supplied.
   B. an increase in supply.
   C. an increase in quantity supplied.
   D. a decrease in supply.
   E. output prices to fall.

10. In a free market, if the price of a good is above the equilibrium price, then
    A. government needs to set a higher price.
    B. suppliers, dissatisfied with growing inventories, will raise the price.
    C. demanders, wanting to ensure they acquire the good, will bid the price lower.
    D. government needs to set a lower price.
    E. suppliers, dissatisfied with growing inventories, will lower the price.

11. The demand curve illustrates that consumers
    A. tend to purchase more of a good as its price rises.
    B. purchase name brand products more frequently than generic products.
    C. tend to purchase more of a good as its price falls.
    D. purchase more of a good as their incomes fall.
    E. purchase more of a good as their incomes rise.

12. One observes that the equilibrium price of coffee falls, and the equilibrium quantity falls.
    Which of the following best fits the observed data?
    A. An increase in demand with supply constant.
    B. An increase in demand coupled with a decrease in supply.
    C. An increase in demand coupled with an increase in supply.
    D. A decrease in demand with supply constant.
    E. Demand constant and an increase in supply.

13. A decrease in supply, holding demand constant, will always result in a(n)
    A. higher equilibrium price.
    B. lower equilibrium price.
    C. larger equilibrium quantity.
    D. larger quantity demanded.
    E. indeterminate change in the equilibrium quantity.

14. If, in a particular market, all unexploited opportunities have been realized, one can conclude
    that
    A. government regulation has proven successful.
    B. the market is in equilibrium.
    C. demanders are unable to find adequate amounts of the good.
    D. excess demand is present.
    E. excess supply is present.

15. Suppose the price of beer increases. One would expect to see in the wine market a(n)
    A. increase in the quantity of wine demanded.
    B. increase in the demand for wine.
    C. decrease in the quantity of wine demanded.
    D. decrease in the demand for wine.
    E. indeterminate change in the wine market.

16. If the wages paid to workers rise, one would expect to see a(n)
    A. increase in quantity supplied.
    B. increase in supply.
    C. increase in demand.
    D. decrease in quantity supplied.
    E. decrease in supply.

17. Which of the following is not true of a demand curve?
    A. It has a negative slope.
    B. It shows the amount consumers are willing and able to purchase at various prices, holding other factors constant.
    C. It relates the price of an item to the quantity demanded of that item.
    D. It relates the price of an item to the demand for that item.
    E. It shows that consumers tend to purchase less of a good as its price rises.

18. When supply for a good decreases, consumers respond by
    A. decreasing their demand.
    B. increasing their preferences for the good.
    C. decreasing their quantity demanded.
    D. increasing their quantity demanded.
    E. purchasing more complementary goods.

19. As the price of a good rises,
    A. firms earn larger profits.
    B. more firms can cover their opportunity costs of producing the good.
    C. firms find they can raise price by even more.
    D. consumers become more willing to purchases the good.
    E. government regulation becomes more justified.

20. In general, when the supply curve shifts to the left and demand is constant, then the
    A. market cannot reestablish an equilibrium.
    B. equilibrium price will fall.
    C. equilibrium quantity will rise.
    D. equilibrium price will rise.
    E. quantity supplied falls.

21. Suppose that both the equilibrium price and quantity of mustard rise. The most consistent explanation for these observations is
    A. a decrease in demand for mustard with no change in supply.
    B. a decrease in the supply of mustard with no change in demand.
    C. a decrease in demand for mustard and a decrease in the supply of mustard.
    D. an increase in demand for mustard with no change in supply.
    E. an increase in the supply of mustard with no change in demand.

22. A market in disequilibrium would feature
    A. a stable price.
    B. consumers able to purchase all they wish at the market price.
    C. a stable quantity.
    D. either excess supply or excess demand.
    E. firms able to sell all they wish at the market price.

23. "As the price of personal computers continues to fall, demand increases." This headline is inaccurate because
   A. a change in the price of personal computers shifts the demand curve.
   B. a change in the price of personal computers shifts the supply curve.
   C. the statement is backwards: increased demand leads to lower prices.
   D. falling prices for personal computers increases quantity demanded, not demand.
   E. falling prices for personal computers increases quantity supplied.

24. A market comprised of a downward sloping demand curve and an upward sloping supply curve is said to be stable because
   A. price will never change.
   B. quantity will never change.
   C. demand will never change.
   D. supply will never change.
   E. at any price other than equilibrium, forces in the market move price towards the equilibrium.

25. Which of the following statements expresses the justification for making efficiency the first goal of economic interaction?
   A. Efficiency gives the poor an incentive to improve their economic status.
   B. Since consensus on what is a fair distribution of goods is impossible, efficiency is the next best goal.
   C. People are not really concerned about the problems of the poor.
   D. It is too difficult to pursue more than one goal at a time.
   E. Efficiency maximizes total economic surplus and thereby allows other goals to be more fully achieved.

Short Answer Problems
(Answers and solutions are given at the end of the chapter.)

1. Demand, Supply, and Market Equilibrium.
The following question tests your understanding of quantity demanded, quantity supplied, and market equilibrium applied to the market for memory chips used in personal computers.

Price of a 128 MB SDRAM Memory Chip	Quantity of 128 MB SDRAM demanded (in millions)	Quantity of 128 MB SDRAM supplied (in millions)
$75	45	6
$100	21	11
$150	15	15
$200	7	23
$225	4	36

   A. As the price of 128 MB memory chips rises, quantity demanded (rises/falls) _____.
      When the price of memory chips falls, quantity supplied (increases/decreases) _____.

B. In this market, an equilibrium occurs at a price of _____. At this price, (quantity demanded/demand) _____ equals (quantity supplied/supply) _____ with _____ million units exchanged.

C. At a price of $225, (supply/quantity supplied) _____ exceeds (demand/quantity demanded) _____ by an amount equal to _____ units. The market is thus experiencing (excess supply/excess demand) _____. As a result, (producers/consumers) _____ will (lower/raise) _____ the price of memory chips.

D. At a price of $100, (demand/quantity demanded) _____ exceeds (supply/quantity supplied) _____ by an amount equal to _____ units. The market is thus experiencing (excess supply/excess demand) _____. As a result, (producers/consumers) _____ will (lower/raise) _____ the price of memory chips.

2. Graphical Analysis of Demand and Supply Curve Shifts

Understanding which variables cause shifts in the demand curve or the supply curve and how these shifts are illustrated in a graph are major objectives of this chapter. The following questions helps to assess your comprehension of demand and supply shifts.

A. A shift from demand curve D_1 to D_2 indicates that (demand/quantity demanded) _____ has (increased/decreased)_____. This shift could be caused by an increase in the price of a (substitute/complement) _____.

B. A shift from supply curve S_2 to S_1 indicates that (supply/quantity supplied) _____ has (increased/decreased)_____. This shift could be caused by an increase in the (price of an input/quality of technology) _____.

3. Changes in Demand/Supply versus Changes in Quantity Demanded/Supplied

To fully understand how markets function, the difference between "changes in demand" and "changes in quantity demanded" must be clear in your mind. A similar distinction applies to supply and must be clear as well. A graph of a market shows the difference most plainly and also allows predictions to be made about market adjustments.

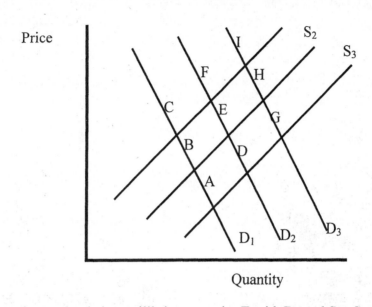

A. Assume the market is in equilibrium at point E with D_2 and S_2. Suppose the market equilibrium changes to point B. This change reflects a (decrease in demand/decrease in quantity demanded) _____ coupled with a (decrease in supply/decrease in quantity supplied) _____.

B. Assume the market is in equilibrium at point E with D_2 and S_2. Suppose the market equilibrium changes to point D. This changes stems from an (increase in demand/increase in quantity demanded) _____ combined with an (increase in supply/increase in quantity supplied) _____.

C. Assume the market is in equilibrium at point H with D_3 and S_2. If demand remains constant and supply decreases, the new equilibrium price will be (higher/lower) _____ and the new equilibrium quantity will be (smaller/larger) _____.

D. Assume the market is in equilibrium at point E with D_2 and S_2. A simultaneous decrease in supply and an increase in demand would move the market to a new equilibrium at point (F/H/I) _____. The equilibrium price (falls/rises) _____ and the equilibrium quantity (falls/rises) _____. Without the aid of the above graph, only the (price/quantity) _____ change is certain to occur.

4. Price Controls and Market Equilibrium

The final problem focuses on your understanding of price controls and the effect they have on the marketplace. Consider the following market data for White Lightin', a famous type of moonshine.

Price of a 32-oz. jug of White Lightin'	Quantity of 32-oz. jugs of White Lightin' demanded (thousands)	Quantity of 32-oz. jugs of White Lightin' supplied (thousands)
$1	100	10
$2	75	35
$3	50	50
$4	25	65
$5	5	95

A. In an unregulated legal environment, the equilibrium price of White Lightin' is ($4/$3) _____ and the equilibrium quantity is (50/65) ____ units.

B. Suppose the government deems White Lightin' a necessity and, to ensure widespread access to it, imposes a price ceiling of $1. Quantity demanded is now (75/100) _____ units, and quantity supplied is (10/50) _____ units, resulting in (excess supply/excess demand) _____.

C. Suppose government rethinks it policy and decides that White Lightin' is not a necessity, but producers of White Lightin' need help to remain in business. Government now imposes a price of $5 (called a price floor). Quantity demanded is now (50/5) _____ units and quantity supplied is (95/65) _____. The market will now experience (excess supply/excess demand) _____.

IV. Economic Naturalist Application

With a little creativity, one can use the model of supply and demand to describe situations not normally thought of as markets. Try developing a demand and supply model for the following interactions: marriage; size of family; illegal drugs; and prostitution. In each case, include the proper price that the supply and demand curves are based upon and also the variables that cause systematic shifts in the demand and supply curves.

V. Go to the Web: Graphing Exercises Using Interactive Graphs

For practice using interactive graphs, please go to the Electronic Learning Session in the Student Center at the Frank/Bernanke web site: http://www.mhhe.com/economics/frankbernanke2.

VI. Self-Test Solutions

Key Terms

1. m
2. d
3. t

4. i
5. f
6. n
7. r
8. k
9. aa
10. o
11. q
12. e
13. h
14. g
15. s
16. y
17. l
18. a
19. b
20. p
21. w
22. z
23. j
24. bb
25. v
26. x
27. c
28. u

Multiple-Choice Questions

1. C
2. B
3. B
4. D
5. D
6. A
7. A
8. C
9. D
10. E
11. C
12. D
13. A
14. B
15. B
16. E
17. D
18. C

19. B
20. D
21. D
22. D
23. D
24. E
25. E

Short Answer Problems

1.
A. falls; decreases
B. $150; quantity demanded; quantity supplied; 15
C. quantity supplied; quantity demanded; 32 million; excess supply; producers; lower
D. quantity demanded; quantity supplied; 10 million; excess demand; consumers; raise

2.
A. demand; increased; substitute
B. supply; decreased; price of an input

3.
A. decrease in demand; decrease in quantity supplied
B. increase in quantity demanded; increase in supply
C. higher; smaller
D. rises; rises; price

4.
A. $3; 50.
B. 100; 10; excess demand.
C. 5; 95; excess supply

Chapter 4
Elasticity

I. Pretest: What Do You Really Know?
Circle the letter that corresponds to the best answer. (Answers appear immediately after the final question).

1. If the demand curve for espresso is $P = 20 - 5Q$, what are total revenues when $P = \$5$?
   A. $15
   B. $25
   C. $30
   D. $35
   E. $50

2. The correct mathematical statement of the price elasticity of demand is
   A. $(\Delta P/P)/(\Delta Q/Q)$.
   B. $(\Delta Q/Q)/(\Delta P/P)$.
   C. $\Delta P/\Delta Q$.
   D. $\Delta Q/\Delta P$.
   E. $(\Delta P/P)/\Delta Q$.

3. Assume the short-run price elasticity of demand for electricity is 0.03 and the long-run elasticity is 1.1. The short-run elasticity is _____ and the long-run elasticity is _____.
   A. elastic; elastic
   B. elastic; inelastic
   C. inelastic; unit elastic
   D. inelastic; elastic
   E. inelastic; inelastic

4. The responsiveness of quantity demanded for good M when the price of good N changes is measured by the
   A. price elasticity of demand.
   B. income elasticity of demand.
   C. price elasticity of supply.
   D. preference elasticity of demand.
   E. cross-price elasticity of demand.

5. If the percentage change in quantity demanded is zero for any percentage change in the price, demand is classified as
    A. inelastic.
    B. perfectly inelastic.
    C. unit elastic.
    D. perfectly elastic.
    E. elastic.

6. Generally speaking, demand for a good will be more inelastic
    A. if few substitutes exist.
    B. when the good represents a large share of the consumer's budget.
    C. in the long run.
    D. when many substitutes exist.
    E. if the good is a necessity.

7. If the percentage change in quantity supplied is greater than the percentage change in price, supply is classified as
    A. perfectly inelastic.
    B. inelastic.
    C. unit elastic.
    D. elastic.
    E. perfectly elastic.

8. If the value of the price elasticity of supply is infinity, supply is categorized as being
    A. perfectly elastic.
    B. elastic.
    C. unit elastic.
    D. inelastic.
    E. perfectly inelastic.

9. If factors of production are relatively immobile, the price elasticity of supply will tend to be
    A. larger.
    B. perfectly elastic.
    C. smaller.
    D. elastic.
    E. unaffected.

10. A normal good will have an income elasticity that is
    A. negative.
    B. positive.
    C. zero.
    D. less than 1.
    E. greater than 1.

Solutions and Feedback to Pretest
For each question you answered incorrectly, we strongly recommend taking the time to review the appropriate material before continuing. In the table below, the relevant textbook pages are listed for each question as well as the pertinent Learning Objective from the following Key Point Review.

Correct Answer	Textbook Page Numbers	Learning Objective
1. A	pp. 101-05	4
2. B	pp. 92-93	1
3. D	pp. 92-93	1
4. E	pp. 105-06	5
5. B	pp. 96-101	3
6. A	pp. 93-96	2
7. D	pp. 106-09	6
8. A	pp. 106-09	6
9. C	pp. 109-13	7
10. B	pp. 105-06	5

II. Key Point Review

Learning Objective 1: Define the price elasticity of demand. List and define the three categories of elasticity.
Having established a negative relationship between price and quantity demanded, now the issue is by *how much* does the quantity demanded change in response to a price change. For example, would a 5 percent increase in the price of food cause a greater than or less than 5 percent decrease in the quantity of food demanded? The **price elasticity of demand** measures the percentage change in quantity demanded as a result of a 1 percent change in the price of the good. Since the change in quantity and the change in price are of opposite signs, the price elasticity is always a negative number. To ease interpretation, one refers to the absolute value of the price elasticity (i.e., ignore the minus sign). A price elasticity of 0.5 is read as "a 1 percent increase in the price of this good results in a one-half percent decline in quantity demanded." Price elasticities are classified in one of three ways. If the price elasticity is greater than one in absolute value, demand is termed **elastic**. If the price elasticity is less than one in absolute value, demand is called **inelastic**. If the price elasticity is exactly one, then demand is called **unit elastic**.

Learning Objective 2: Discuss the factors affecting the size of the price elasticity of demand. Cite some actual estimates of the price elasticity of demand.
Why would one good have elastic demand and another have inelastic demand? Several factors influence the size of the price elasticity of demand and therefore whether it is elastic or inelastic. First, and most important, is the number and degree of closeness of substitute goods. If a good has many substitutes the price elasticity of demand will be relatively large. A good with few substitutes will have a relatively small demand elasticity. As an illustration of how substitutes affect the size of the price elasticity of demand, consider the market for peanut butter. One can

ignore the brand names of peanut butter and think of it as a single good or one can think of each individual brand name as a unique good. The elasticity of demand for a specific brand name peanut butter must be larger than the elasticity for peanut butter itself. For a specific brand name peanut butter, one can substitute all other brands of peanut butter (making the elasticity larger). Presumably, one brand name peanut butter is a reasonable substitute for another brand name. For the single good, peanut butter, the number and degree of closeness of substitutes is considerably less: lunch meats, other sandwich spreads, or Spam (making the elasticity smaller).

The second factor determining the size of demand elasticity involves the importance of the item in the consumer's budget. Rent (or a mortgage payment) is the largest single expenditure most consumers make. If rents were to increase by 50 percent, consumers would have to make large changes in their lifestyles to accommodate the price increase. Few would remain in their existing apartment. However, a 50 percent increase in the price of toothpicks would likely cause only minor changes in the number of toothpicks purchased. Thus, the consumer's response to the toothpick price change would be small and hence demand for toothpicks would be relatively inelastic. The consumer's response to the rent change would result in large changes, and hence demand for apartments would be relatively elastic. The more important the item is in the consumer's budget, the more elastic demand for the item will be.

The final factor is time. The longer consumers have to adjust to a price change, the more elastic their demand will be. For example, if the price of gasoline doubled tonight, most consumers would likely make the same driving choices tomorrow as they did today. But 2 years from now, consumers might have purchased a more fuel-efficient car, moved closer to work or school, started a car pool, and so on. Thus, demand in the short run would be relatively inelastic but in the long run it would be relatively elastic. The empirical results presented in the textbook indicate that demand for automobiles is elastic (1.63) while demand for coffee is inelastic (0.25).

Hint: Economists use the terms elastic and inelastic in several ways. The first is to classify a numerical value. When an actual estimate is available one can definitely categorize demand as elastic (greater than 1) or inelastic (less than 1). The second and more common usage is too describe how a given factor affects the size of numerical value. Regardless of whether the estimated value is greater than 1 or less than 1, any factor that increases the size of the estimate results in demand that is *more elastic* or *less inelastic*. Factors that decrease the size of the elasticity value cause demand to be *more inelastic* or *less elastic*. Thus, when one says demand has become more elastic, the degree of consumer responsiveness to price changes has grown but does not guarantee that demand is elastic. Finally, when good A is said to be *relatively elastic* and good B is *relatively inelastic* it means the size of good A's elasticity exceeds good B's value. It does not mean, necessarily, that good A has elastic demand while good B has inelastic demand.

Learning Objective 3: Calculate the price elasticity of demand using a linear demand curve. Discuss the pattern of the elasticity along a linear demand curve. Define the two special cases of the price elasticity of demand.

The calculation of a price elasticity of demand requires the application of a formula. Consider a linear (straight line) demand curve of the form $P = b - m \times Q$, where b is the "y-intercept" and m is the slope. The price elasticity is calculated as $\varepsilon = (1/m) \times (P/Q)$. Again, one ignores the minus sign associated with the slope, which has the same effect as leaving the minus sign in place and then taking the absolute value. An interesting feature of the price elasticity of demand along a linear demand curve involves the way it changes. Starting at the y-intercept, where prices are relatively high and quantity demanded is relatively small, the measured price elasticity is elastic (greater than 1). As one move down the demand curve to lower prices and greater quantities demanded, the measured price elasticity gets progressively smaller (more inelastic). In fact at the midpoint price-quantity combination, the price elasticity is exactly 1. Thereafter, it is inelastic. So while the slope of the linear demand curve is constant, the price elasticity is not constant, growing smaller as one moves down the demand curve. For a horizontal demand curve, the slope is zero and hence the elasticity is infinite ($1/0 = \infty$). If the price elasticity of demand is infinite, then one has **perfectly elastic demand**. A vertical demand curve has an infinite slope and thus its price elasticity is zero ($1/\infty = 0$). **Perfectly inelastic demand** occurs when the price elasticity equals zero.

Learning Objective 4: Define total revenues and total expenditures. Explore the relationship between the price elasticity of demand and total revenues.

The product of a firm's per unit price and the quantity sold measures the firm's **total revenue**. The sum of all expenditures made by consumers for a good or service defines **total expenditures**. The two measures must be identical: the amount of dollars the firm collects must be equal to the amount buyers spent. Suppose demand for a particular product is given by $P = 10 - 3*Q$ with a price of $4. Substituting for P, one finds Q = 2. Total revenues equal $8 (= $4*2) which is also the extent of total expenditures. The relationship between changes in total revenues and changes in price depends on the price elasticity of demand. A firm that faces inelastic demand will find that price reductions lower total revenues, while a price increase will enlarge the pool of revenues. When demand is inelastic, the %ΔQ is always smaller in absolute value than the %ΔP. The firm is better off by raising its price because quantity demanded will not fall by much. A price decrease, on the other hand, will result in lower revenues because consumers will not purchase much more of the good in question. A firm facing elastic demand forms the exact opposite conclusion. Elastic demand means the absolute value of %ΔQ is always larger than %ΔP. Now the firm is better off to offer the consumer a lower price, which stimulates a larger increase in quantity demanded and thereby enlarges the firm's total revenues. A price hike will reduce quantity demanded by more than the price increase, leading to smaller total revenues.

Learning Objective 5: Define and interpret the cross-price elasticity of demand and the income elasticity of demand.

The **cross-price elasticity of demand** measures the percentage change in quantity demanded of one good when the price of another good changes by 1 percent. Recall that two goods can be used in place of each other (substitutes) or they can be used together (complements). If two goods are substitutes, their cross-price elasticity must be a positive number. If two goods are complements, the cross-price elasticity must be negative. The **income elasticity of demand** measures the percentage change in quantity demanded of a good when incomes change by 1 percent. If an increase in income causes an increase in quantity demanded (a normal good), then the income elasticity of demand will be positive. If a good is inferior—an increase in income causes a decline in quantity demanded—then the income elasticity will be negative.

Note: Unlike the price elasticity of demand, one cannot ignore the minus sign for either the cross-price or income elasticities. The sign of these elasticities allows for proper classification. Additionally, the definitions apply in either direction: substitutes must have a positive cross-price elasticity and a positive cross-price elasticity means the two goods are substitutes. Be careful: if the test question indicates the cross-price elasticity for TVs and cable services is positive then TVs and cable services are substitutes. The sign of the cross-price and income elasticities determines the relationship; resist the temptation to indicate they are complements even though it is the correct relationship

Learning Objective 6: Define and calculate the price elasticity of supply. List and define the categories of the price elasticity of supply and enumerate the special cases.
The **price elasticity of supply** for a good or service is the percentage change in quantity supplied in response to a 1 percent change in the good's price. For a general supply curve of the form $P = \alpha + \beta \times Q$, the formula is $((1/\beta) \times (P/Q))$. Since prices and quantities are always positive and the slope of the supply (β) is positive, the price elasticity of supply is always positive. One noteworthy special case to keep in mind is, for supply curves of the form $P = \beta \times Q$, the price elasticity of supply is always 1 regardless of the price-quantity combination. When the supply curve includes an intercept term ($\alpha > 0$), then the value of the price elasticity varies: at larger and larger quantity levels, the size of the price elasticity of supply declines and supply becomes more inelastic. A numerical value between zero and one is termed inelastic supply; a value between one and infinity is termed elastic supply. A **perfectly inelastic supply** curve is vertical and has an elasticity of zero. A **perfectly elastic supply** curve is horizontal and has an elasticity of infinity.

Learning Objective 7: Discuss the factors affecting the size of the price elasticity of supply.
The easier it is to acquire additional units of the factors of production needed to produce a good, the greater the price elasticity of supply. The ease with which additional units can be acquired can be thought of in three different ways. The first is the flexibility of the factors of production. If production of a good uses factors widely available in other industries, then it will be relatively easy to entice additional units away from their current uses, making supply relatively elastic. The second is the degree of mobility the factors possess. If factors can be easy transported from region to region, then supply will be more elastic. The third is the degree to which alternative factors can be used in place of the current factor. If many alternatives are present, then supply will again be more elastic. Finally, the time frame considered influences the size of the elasticity. Changes in factor flexibility, mobility, or alternatives do not occur rapidly over a short period. But given a sufficient amount of time, large-scale changes can and do take place. Thus, all price elasticities of supply will be smaller over the short run and grow larger over the long run.

III. Self-Test

Key Terms
Match the term in the right-hand column with the appropriate definitions in the left-hand column by placing the letter of the term in the blank in front of its definition. (Answers are given at the end of the chapter.)

1. ____ The quantity resulting from multiplying the firm's per unit price times the number of units sold.

2. ____ When a 1 percent change in price results in a less than 1 percent change in quantity demanded.

3. ____ Demand for which any change in price results in no change in quantity demanded.

4. ____ A measure of the responsiveness of quantity demanded to a 1 percent change in price.

5. ____ The quantity resulting from adding all consumer expenditures of a good or service.

6. ____ A measure of the responsiveness of quantity demanded for one good when another good's price changes by 1 percent.

7. ____ Demand for which the price elasticity of demand is infinite.

8. ____ When a 1 percent change in price results in a greater than 1 percent change in quantity demanded.

9. ____ A measure of the responsiveness of quantity demanded to a 1 percent change in consumer incomes.

10. ____ A measure of the responsiveness of quantity supplied to a 1 percent change in price.

11. ____ When the quantity supplied does not change when a change in the price occurs.

12. ____ When a 1 percent change in price results in a 1 percent change in quantity demanded.

13. ____ When the price elasticity of supply equals infinity.

a. cross-price elasticity of demand

b. elastic

c. income elasticity of demand

d. inelastic

e. perfectly elastic demand

f. perfectly elastic supply

g. perfectly inelastic demand

h. perfectly inelastic supply

i. price elasticity of demand

j. price elasticity of supply

k. total expenditures

l. total revenues

m. unit elastic

Multiple-Choice Questions
Circle the letter that corresponds to the best answer. (Answers are given at the end of the chapter.)

1. Suppose that as price falls from $10 to $9, quantity demanded rises from 1 to 2 units and as price falls from $2 to $1, quantity demanded increases from 9 to 10 units. Measuring the price elasticity at the $10 to $9 points versus the $2 to $1 points will show the
A. two elasticities to be the same.
B. $10 to $9 elasticity to be smaller.
C. $2 to $1 elasticity to be more elastic.
D. $10 to $9 elasticity to be more elastic.
E. $2 to $1 elasticity to be larger.

2. The reason firms that face elastic demand should lower price to increase total revenues is that

A. demand curves are downward sloping.
B. consumers prefer lower prices.
C. the percentage increases in sales will be larger than the percentage decrease in price.
D. more consumers will try their products.
E. the percentage increase in sales will be smaller than the percentage decrease in price.

3. If demand for socks is $P = 32 - 5*Q$, the price elasticity of demand is _____ at $P = \$2$.
   A. 5
   B. 2
   C. 0.5
   D. 0.2
   E. 067

4. From the 1981 introduction of the IBM PC to the fall of 2003, the price elasticity of demand for IBM PC has
   A. fallen due to the growth of substitutes, e.g., Dell and Gateway.
   B. increased due to the lower price of IBM computers.
   C. increased due to the growth of substitutes, e.g., Dell and Gateway.
   D. fallen because consumers started to switch from PCs to handhelds.
   E. increased due to a reduction in demand for PCs.

5. A perfectly elastic demand curve has a slope of _____ while a perfectly inelastic demand curve has a slope of _____.
   A. infinity; 0
   B. 1; infinity
   C. 0; 1
   D. 0; infinity
   E. infinity; 1

6. If the elasticity of demand for the latest Avril Lavigne CD is −1.4, this means
   A. few substitutes exist.
   B. a 1% increase in the price leads to a 14% reduction in quantity demanded.
   C. a 10% decrease in the price leads to a 140% increase in quantity demanded.
   D. a 5% increase in the price leads to a 7% decrease in quantity demanded.
   E. a 5% increase in the price leads to a 7% increase in quantity demanded.

7. The proper sequence of elasticity categories from least responsive to most responsive is
   A. perfectly inelastic, perfectly elastic, inelastic, elastic.
   B. elastic, perfectly elastic, perfectly inelastic, inelastic.
   C. perfectly inelastic, inelastic, perfectly elastic, elastic.
   D. perfectly inelastic, inelastic, elastic, perfectly elastic.
   E. perfectly elastic, elastic, inelastic, perfectly inelastic.

8. The most important factor influencing the size of the price elasticity of supply is the
   A. price elasticity of demand.
   B. number of firms.

C. number of consumers.

D. ease with which additional units of factors of production can be acquired.

E. age of the industry.

9. Suppose a 1 percent decrease in the price of a good results in a 5 percent decrease in the quantity supplied. Thus, supply is
   A. perfectly inelastic.
   B. perfectly elastic.
   C. inelastic.
   D. elastic.
   E. unit elastic.

10. Supply curves of the form $P = b*Q$, where $b > 0$, will always have a price elasticity of supply
    A. equal to 0.
    B. that becomes more elastic at higher levels of output.
    C. equal to 1.
    D. that becomes more inelastic at higher levels of output.
    E. equal to b.

11. If the local electricity utility wants to raise revenues, it should _____ its price because demand for electricity is likely to be _____.
    A. lower; inelastic
    B. raise; elastic
    C. lower; elastic
    D. raise; inelastic
    E. lower; perfectly inelastic

12. A price elasticity of demand of 0.3 means that a
    A. 10 percent increase in the price results in a 3 percent increase in quantity demanded.
    B. 3 percent increase in the price results in a 3 percent decrease in quantity demanded.
    C. 10 percent increase in the price results in a 3 percent decrease in demand.
    D. 10 percent increase in the price results in a 3 percent decrease in quantity demanded.
    E. 10 percent increase in the price results in a 3 percent increase demand.

13. The development of small satellite dish units in the 1990s caused the price elasticity of demand for cable TV to
    A. grow more inelastic.
    B. become less elastic.
    C. grow more elastic.
    D. become smaller in absolute value.
    E. shift to the left.

14. The cross-price elasticity for bread and butter is estimated to be 0.5, implying they are
    A. normal goods.
    B. substitutes.
    C. elastic goods.

D. complements.
E. unrelated.

15. The income elasticity of demand for chicken noodle soup is found to be –0.7, suggesting it
    A. is a normal good.
    B. has inelastic demand.
    C. is a superior good.
    D. has elastic demand.
    E. is an inferior good.

16. The long-run price elasticity of supply for a particular good will be _____ its short-run elasticity.
    A. smaller than
    B. more inelastic than
    C. larger than
    D. less elastic than
    E. equal to

17. If the numerical value of the price elasticity of supply is zero, supply is categorized as being
    A. perfectly elastic.
    B. elastic.
    C. unit elastic.
    D. inelastic.
    E. perfectly inelastic.

18. The supply curve for yogurt is P = 4*Q. When price is $8, the price elasticity of supply is
    A. 8.
    B. 4.
    C. 2.
    D. 1.
    E. 0.25.

19. For which of the demand elasticities is the sign (+ or -) important in interpreting the meaning?
    A. Only the price elasticity of demand.
    B. Both the price elasticity of demand and the income elasticity of demand.
    C. Both the income elasticity of demand and the cross-price elasticity of demand.
    D. Only the cross-price elasticity of demand.
    E. All three elasticities (price, income, and cross-price).

20. A cross-price elasticity of –1.2 indicates the two goods are
    A. inferior.
    B. elastic.
    C. complements.
    D. substitutes.
    E. normal.

Short Answer Problems
(Answers and solutions are given at the end of the chapter.)

1. Interpretation of Estimated Price Elasticities of Demand
The following question asks you to explore your intuition about the price elasticity of demand. The following table is taken from Baye, Jansen, and Lee, "Advertising Effects in Complete Demand Systems," *Applied Economics* 24 (1992), pp.1087-96. The figures are presented as they appeared; just take the absolute value of the entries to get positive values.

Item	Short-Run Price Elasticity of Demand	Long-Run Price Elasticity of Demand
Transportation	-0.6	-1.9
Food	-0.7	-2.3
Alcohol and Tobacco	-0.3	-0.9
Recreation	-1.1	-3.5
Clothing	-0.9	-2.9

    A. Consider the short-run estimates in column 2. Classify the items on the basis of elasticity. The results show consumers are less responsive to changes in the price of transportation than to changes in the price of food. Does this mean transportation is a greater necessity than food? That alcohol and tobacco are more necessary than transportation and food?

    B. Looking again at the column 2, you see that the short-run estimate for Clothing is inelastic. Do you believe the demand for Levi's blue jeans is also inelastic? Why?

    C. The long-run estimates appear in column 3. Are the estimates for the long run consistent with what you know, i.e., the elasticity for food in the short run compared with its long-run estimate. What implications for the discussion of necessities versus wants do these results hold?

2. Pricing Policies, Total Revenues, and the Price Elasticity of Demand
Your understanding of the impact of a price change on total revenues will be tested as well as your ability to calculate total revenues and the price elasticity of demand. Suppose the demand curve for a firm is given by $P = 1,000 - .5*Q$.

    A. If the firm's current price is $650, calculate the firm's total revenues and the price elasticity of demand.

    B. Suppose two factions have developed in the marketing department: one camp wants to raise a price by 10 percent while the other advocates a 10 percent reduction. Presume increased total revenues is the firm's goal. Calculate the value of total revenues under each of the possible price changes.

    C. Which value is larger and therefore which price change should be adopted? Does this answer agree with the generalizations made about the size of the price elasticity and the proper price change to increase revenues?

    D. Finally, assume the firm introduces a new feature that makes its product much more effective than the competition. The rightward shift of the demand curve can be expressed with a new equation: P = 2,000 - .5*Q. Calculate the price elasticity of demand at the original price of $650 using the new demand curve. In what direction (more or less elastic) does the elasticity move? Does this seem reasonable?

3. Price Elasticity of Supply

This question will review your understanding of how to calculate the price elasticity of supply and, once calculated, how to classify the result.

   A. Given the following supply curve P = 6×Q, when P = $5, the price elasticity of supply is _____. When P = $7, the price elasticity is _____.
   B. Given the following supply curve P = 10 + 8×Q, when P = $11, the price elasticity of supply is _____. When P = $15, the price elasticity is _____.
   C. When the price elasticity of supply is greater than zero but less than one, supply is termed (elastic/inelastic) _____. When the price elasticity of supply exceeds one but is less than infinity, supply is called (elastic/inelastic) _____.

IV. Economic Naturalist Application

Analyze the price elasticity of demand for various illegal activities and goods. Is demand for illegal drugs elastic or inelastic? What about specific illegal drugs, e.g., crack, heroin, and ecstasy? How about drugs that are legal like alcohol and nicotine? Be sure to consider the substitution possibilities as well as the criminal consequences when designing your answer.
Answer:

V. Go to the Web: Graphing Exercises Using Interactive Graphs

> In the next chapter, the ideas of "needs" versus "wants" will be explored. Most likely, you will be surprised by the narrow view economists take towards "needs": very few items are on the list. Most people would claim their auto is a necessity. If true, the size of the elasticity for autos should be small (relatively inelastic). Search the Web for elasticity estimates for autos (look for estimates that combine both new and used into one estimate). Do the elasticity estimates agree with the concept of necessity? Repeat the exercise for items you consider necessities.
> Answer:

To review the answer to this question and learn more about the use of economic theory to analyze this issue (and other macroeconomic issues), please go to Electronic Learning Session in the Student Center at the Frank/Bernanke web site: hppt://www.mhhe.com/economics/frankbernanke2.

VI. Self-Test Solutions

Key Terms

1. l
2. d
3. g
4. i
5. k
6. a
7. e
8. b
9. c
10. j
11. h
12. m
13. f

Multiple-Choice Questions

1. D
2. C
3. E $2 = 32 -5*Q => Q = 6$ substituting, elasticity $= (1/5)*(2/6) = 1/15 = 0.067$
4. C
5. D
6. D
7. D

8. D
9. D
10. C
11. D
12. D
13. B
14. B
15. E
16. C
17. E
18. D   see 2 above, the steps are the same
19. C
20. C

Short Answer Problems

1.
A. Recreation is elastic, all the rest are inelastic. No, there are apparently better substitutes for food than transportation. No, again there are apparently closer substitutes for food and transportation than for alcohol and tobacco.
B. Probably not. While the number of substitutes for clothing are limited, the number of substitutes for Levi's blue jeans is quite large. All other blue jeans manufacturers products plus all slack and pant manufacturers.
C. Yes, all the long-run elasticities are larger than their short-run counterparts, exactly as intuition would suggest. Consumers show significant long-run responsiveness to price changes. Notice that the one inelastic long-run estimate, alcohol and tobacco, is nearly unit elastic.

2.
A. $650 = 1,000 - 5*Q \Rightarrow Q = 70$; $TR = 650*70 = 45,500$; $\varepsilon = |(1/-5)*(650/70)| = 1.86$
B. For 10% increase: $650*(1.10) = 715$; $715 = 1,000 - 5*Q \Rightarrow Q = 57$; $TR = 715*57 = 40,755$.
For 10% decrease: $650*(.90) = 585$; $585 = 1,000 - 5*Q \Rightarrow Q = 83$; $TR = 585*83 = 48,555$.
C. The price decrease. Yes, demand is elastic so to increase total revenues, one lowers the price.
D. $650 = 2,000 - 5*Q \Rightarrow Q = 270$; $\varepsilon = |(1/-5)*(650/270)| = 0.48$. Demand is now more inelastic (less elastic). Yes, the degree of closeness of the substitute goods is smaller owning to the new feature.

3.
A. 1; 1
B. 11; 3
C. inelastic; elastic

Chapter 5
Demand: The Benefit Side of the Market

I. Pretest: What Do You Really Know?
Circle the letter that corresponds to the best answer. (Answers appear immediately after the final question).

1. The extra utility gained from consuming an extra unit of a good measures its
   A. total utility.
   B. average utility.
   C. marginal utility.
   D. total satisfaction.
   E. diminishing utility.

2. For two goods, A and B, the rational spending rule is expressed as
   A. $MU_A = MU_B$.
   B. $P_A = P_B$.
   C. $(MU_A / P_B) = (MU_B / P_A)$.
   D. $(MU_A / MU_B) = (P_B / P_A)$.
   E. $(MU_A / P_A) = (MU_B / P_B)$.

3. The market demand curve is
   A. the vertical summation of all the demand curves of individuals.
   B. positively sloped for some goods.
   C. the horizontal summation of all the demand curves of individuals.
   D. found by adding up all the different prices consumers would pay for a given quantity.
   E. unaffected by changes in consumers' incomes.

4. After subsistence levels of food, shelter, and clothing are provided,
   A. all other goods and services are "needs."
   B. many goods and services are "needs."
   C. all other goods and services are "wants."
   D. a few goods and services are "needs."
   E. all other goods and services are "luxuries."

5. The fact that the average price of a gallon of gasoline in England is much higher than the price in the U.S. would lead to which of the following predictions?
   A. Average miles per gallon for new cars would be lower in England.
   B. English drivers would tend to drive a greater average number of miles.
   C. American drivers would tend to make fewer trips with more stops.
   D. Sport Utility Vehicles will be less popular with consumers in England.
   E. Air pollution from automobiles will be worse in England.

6. The law of demand indicates that as the cost of an activity
   A. falls, less of the activity will occur.
   B. falls, the level of the activity will increase at all possible costs.
   C. rises, more of the activity will occur.
   D. rises, the level of the activity will decrease at all possible costs.
   E. falls, more of the activity will occur.

7. Purchasing goods so that the ratio of marginal utility to price is equal across all goods results in the
   A. greatest total utility.
   B. lowest expenditure on goods.
   C. greatest average utility.
   D. greatest expenditure on goods.
   E. equal expenditures for all goods.

8. For most goods, as the number of units consumed increases, total utility _____, while marginal utility _____.
   A. increases; decreases
   B. decreases; increases
   C. increases; increases
   D. decreases; decreases
   E. peaks; bottoms out

9. Which of the following statements is false?
   A. Goods and services are valuable to consumers because they generate utility.
   B. Four hamburgers generate more total utility than three hamburgers.
   C. Utility cannot be quantified.
   D. The fourth hamburger increases total utility by more than the third hamburger.
   E. The marginal utility from an extra movie is likely to be different than the marginal utility from an extra automobile.

10. When the price of a good falls, the ratio of the marginal utility of that good divided by its price _____ and as a result, consumers purchase _____.
   A. rises; more
   B. falls; more
   C. rises; less
   D. falls; less
   E. does not change; the same quantity

Solutions and Feedback to Pretest
For each question you answered incorrectly, we strongly recommend taking the time to review the appropriate material before continuing. In the table below, the relevant textbook pages are listed for each question as well as the pertinent Learning Objective from the following Key Point Review.

Correct Answer	Textbook Page Numbers	Learning Objective
1. C	pp. 120-23	2
2. E	pp. 124-32	3
3. C	pp.132-33	4
4. C	pp. 118-20	1
5. D	pp. 118-20	1
6. E	pp. 118-20	1
7. A	pp. 124-32	3
8. A	pp. 120-23	2
9. D	pp. 120-23	2
10. A	pp. 124-32	3

II. Key Point Review

Learning Objective 1: State the Law of Demand. Distinguish between needs and wants based on the criteria developed in the textbook.
The **law of demand** suggests that people will do less of what they want to do when the cost of doing it rises. The law applies to conventional consumer goods (e.g., TVs) and to unconventional items (e.g., close campus parking spaces). In all cases, the relationship between quantity demanded and the cost of the good or service is negative. One must make a sharp distinction between needs and wants. The list of needs is short, including only subsistence levels of food, water, shelter, and clothing. Once the subsistence levels are fulfilled everything else consumers purchase is a want. No one needs electricity because no one will die if it is withdrawn. To be sure, electricity is a very useful good and countless electrical appliances exist, helping to improve or simplify life. However, being highly useful and quite common is not enough to elevate a good or service to the status of a necessity. The origins of human wants are dimly understood. Some are clearly biological (e.g., food and water) while others are related to social influences. Whatever the relative importance of genetics versus social factors, the wants, preferences, and tastes of consumers are transformed into expressions of demand for various goods and services.

Learning Objective 2: Describe the concept of utility. Express the goal consumers are thought to be pursuing. Define marginal utility and explain the Law of Diminishing Marginal Utility.
The satisfaction buyers receive from the act of consuming is termed utility. Consumers are presumed to set utility maximization as the goal governing their behavior. Assume the degree of consumption satisfaction could be explicitly measured in units called "utils." As an individual consumes more of any particular good, the amount of total utility will rise. The size of the

increase in total utility as consumption rises is our primary focus. **Marginal utility** is the extra utility one gets from consuming an extra unit of a good. Let automobiles be the good whose consumption is going to be varied. The first auto causes a sizable increase in total utility because self-determined mobility makes life much more convenient. Adding a second car would also result in an increase in total utility. The size of the increase, however, must be smaller than the increase for the first auto. Even in the context of a family with several drivers, the first car will always be more valuable (increased total utility) then the second, third, or fourth auto. Thus, as consumption of a good increases, the marginal utility from the additional units declines. Declining marginal utility is so common it has been declared a law. The **law of diminishing marginal utility** holds that at some point the additional utility from additional consumption will begin to grow smaller.

> **Hint:** Be careful not to confuse declining with negative. Marginal utility is initially positive and with each extra unit gets smaller - it is declining. At some point the marginal utility may become negative, e.g., the last helping of food at the all-you-can-eat dinner. Also, exceptions to the law of diminishing marginal utility clearly exist.

Learning Objective 3: Define the optimal combination of goods and the Rational Spending Rule. Explain how the application of the Rational Spending Rule leads to the optimal combination of goods. Discuss substitution and income effects in terms of the Rational Spending Rule. Define nominal and real prices.

The **optimal combination of goods** defines the mix of goods that yield the greatest total utility without violating the consumer's income constraints. The optimal combination directly results from the consumer's efforts to maximizes his or her utility. But as all too obvious, the consumer's choices must be made with a limited amount to spend on goods and services. How then does the consumer find the optimal combination in the face of limited or fixed income? By applying the rational spending rule. The **rational spending rule** suggests that spending should be allocated across goods so that the marginal utility per dollar spent is identical for all goods. Formally, the rule is $MU_A/P_A = MU_B/P_B$ where MU_i is the marginal utility for the two goods A and B and P_i is the price of the two goods.

The rational spending rule allows for a more precise description of how changes in prices and incomes change consumption decisions. When the price of good A falls, the ratio MU_A/P_A rises and disrupts the optimal combination of A and B. To restore utility maximization, changes in MU_A and MU_B must occur since consumers cannot alter prices. To change the marginal utilities, one must consume either more or less of the goods. If P_A falls, then MU_A must also fall to return the ratio to its original value. To make MU_A decline, one needs to purchase more A (by the law of diminishing marginal utility). Thus, when the price of A falls, consumers purchase more A in order to restore the point of utility maximization. The consumer could also have taken a direct path to reestablish equilibrium. Continuing to purchase the same amount of A after the price decrease frees up dollars to spend on B. Buying more B serves to lower MU_B, causing the ratio of MU_B/P_B to fall. Hence, restoring the point of utility maximization can also be accomplished by leaving purchases of A alone and buying increased amounts of B. Of course, the consumer can do a little of both to achieve equilibrium. Thinking back to Chapter 3, the reasoning behind the first path (buy more A when the price of A declines) is the essence of the demand curve. The second path (buy more B when the price of A declines) is the essence of shifting the demand curve for B when the price of a substitute good (A) changes. If income increases, then the range of available combinations expands. The rational spending rule is still in force; the numerical value of the point of utility maximization is lower.

 Note: The above discussion involves difficult material; be sure to work Problem 1 in the Short Answer section to ensure a firm understanding of how the rational spending rule works.

Finally, with so much emphasis on the role of prices, clarity about the different kinds of prices is essential. The **nominal price** of a good is its absolute price in dollar terms: it is the price of the product in the store. The **real price** is the dollar price of a good relative to the average dollar prices of all other goods: it is the amount of purchasing power used when one buys the good. Only the real price of a good exerts influence on the decisions made by consumers. Consider the behavior of the nominal and real price of a gallon of gasoline. In 1980, a gallon of gasoline had a nominal price of $1.25. Adjusting for inflation (see the inflation calculator at http://woodrow.mpls.frb.fed.us/research/data/us/calc/), the equivalent nominal price in 2003 would be $2.79. With a nominal price of only $1.59 in 2003, the amount of purchasing power sacrificed to buy a gallon of gas today versus 1980 is dramatically lower. One can also work the problem another way: $1.59 in 2003 would buy 71 cents worth of goods in 1980. Either way, the cost of a gallon of gas is much lower in 2003 than in 1980, which helps to explain the rapid growth of SUVs.

Learning Objective 4: Understand how the market demand curve is derived from the demand curves of individual consumers.
From the demand curves for individuals comes the market demand curve. Horizontally summing all the buyers' demand curves for a good at each and every price results in the market demand curve. For example, if Roy is willing to purchase 11 units of food at a price of $5 and Dustin is willing to purchase 6 units, then their combined demand for food at a price of $5 is 17 units. By including all of the relevant buyers and considering all possible prices, one generates the market demand curve.

Learning Objective 5: Define consumer surplus and know how to calculate its value. Identify the area of consumer surplus in a demand diagram.
The difference between the consumer's reservation price and the actual price paid defines **consumer surplus**. While defined in terms of a single individual, the concept of consumer surplus extends to the market as a whole. Consumer surplus for the entire market is simply the sum of the consumer surplus accruing to each buyer. Graphically, it is the area underneath the demand curve and above the market price, making a triangle. The formula for calculating the are of a triangle is Area = ½ (length)(height).

III. Self-Test
Key Terms
Match the term in the right-hand column with the appropriate definitions in the left-hand column by placing the letter of the term in the blank in front of its definition. (Answers are given at the end of the chapter.)

1. ____ The extra utility that results from consuming an extra unit of a good.

2. ____ The dollar price of a good relative to the average dollar prices of all other goods.

3. ____ As the cost of an activity rises, individuals will engage in less of the activity.

4. ____ When spending is allocated across goods such that the marginal utility per dollar spent is identical.

5. ____ The absolute price of a good in dollar terms.

6. ____ The difference between the consumer's reservation price and the actual price paid.

7. ____ As additional units of a good are consumed, the additional utility from each unit declines.

8. ____ The mix of goods that yields the greatest total utility to the consumer without exceeding his or her budget constraints.

a. consumer surplus

b. law of demand

c. law of diminishing marginal utility

d. marginal utility

e. nominal price

f. optimal combination of goods

g. rational spending rule

h. real price

Multiple-Choice Questions
Circle the letter that corresponds to the best answer. (Answers are given at the end of the chapter.)

1. If Karen's marginal utility from her 13th pair of shoes is 15, then the marginal utility from her 14th pair would be
   A. more than 15.
   B. exactly 15.
   C. less than 15.
   D. exactly 14.
   E. less than 14.

2. A consumer purchases quantities of good A and good B in accordance with the rational spending rule. An increase in the price of good A will cause the consumer to
   A. buy more A to restore the rational spending rule.
   B. buy less B to restore the rational spending rule.
   C. do nothing; he or she is unaffected by the price change.
   D. buy less A to restore the rational spending rule.
   E. buy more of both A and B to restore the rational spending rule.

3. Assume that consumers in both Texas and Montana have identical incomes and preferences but the price of ice cream is higher in Montana. The rational spending rule would predict that
   A. consumers in Texas will eat more ice cream.
   B. consumers in Montana will eat more ice cream.

C. consumers in both Texas and Montana will eat less ice cream.

D. consumers in both Texas and Montana will eat more ice cream.

E. consumers in Texas will eat less ice cream.

4. John, Don, and Mary are willing and able to purchase 5, 7, and 3 units of canned cat food, respectively, when the price is $1.50. If they are the only consumers, the market quantity demanded at a price of $1.50 is

A. 15.

B. 10.

C. 7.

D. 5.

E. 3.

5. Which of the following is *not* true of the law of demand?

A. It is based on the cost-benefit principle.

B. It predicts a negative relationship between costs and benefits.

C. It applies only to monetary costs

D. It is rarely violated.

E. It requires demand curves to be downward sloping.

6. Taking a limousine to a five star restaurant in New York is a

A. necessity to Donald Trump but a luxury to Joe Average.

B. necessity to both Joe Average and Donald Trump.

C. luxury to both Joe Average and Donald Trump.

D. want to Donald Trump and a luxury to Joe Average.

E. want to both Joe Average and Donald Trump.

7. Assume one has $30 in income and the price of a loaf of bread is $1.50 and the price of a jar of peanut butter is $3. If one's income rises to $45, one can now buy a maximum of _____ loaves of bread or a maximum of _____ jars of peanut butter.

A. 5; 25

B. 10; 40

C. 15; 30

D. 20; 20

E. 30; 15

8. If the marginal utility of the 3rd cup of coffee is 23 and the marginal utility of the 4th cup is 15, then

A. it is optimal for the consumer to have 3 cups of coffee.

B. the price of a cup of coffee must be relatively low.

C. it is optimal for the consumer to have 4 cups of coffee.

D. the law of diminishing marginal utility is evident.

E. the price of a cup of coffee must be relatively high.

9. Which of the following statements about total utility is *false*?

A. Total utility can't be measured.

B. The increase in total utility from the first unit consumed usually exceeds the increase from the second unit consumed.

C. Total utility increases as more units of a good are consumed.

D. The increase in total utility from the second unit consumed exceeds the increase from the first unit consumed.

E. At some point, the increase in total utility from consuming an extra unit begins to get smaller.

10. Which of the following statements is not an example of the law of demand?

A. I think I'll wait to leave for work at 9:30 a.m. so that traffic is not so heavy.

B. The local record store has all their CD's on sale; I'm going to buy some right now.

C. With unemployment so high, I can't find a job. I think I'll enroll at the local college.

D. The increase in apartment rents is causing me to consider renting out our spare bedroom.

E. The Internet has increased the amount of information I collect before making a purchase.

11. If a consumer is willing to purchase one unit of a good for $10 but finds he or she can buy it for $2.50, he or she has a consumer surplus of

A. $12.50.

B. $7.50.

C. $5.

D. $6.25.

E. $2.50.

12. Let A represent the vertical intercept of a demand curve, B is the point on vertical axis representing the price being charged ($A > B$), and C is the point on the horizontal axis representing the purchases of consumers at the price B. The area of consumer surplus is calculated as

A. $(A - B) \times C$.

B. $\frac{1}{2} \times (A - B) \times C$.

C. $A \times C$.

D. $\frac{1}{2} \times A \times C$.

E. $\frac{1}{2} \times (A - B)$.

13. In general, if the marginal utility of the nth unit of a good is X, then the marginal utility of the n-1 unit is

A. less than X.

B. equal to X.

C. equal to X/n-1.

D. greater than X.

E. impossible to gauge without numbers.

14. Assume the consumer is correctly applying the rational spending rule for goods X and Z. If the consumer's income increases, purchases of X and Z rise because

A. the marginal utility of X decreases.

B. the price of Z falls.

C. the marginal utility of Z decreases.

D. combinations of X and Z that could not be considered before now become available.

E. the price of X increases.

15. The rational spending rule is derived from the consumer's efforts to
    A. maximize expenditures.
    B. maximize utility.
    C. minimize expenditures.
    D. obtain the lowest possible price.
    E. maximize the number of units purchased.

16. Summing the quantities of butter all consumers are willing and able to purchase at different prices results in
    A. total expenditures for butter.
    B. total revenues.
    C. the market demand curve for butter.
    D. the market supply curve for butter.
    E. an upward sloping relationship.

17. As discussed in the textbook, the chronic shortage of water in southern California is due to
    A. the necessity of water.
    B. the lack of prohibition of lawn watering.
    C. the extensive agricultural production.
    D. the artificially low price of water.
    E. a greater than average taste for bathing.

18. When the price of a good rises, the ratio of the marginal utility of that good divided by its price _____ and as a result, consumers purchase _____.
    A. rises; more
    B. falls; more
    C. rises; less
    D. falls; less
    E. does not change; the same quantity

19. According to the textbook, the homes of the wealthy in Seattle average in excess of 10,000 square feet while the homes of the wealthy in New York City average less than 5,000 square feet. The difference is primarily due to
    A. greater "tastes" for space in Seattle.
    B. a ban on construction of new homes in excess of 5,000 square feet in NYC.
    C. a significantly higher price for land and construction in NYC.
    D. greater "tastes" for crowding in NYC.
    E. property tax abatements granted to new homes with at least 10,000 square feet in Seattle.

20. Goods and services are valuable to consumers
    A. because consumers need them.
    B. only if they were purchased on sale.
    C. if they are very expensive.

80

D. only if they are name brand items.

E. because they produce utility for the consumer.

Short Answer Problems
(Answers and solutions are given at the end of the chapter.)

1. Calculating Total and Marginal Utilities

The basics of computing the total utility (TU) and marginal utility (MU) measures are covered in this question. Complete this one before moving on to Question 2. The table below contains data for Stan's total and marginal utilities as the amount of consumption changes.

Quantity of Good X	Total Utility	Marginal Utility
0	0	n/a
1	40	
2	60	
3		10
4	75	
5		0
6	70	

A. Fill in the missing values for total utility and marginal utility.

B. This good exhibits the law of diminishing marginal utility with the ($2^{nd}/3^{rd}$) _____ unit.

C. The value of marginal utility for the last unit is (positive/negative) _____, suggesting Stan would be better off by (not consuming/consuming) _____ the 6th unit.

2. Applying the Rational Spending Rule

Answering this question will help you with the mechanics of the rational spending rule. The following table has data on: (1) Megan's total utility (TU_i) from the consumption of goods X, Y, and Z, (2) a column to record the values of the marginal utilities (MU_i), and (3) a column to calculate the ratio of the marginal utilities to price (MU_i)/P_i.

	Good X			Good Y			Good Z		
Quantity	TU_X	MU_X	MU_X/P_X	TU_Y	MU_Y	MU_Y/P_Y	TU_Z	MU_Z	MU_Z/P_Z
0	0	n/a	n/a	0	n/a	n/a	0	n/a	n/a
1	14			30			40		
2	26			54			76		
3	36			72			108		
4	44			84			136		
5	50			90			160		
6	54			90			180		
7	56			84			196		
8	56			72			208		
9	54			54			216		

A. Calculate the marginal utilities for X, Y, and Z.

B. Given that $P_X = \$2$, $P_Y = \$6$, and $P_Z = \$16$, compute the ratio of marginal utility to price for all three goods.

C. Assume that Megan has $88 to spend. Apply the rational spending rule, i.e., locate the combination of X, Y, and Z where the extra utility from the last dollar spent is equal for all three goods. If you have difficulty answering this, review the formula for the rational spending rule and remember that Megan can't overspend but she can underspend.

D. Let the price of good X double to $4. Based on the rational spending rule, how do you predict Megan will alter her choices of X, Y, and Z. Can you numerically confirm your prediction?

3. Market Demand

Here the deriving of the market demand curve from the individual consumer's demand curves is reviewed. The following table contains the individual demand curves for three consumers.

Price	Jim Bob's Demand Curve	Joe Bob's Demand Curve	Bob Bob's Demand Curve
$1	5	18	5
$2	3	15	4
$3	1	12	3
$4	0	9	2
$5	0	6	1

A. From the table it is clear that all 3 consumers purchase (more/less) _____ as the price rises. The change in behavior is called a (change in quantity demanded/change in demand) _____.

B. If the three consumers make up the entire market for this good, then at a price of $1, market quantity demanded is _____ units.

C. If the three consumers make up the entire market for this good, then at a price of $3, market quantity demanded is _____ units.

D. If the three consumers make up the entire market for this good, then at a price of $5, market quantity demanded is _____ units.

4. Consumer Surplus

Your skill at computing consumer surplus is measured by this question. Suppose market demand for a service is given by $P = 500 - 0.2 \times Q$.

A. If price equals $400, the amount of consumer surplus is _____.

B. Compared to a price of $400, if the price falls to $300, consumer surplus (rises/falls) _____ by an amount equal to _____ dollars.

C. Compared to a price of $400, if the price rises to $450, the amount of consumer surplus is _____, which is an (increase/decrease) _____ of _____ dollars.

IV. Economic Naturalist Application

Think about an item you really want to own but have resisted purchasing because the price is relatively high. Suppose the item goes on sale for 50 percent off and you choose to buy it, proclaiming to your friends and family that you "saved a great deal of money." Since it is impossible to buy something and save money simultaneously, why did the purchase occur during the sale? Did the extent of consumer surplus change? In fact, reflect on occasions where you bought something and felt you "really got a good deal." Is a "really good deal" just shorthand for a larger than expected amount of consumer surplus? Keep changes in consumer surplus in the back of your mind as you make purchases during the semester.

Answer:

V. Go to the Web: Graphing Exercises Using Interactive Graphs

The law of diminishing marginal utility fails to apply to some goods and services. Consider your favorite CD. Was the marginal utility of your second playing less than the first? The 10th playing? Did you consider the CD to be one of your favorites after just the first playing? Thinks of other examples where the law of diminishing marginal utility may be violated.

Answer:

To review the answer to this question and learn more about the use of economic theory to analyze this issue (and other macroeconomic issues), please go to Electronic Learning Session in the Student Center at the Frank/Bernanke web site: hppt://www.mhhe.com/economics/frankbernanke2.

VI. Self -Test Solutions

Key Terms
1. d
2. h
3. b
4. g
5. e
6. a
7. c
8. f

Multiple-Choice Questions
1. C
2. D
3. A
4. A
5. C
6. E
7. E
8. D
9. D
10. D
11. B
12. B
13. A
14. D
15. B
16. C
17. D
18. D
19. C
20. E

Short Answer Problems

1.

Quantity of Good X	Total Utility	Marginal Utility
0	0	n/a
1	40	40
2	60	20
3	70	10
4	75	5
5	75	0
6	70	-5

A. See table

B. 2nd

C. negative; not consuming

2.

Q	Good X			Good Y			Good Z		
	TU_X	MU_X	MU_X/P_X	TU_Y	MU_Y	MU_Y/P_Y	TU_Z	MU_Z	MU_Z/P_Z
0	0	n/a	n/a	0	n/a	n/a	0	n/a	n/a
1	14	14	7.0	30	30	5.0	40	40	2.50
2	26	12	6.0	54	24	4.0	76	36	2.25
3	36	10	5.0	72	18	3.0	108	32	2.00
4	44	8	4.0	84	12	2.0	136	28	1.75
5	50	6	3.0	90	6	1.0	160	24	1.50
6	54	4	2.0	90	0	0.0	180	20	1.25
7	56	2	1.0	84	-6	-1.0	196	16	1.00
8	56	0	0.0	72	-12	-2.0	208	12	0.75
9	54	-2	-1.0	54	-18	-3.0	216	8	0.50

A. See table.

B. See table.

C. To answer this, one must find where the three <u>ratios</u> (not quantities) are equal. The only values common to all three ratios: 2.0 and 1.0. Next, one checks to see if Megan can afford either bundle. When the ratios equal 2.0, Megan would spend (6×$2) + (4×$6) + (3×$16) = $84, which is less than her income of $88. When the ratios equal 1.0, Megan would spend (7×$2) + (5×$6) + (7×$16) = $156. She will pick the bundle where the ratios are all 2.0.

D. To solve this, one must recalculate the MU_X/P_X column with P_X = $4. Then one repeats the steps in part C. The only affordable solution is where the ratios again equal 2.0, but now Megan is buying less X and spending all of her income.

3.

A. less; change in quantity demanded

B. 28

C. 16

D. 7

4.

A. 400 = 500 - 0.2*Q => Q = 500; CS = (.5)*(500)*(500-400) = 25,000

B. rises; 300 = 500 - 0.2*Q => Q = 1,000; CS =(.5)*(1,000)*(500-300) = 100,000; thus, CS increased by 75,000

C. 450 = 500 – 0.2*Q => Q =250; CS = (.5)*(250)*(500-450) = 6,250; decrease; 18,750

Chapter 6
Perfectly Competitive Supply: The Cost Side of the Market

I. Pretest: What Do You Really Know?
Circle the letter that corresponds to the best answer. (Answers appear immediately after the final question).

1. The primary objective of all private firms is to
    A. revenue maximize.
    B. profit maximize.
    C. cost minimize.
    D. output maximize.
    E. input minimize.

2. A price taker confronts a demand curve that is
    A. vertical at the market price.
    B. upward sloping.
    C. downward sloping.
    D. horizontal at the market price.
    E. elastic.

3. The law of diminishing marginal returns
    A. is a long-run concept.
    B. applies only to small- and medium-sized firms.
    C. is a short- and long-run concept.
    D. applies only to large firms.
    E. is a short-run concept.

4. Which of the following factors of production is likely to be fixed in the short run?
    A. The location of the firm.
    B. The number of employee-hours.
    C. The amount of electricity consumed.
    D. The amount of paper used.
    E. The amount of RAM installed in the network server.

5. In the graph of average costs, marginal costs, and price the profit-maximizing solution for a perfect competitor is found where
   A. marginal costs equal average costs.
   B. marginal costs equal price.
   C. average costs equals price.
   D. average costs are the least.
   E. the difference between marginal costs and price is the largest.

6. If the firm produces an output level where price is less than marginal costs, then the firm should
   A. raise its price.
   B. pay less to its fixed factors of production.
   C. contract output to earn greater profits or smaller losses.
   D. expand output to earn greater profits or smaller losses.
   E. leave its output decision unchanged.

7. The upward-sloping portion of the marginal cost curve is the firm's
   A. production function.
   B. total cost curve.
   C. supply curve.
   D. diminishing marginal returns curve.
   E. profit curve.

8. The difference between the price a firm receives and the firm's reservation price is termed
   A. producer surplus.
   B. profit.
   C. a normal rate of return.
   D. corporate greed.
   E. loss.

9. The price of output to a firm is $9 and the marginal cost of the last unit produced is $8.50. This means the
   A. extra benefit of the last unit produced is less than the extra cost.
   B. firm should lower its output to increase profits.
   C. firm is earning an average profit of $0.50.
   D. extra benefit of the last unit produced is greater than the extra cost.
   E. firm is earning profits.

10. In order for a firm to choose to produce a positive amount of output, it must be the case that
    A. total revenues are greater than total costs.
    B. total revenues are greater than fixed costs.
    C. total revenues equal total costs.
    D. total revenues are greater than or equal to variable costs.
    E. total revenues minus total costs are greater than variable costs.

Solutions and Feedback to Pretest
For each question you answered incorrectly, we strongly recommend taking the time to review the appropriate material before continuing. In the table below, the relevant textbook pages are listed for each question as well as the pertinent Learning Objective from the following Key Point Review.

Correct Answer	Textbook Page Numbers	Learning Objective
1. B	pp. 145-47	1
2. D	pp. 145-47	1
3. E	pp. 147-49	2
4. A	pp. 147-49	2
5. B	pp. 151-55	5
6. C	pp. 149-51	4
7. C	pp. 151-55	5
8. A	pp. 160-61	7
9. D	pp. 149-51	4
10. D	pp. 149-51	4

II. Key Point Review

Learning Objective 1: Define the following terms: profit, a profit-maximizing firm, a perfectly competitive industry, a price taker, and an imperfectly competitive firm. Understand how the nature of the firm's demand curve determines whether the firm is a perfect or imperfect competitor.

Chapter 6 explores in detail the inner workings of the firm. The motivational assumption ascribed to private firms is to earn a profit for their owners. **Profit** is the difference between total revenues the firm collects and the explicit and implicit costs incurred by the firm to produce the good or service. Firms that take earning maximum profit as their primary objective are **profit-maximizing firms**. A **price taker** is a firm that has no ability to influence the price it receives for its output. **Perfectly competitive industries** are comprised entirely of price takers. The other category of firm structure is called an **imperfectly competitive firm**: a firm that has some degree of control over the market price of their output.

The closest example of a perfectly competitive industry is agricultural goods. Any particular corn farmer faces two specific facts: first, he contributes a minuscule fraction of the entire worldwide production of corn, and second, his corn is no better or worse than the corn grown by all other corn farmers. The combination of smallness and a standardized product means any attempt to charge a higher price for his corn would only result in a complete loss of sales. In the international market for corn, where all demanders and all suppliers interact, an equilibrium quantity and price for corn is established. To the individual corn farmers, the international price of corn is the price they take. These individual firms can sell as much or as little corn as they wish at the market price. As a result, the demand curve for the individual firms is perfectly elastic (horizontal) at the market price. Since the price taker has no control over price, maximizing profits comes down to one decision: how much to produce. To fully develop profit maximization, a rudimentary understanding of the mechanics of production is necessary

Learning Objective 2: Define the listed terms: factor of production, the short run, the long run, a fixed factor of production, and a variable factor of production,. Explain and apply the law of diminishing returns.

Production theory emphasizes the connection between the firm's output and its usage of **factors of production**—the inputs the firm uses to produce its output. The time horizon is an important factor in determining which factors of production are available for alteration. The **short run** is a period in which at least some of the firm's factors of production cannot be altered. The **long run** is a period of sufficient duration for all factors of production to be variable. For most firms, the location, size, and level of technology of their production facility are **fixed factors of production** in the short run.   The number of employees and the amount of electricity are **variable factors of production** in the short run. Of course, all factors are variable in the long run. When the firm is producing in the short run with fixed and variable factors of production, an important regularity is apparent. Imagine a firm is considering increasing production in 100-unit increments, i.e., 100 versus 200 versus 300. The **law of diminishing marginal returns** states that at some point, larger and larger amounts of the variable factors will be necessary to achieve a given increase in output. For example, to produce the first 100 units, the firm may need only three employees. But to produce the second 100 units (200 total), the firm may need to hire four employees (7 total). The third 100 units might require 6 additional employees. The reason for the law of diminishing marginal returns stems, typically, from congestion of the fixed factors of production.

Learning Objective 3: Define the following: fixed costs, variable costs, total costs, and marginal costs.

The two types of factors of production give rise to two types of costs. When the amount of cost incurred is independent of the amount of output the firm produces, then it is classified as a **fixed cost**. Fixed factors of production generate fixed cost: the rent for office space is due whether output is large or small. **Variable costs** depend directly on the amount of output the firm produces and result from the use of variable factors of production. The amount of overtime the firm pays to its workers can be zero or positive, depending on the urgency to produce output. The sum of fixed and variable costs results in **total costs**. Finally, the extra total cost incurred when extra output is produced is termed **marginal costs**.

Learning Objective 4: Explain how the profit maximizing level of output is reached. Distinguish between the impact of a change in variable costs and the impact of a change in fixed costs on the profit maximization decision. Discuss the condition under which the firm chooses to shutdown rather than operate.

According to the Cost-Benefit Principle introduced in Chapter One, an activity should be pursued up to the point where the additional benefit of more activity equals the additional cost of more activity. For the perfectly competitive firm, the activity is producing output, the benefit is the additional revenue collected and the cost is the additional dollars expended for variable factors. For a price taker, the extra revenue from selling an extra unit of output is exactly the market price. The extra cost of producing an extra unit of output is its marginal cost, the increase in total costs as an additional unit is produced. The Cost-Benefit Principle, applied to a price taker, indicates that to maximize profits, production should be increased until price equals the marginal costs of the last unit produced. When the law of diminishing marginal returns is present, the marginal costs of producing additional units of output will be positively sloped. Changes in the cost of fixed factors alter the size of profits or losses but they do not influence marginal costs, and hence the optimal output level does not change. Changes in the costs of variable factors of production alter marginal costs and therefore change the profit maximizing level of output. Finally, note that it is not always better for the firm to remain in business. If the firm can not collect adequate revenues at the current market price to pay its variable factors of production, it will choose to shut down. For example, a firm that collects $700 in revenues and has $500 of variable expenses and $300 of fixed expenses will be better off operating (-$100 versus -$300); but if the variable expenses had been $800, it would be better to shut down (-$400 versus -$300).

Learning Objective 5: Define average variable costs, average total costs, and a profitable firm. Find the profit-maximizing level of output in the context of a graph. Describe how one calculates profits or losses in the graph. Interpret the meaning of the marginal cost curve as it relates to the concept of supply.

Typically, average measures are more convenient than total measures when thinking about profit maximization: a CEO may not have a precise recollection of the firm's total revenues but probably does know the price (average revenues) the firm charges. **Average variable costs (AVC)** results from dividing variable costs by the amount of output the firm produces. Taking total costs and dividing by the amount of output the firm produces generates **average total costs (ATC)**. A **profitable firm** is one for which total revenues exceed total costs or average revenues (price) exceeds average total costs.

When a graph of average costs and price is presented, the question of how much to produce to maximize profits is answered the same way as above: where the extra benefits equal the extra costs. Marginal costs provides the extra cost information and price supplies the extra benefit measurement. Thus, profit maximization occurs at the output level where the price line intersects the marginal cost curve. As before, profit maximization does not guarantee a profit; it may illustrate the smallest loss. Finding the extent of profits or losses requires three steps. First, identify the profit-maximizing level of output (price equals marginal costs). Second, moving vertically up from the profit-maximizing output, note the intersection of at the ATC curve and the price line. If you encounter the ATC curve first, then the firm is earning a profit. If you reach the price line first then the firm has losses. Third, from the points of intersection move horizontally to the left until you strike the vertical axis (the line at the price is already there but in future models it won't be, so practice marking it even if you don't actually redraw the line). The area of total profits or losses is now enclosed by the two point on the vertical axis and the two points of intersection from step two.

Note: Locating the output level that achieves profit maximization is difficult, so be sure to practice questions 2, 3, and 4 in the Problems section.

The final point to make connects profit-maximization behavior to the concept of the supply curve introduced in Chapter 3. As the price of the firm's output rises, the intersection of price and marginal costs moves in a northeastern direction along the marginal cost curve. When you mark the new profit maximizing level of output has price rises it will be to the right of the original level of output. Likewise, if price falls, the intersection moves in a southwestern direction along the marginal cost curve. Now the profit maximizing level of output will be smaller or to the left of the starting point. The marginal cost curve is tracking a direct relationship between changes in price and the resulting output decision of the firm. The supply curve is, therefore, the direct result of the firm's efforts to profit maximization. Construction of the market supply curve is accomplished by summing the marginal cost curves of all the firms at each and every price.

Note: This is why it is incorrect to say that firms produce more when the price rises so as to earn larger profits. They may just be incurring smaller losses. In either case, when price rises, the firm improves its condition by producing more.

Learning Objective 6: Discuss the determinants of supply in light of the profit maximizing model

With the development of marginal costs, the firm's supply curve and the market's supply curve finished, the determinants of supply (variables that shift the entire supply curve to the left or right) discussed in Chapter 3 can be analyzed more fully. Technological innovations reduce costs by improving efficiency, shifting the firm's marginal cost curve and hence the market supply curve to the right. As the prices of variable factors of production rise, the cost of producing any particular additional unit of output will rise, shifting the marginal cost curves and therefore the market supply curve to the left. When more firms join the industry, greater amounts of the good will be available at any and all prices, shifting market supply to the right. If producers form expectations that the market price will be higher in six months, they will withhold production today, shifting the market supply curve to the left. Finally, and perhaps most importantly, changes in prices of other goods and services can lead to a shift in the supply curve. For example, if the price of corn skyrockets, some wheat farmers may choose to leave the wheat market and enter the corn market, which would shift the market supply curve for wheat to the left and the market supply curve for corn to the right.

Learning Objective 7: Define and calculate the producers surplus.

The difference between the firm's reservation price and the actual price defines **producer surplus**. Producer surplus for the entire market is simply the sum of the producer surplus accruing to each seller. Graphically, it is the area above the supply curve and below the market price, making it a triangle. The formula for calculating the area of a triangle is as follows:

$$\text{Area} = \tfrac{1}{2} (\text{length})(\text{height}).$$

III. Self-Test

Key Terms
Match the term in the right-hand column with the appropriate definitions in the left-hand column by placing the letter of the term in the blank in front of its definition. (Answers are given at the end of the chapter.)

1. ____ A period in which all factors of production used by the firm can be altered.

2. ____ A firm that takes the market price as given, i.e., the firm has no ability to set the price of its output.

3. ____ The sum of variable costs and fixed costs.

4. ____ A firm that has some ability to set the price of its output.

5. ____ The difference between total revenues and total explicit and implicit costs.

6. ____ The result of dividing a firm's variable costs by the amount of output the firm made.

7. ____ A period in which at least one factor of production used by the firm cannot be altered.

8. ____ Costs that are invariant to the firm's level of output.

9. ____ In the short run, as additional units of a variable factor of production are used, the additional output generated begins to decline at some point.

10. ____ A market comprised entirely of price-taking firms.

11. ____ The extra cost incurred when the firm produces an extra unit of output.

12. ____ A factor of production whose level of usage depends on the amount of output the firm produces, e.g., labor.

13. ____ The difference between the price the firm receives and its reservation price.

14. ____ The result of dividing a firm's total costs by the amount of output the firm made.

15. ____ A firm that takes profit maximization as it primary goal.

16. ____ A factor of production whose level of usage does not depend on the amount of output the firm produces, e.g., square footage of the office.

17. ____ Any input the firm uses in order to produce its output.

18. ____ When the level of a cost incurred by the firm depends on the size of the firm's output.

19. ____ A firm for which total revenues exceed total costs.

a. average total cost (ATC)

b. average variable cost (AVC)

c. factor of production

d. fixed cost

e. fixed factor of production

f. imperfectly competitive firm

g. law of diminishing returns

h. long run

i. marginal cost

j. perfectly competitive market

k. price taker

l. producer surplus

m. profit

n. profitable firm

o. profit-maximizing firm

p. short run

q. total cost

r. variable cost

s. variable factor of production

Multiple-Choice Questions
Circle the letter that corresponds to the best answer. (Answers are given at the end of the chapter.)

1. An imperfectly competitive firm is one that
   A. has some degree of influence over the price it charges for its output.
   B. finds it difficult to compete.
   C. charges any price it wishes.
   D. revenue maximizes.
   E. confronts a perfectly inelastic demand curve.

2. To produce 150 units of output, the firm must use 3 employee-hours. To produce 300 units of output the firm must use 8 employee-hours. Apparently, the firm is
   A. more profitable.
   B. in the long run.
   C. experiencing diminishing marginal returns.
   D. not using any fixed factors of production.
   E. failing to profit maximize.

3. To maximize profits, the firm should produce the output level where
   A. total costs are the lowest.
   B. variable costs are the lowest.
   C. total revenues are the largest.
   D. price equals marginal costs.
   E. marginal costs are the lowest.

4. The shutdown condition for a firm occurs where
   A. total revenues are less than the total cost of fixed and variable factors of production.
   B. total revenues are less than the cost of variable factors of production.
   C. total revenues are less than the cost of fixed factors of production.
   D. profits are negative.
   E. profits are zero.

5. An increase in the price the firm receives for its output will cause the firm to
   A. expand output and earn greater profits or smaller losses.
   B. expand output and earn greater profits.
   C. leave output unchanged and earn greater profits.
   D. leave output unchanged and earn greater profits or smaller losses.
   E. contract output and earn greater profits.

6. Suppose a firm is collecting $1345 in total revenues and the total cost of its fixed factors of production rise from $200 to $300. One can speculate that the firm will
   A. expand output.
   B. raise price.
   C. earn greater profits or smaller losses.
   D. contract output.

E. earn smaller profits or greater losses.

7. Suppose a firm is collecting $1250 in total revenues and the total costs of its variable factors of production are $1000 at its current level of output. One can predict that the firm will
   A. shut down.
   B. earn a profit.
   C. earn a loss.
   D. continue to operate.
   E. raise its price.

8. Assuming the firm is experiencing diminishing marginal returns to its variable factors of production, as output price falls the firm will
   A. produce more.
   B. earn profits.
   C. produce less, possibly choosing to shut down.
   D. earn losses.
   E. shutdown.

9. Improvement in production technology causes an increase in
   A. the quantity supplied by firms and an increase in market supply.
   B. supply by firms and an increase in the market quantity supplied.
   C. the quantity supplied by firms and an increase in the market quantity supplied.
   D. supply by firms and an increase in market supply.
   E. supply by firms and no change in market supply.

10. If the firm's demand curve is perfectly elastic, the firm must be
    A. a monopoly.
    B. an imperfect competitor.
    C. an oligopoly.
    D. a perfect competitor.
    E. a revenue maximizer.

11. Of the following characteristics, which one applies to a perfectly competitive firm?
    A. It always earns a profit.
    B. It seeks only to minimize costs.
    C. It can sell all it wants at the market price.
    D. It will never earn a profit.
    E. It has a narrow range of prices it can charge for its output.

12. Which of the following is most likely to be a fixed factor of production at a university?
    A. The number of personal computers.
    B. The number of books in the library.
    C. The number of professors and lecturers.
    D. The amount of chalk.
    E. The size of the college of liberal arts building.

13. Which of the following is most likely to be a variable factor of production at a university?
    A. The number of administrative assistants and student graders.
    B. The size of the basketball arena or football stadium.
    C. The school mascot.
    D. The acreage of the campus.
    E. The location of the university.

14. Congestion of the fixed factors of production at the firm explains
    A. high employee turnover.
    B. increased workplace violence.
    C. the law of diminishing marginal returns.
    D. decreased employee morale.
    E. increased self-employment.

15. Suppose 40 employee-hours can produce 80 units of output. Assuming the law of
    diminishing marginal returns is present, to produce 160 units of output will require
    A. an additional 40 employee-hours.
    B. a total of 80 or less employee-hours.
    C. less than 40 additional employee-hours.
    D. a total of 81 or more employee-hours.
    E. a total of 80 employee-hours.

16. Assume that the firm uses 13 employee-hours and an office to produce 100 units of output.
    The price of output is $5, the wage rate is $10, and rent is $200. The firm has total labor costs
    of
    A. $500.
    B. $300.
    C. $200.
    D. $130.
    E. $10.

17. Assume that the firm uses 13 employee-hours and an office to produce 100 units of output.
    The price of output is $5, the wage rate is $10, and rent is $200. The firm will earn a _____
    of _____.
    A. profit; $500
    B. loss; $200
    C. profit; $370
    D. loss; $170
    E. profit; $170

18. Marginal cost is calculated as
    A. total revenue minus total costs.
    B. the change in output divided by the change in total costs.
    C. the percentage change in total costs divided by the percentage change in output.
    D. the change in total costs divided by the change in output.

E. total revenue minus fixed costs.

19. As price increases, perfectly competitive firms find it is
    A. beneficial to produce more units of output.
    B. more difficult to sell their product.
    C. beneficial to produce less units of output.
    D. less difficult to sell their product.
    E. more important to consider the role of fixed costs.

20. The marginal cost curve is the firm's supply curve because it shows
    A. an inverse relationship between price and output.
    B. the amount of profit at each level of output.
    C. the extra profit at each level of output.
    D. a negative relationship between price and output.
    E. that a profit maximizing firm will produce more as price rises.

Short Answer Problems
(Answers and solutions are given at the end of the chapter.)

1. Production Theory
The question here helps to clarify your understanding of the difference between the short and long run and between fixed and variable factors of production. The data show the firm's output using two factors of production. The factors of production are measured in units, not prices.

Output	Labor (Hours)	Office Space (sq. ft.)
0	0	1000
25	5	1000
65	10	1000
95	15	1000
115	20	1000
125	25	1000
130	30	1000

A. The firm must be operating in the (short run/long run) _____ because (office space/labor) _____ is a (fixed/variable) _____.
B. Increasing labor from 5 to 10 hours causes output to rise by (65/40) _____ units.
C. Increasing labor from 10 to 15 hours causes output to rise by (30/25) _____ units.
D. Based on the answers to parts B and C, the firm begins to experience the law of diminishing marginal returns at (10/15) _____ hours of labor usage.

2. Profit Maximization
The following exercise reviews calculation of total revenues, total costs and profits for a firm.

Output	Employee Hours	Output Price	Rent	Wage Rate	Total Revenues	Total Costs	Profits/ Losses
0	0	$3	$75	$4			
15	3	$3	$75	$4			
30	7	$3	$75	$4			
45	12	$3	$75	$4			
60	18	$3	$75	$4			
75	25	$3	$75	$4			
90	37	$3	$75	$4			

A. Calculate the values for total revenues, total costs, and profits or losses (use a minus sign for losses).

B. For the data in table, the profit-maximizing level of output is (75/90) _____ units, with a profit of ($47/$50) _____.

C. Suppose that the rent on the office space the firm is using increased from $75 to $95 while all other variables remain unchanged. The new profit-maximizing level of output is (60/75) _____ units with a (profit/loss) _____ of ($30/-$30) _____.

D. The results in part C indicate that when the cost of a (fixed/variable) _____ factor of production changes, the optimal level of production (remains the same/changes) _____, but the level of profits or losses (remains the same/changes) _____.

E. Suppose the price the firm receives increases from $3 to $5, while all other variables are at the original values. The new profit-maximizing level of output is (75/90) _____ with a profit of ($227/$200) _____.

3. Marginal Costs and the Supply Curve

The relationship between total costs, marginal costs, and profit maximization is examined in this question.

Output	Employee Hours	Rent	Wage Rate	Total Costs	Marginal Costs
0	0	$20	$4		
20	2	$20	$4		
40	5	$20	$4		
60	9	$20	$4		
80	14	$20	$4		
100	20	$20	$4		

A. Calculate the total costs and marginal costs for all 6 output levels. Calculate marginal costs by taking the difference in total costs for two successive output levels, e.g., the marginal costs of 40 units of output is found by subtracting the total cost of 20 units from the total cost of 40 units and dividing by 20.

B. If the price of the firm's output is 85 cents, the firm should (shut down/operate) _____ and will produce (0/40/60) _____ units, resulting in a (profit/loss) _____ of _____.

C. If the price of output is $1.10, the firm will produce (60/80/100) _____ units and earn a (profit/loss) _____ of _____.

D. Based on parts B and C, as the price the firm receives rises from 85 cents to $1.10, the firm responds by (producing more/cutting costs) _____, illustrating a (positive/negative) _____ relationship between price and quantity supplied.

E. Finally, if the price of the firm's output was 25 cents, the firm would (shut down/operate) _____ because (profits/losses) _____ would be (smaller/larger) _____ than if the firm choose to (shut down/operate) _____.

4. Average Costs

Your proficiency using the graph of average costs, marginal costs, and price to locate and identify different points involved in the profit maximization is evaluated here. The firm is a price taker and the market price of the good is P.

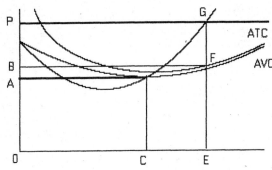

A. In the graph, the ATC and AVC are (growing closer together/a constant distance from each other) _____, which is (sometimes true/always true) _____.
B. The distance that represents the lowest price the firm can endure without shutting down is (EF/0A) _____.
C. The profit-maximizing level of output is measured by the distance (0C/PG) _____. At the profit maximizing output, ATC are (0A/EF/AB) ____.
D. The profit-maximizing level of output earns the firm a (profit/loss) _____ equal to the area of (0PGE/BPGF/GF) _____.
E. If the market price were to increase, the intersection of the new, higher price and the MC curve would be to the (right/left) _____ of the current intersection, resulting in a (larger/smaller) _____ output and a (larger/smaller/can't predict) _____ amount of profit.

IV. Economic Naturalist Application

Returning again to the market for illegal drugs, do you think it is a perfectly competitive industry? Discuss the following factors: the number of sellers, the degree of product standardization, and the easy of entry and exit. Would legalization result in a more or less perfectly competitive environment?
Answer:

V. Go to the Web: Graphing Exercises Using Interactive Graphs

As noted earlier, the mechanics of finding the profit maximizing output level involves several steps using a table or graph. Most students will need to practice these steps several times. Try the following: how would an improvement in the efficiency of the labor input be similar to a reduction in the wage rate paid to the labor input? How would it be different?
Answer:

To review the answer to this question and learn more about the use of economic theory to analyze this issue (and other macroeconomic issues), please go to Electronic Learning Session in the Student Center at the Frank/Bernanke web site: hppt://www.mhhe.com/economics/frankbernanke2.

VI. Self-Test Solutions

Key Terms
1. h
2. k
3. q
4. f
5. m
6. b
7. p
8. d
9. g
10. j
11. i
12. s
13. l
14. a
15. o
16. e
17. c
18. r
19. n

Multiple-Choice Questions
1. A
2. C
3. D
4. B
5. A
6. E
7. D
8. C
9. D
10. D
11. C
12. E
13. A
14. C
15. D
16. D
17. C
18. D
19. A
20. E

Short Answer Problems

1.
A. short run; office space; fixed
B. 40.
C. 30
D. 10

2.

Output	Employee Hours	Rent	Output Price	Wage Rate	Total Revenues	Total Costs	Profits/ Losses
0	0	$75	$3	$4	$0	$75	-$75
15	3	$75	$3	$4	$45	$87	-$42
30	7	$75	$3	$4	$90	$103	-$13
45	12	$75	$3	$4	$135	$123	$12
60	18	$75	$3	$4	$180	$147	$33
75	25	$75	$3	$4	$225	$175	$50
90	37	$75	$3	$4	$270	$223	$47

A. See table
B. 75; $50
C. 75; $30
D. fixed; remains the same; changes
E. 90; $227

3.

Output	Employee Hours	Rent	Wage Rate	Total Costs	Marginal Costs
0	0	$20	$4	$20	NA
20	2	$20	$4	$28	$0.40
40	5	$20	$4	$40	$0.60
60	9	$20	$4	$56	$0.80
80	14	$20	$4	$76	$1.00
100	20	$20	$4	$100	$1.20

A. See table
B. operate; 60; loss; $5
C. 80; profit; $12
D. producing more; positive
E. shutdown; losses; smaller; operate

4.
A. growing closer together; always true
B. 0A
C. PG; EF
D. profit; 0PGE
E. right; larger; larger

Chapter 7
Efficiency and Exchange

I. Pretest: What Do You Really Know?

Circle the letter that corresponds to the best answer. (Answers appear immediately after the final question).

1. If a market is in equilibrium then
   A. supply equals demand.
   B. the price is "too high."
   C. all mutually beneficial transactions between buyers and sellers have taken place.
   D. the price is "too low."
   E. some mutually beneficial transactions between buyers and sellers have not taken place.

2. The resulting reduction in the total economics surplus due to any price blocking policy is
   A. producer surplus.
   B. deadweight loss.
   C. total economics surplus.
   D. conspicuous consumption.
   E. consumer surplus.

3. Which of the following is *not* required for the market equilibrium to be efficient?
   A. Consumers and producers must be well informed.
   B. The market must be perfectly competitive.
   C. The equilibrium price must be considered fair and just.
   D. The supply curve must include all the costs of production.
   E. The demand curve must include all the benefits of consumption.

4. A price ceiling will cause
   A. producer surplus to fall.
   B. total economic surplus to rise.
   C. quantity supplied to exceed quantity demanded.
   D. quantity supplied to increase.
   E. demand to increase.

5. A first-come, first-served allocation mechanism results in a(n)
    A. efficient equilibrium.
    B. efficient equilibrium if you get served.
    C. inefficient equilibrium.
    D. inefficient equilibrium if you don't get served.
    E. efficient equilibrium if you don't get served.

6. A tax of $1 on each unit a producer sells will
    A. shift supply to the right.
    B. decrease quantity supplied.
    C. shift supply to the left.
    D. increase quantity supplied.
    E. decrease demand.

7. The more inelastic demand is, the _____ the burden of the tax borne by _____.
    A. smaller; consumers
    B. larger; consumers
    C. larger; producers
    D. larger; consumers and producers
    E. smaller; consumers and producers

8. If a per unit tax is imposed, the more elastic demand is, the
    A. less likely the deadweight loss will be affected.
    B. smaller the deadweight loss.
    C. larger the deadweight loss to consumers.
    D. smaller the deadweight loss to producers.
    E. larger the deadweight loss.

9. Total economic surplus is
    A. the ratio of consumer surplus or producer surplus.
    B. the difference between consumer surplus and producer surplus.
    C. the difference between tax revenues and government expenditures.
    D. the sum of consumer and producer surpluses.
    E. minimized at the point of market equilibrium.

10. Choosing efficiency as the first social goal and equity as the second means
    A. when equity is considered, the surplus available is as large as possible.
    B. society is unconcerned with the problems of the underprivileged.
    C. society will become more materialistic.
    D. greater income inequality.
    E. the rich get richer and the poor get poorer.

Solutions and Feedback to Pretest
For each question you incorrectly answered, we strongly recommend taking the time to review the appropriate material before continuing. In the table below, the relevant textbook pages are

listed for each question as well as the pertinent Learning Objective from the following Key Point Review.

Correct Answer	Textbook Page Numbers	Learning Objective
1. C	pp. 168-71	1
2. B	pp. 172-80	2
3. C	pp. 168-71	1
4. A	pp. 172-80	2
5. C	pp. 172-80	2
6. C	pp. 182-83	4
7. B	pp. 186-87	6
8. E	pp. 183-85	5
9. D	pp. 183-85	5
10. A	pp. 168-71	1

II. Key Point Review

Learning Objective 1: Define efficiency and explain its meaning in the context of a supply and demand graph. List other important social goals and defend the placement of efficiency as the first social goal.

When a market achieves equilibrium, the resulting price and quantity are said to be **efficient (or Pareto-efficient)**: no reallocation is available that benefits some individuals without harming others. If the market equilibrium is efficient, maximizing total economic surplus, why then are some people unable to acquire minimal amounts of housing? Because the concept of efficiency takes the factors that influence supply and demand as given. Given the distribution of income, the housing market equilibrium is efficient. If the distribution of income is such that some have low incomes, then it is likely that they will suffer from a lack of access to housing. Ignoring the housing needs of low-income consumers is not an implication of efficiency. Efficiency focuses attention on what is actually wrong: a lack of income. The economist would prefer to see a government housing subsidy for low-income consumers rather than rent controls because the subsidy attacks the problem directly without distorting the efficiency of the market. By making efficiency the first goal of society, the total economic surplus is maximized, allowing for the greatest possible ability to address other social goals.

Learning Objective 2: Discuss and analyze the following policies that thwart price adjustments: price ceilings, price subsides, and first-come, first-served pricing.

Price controls are legally mandated prices, designed to prevent the development of the equilibrium price in the name of some social goal. A price ceiling is a law or regulation that prevents sellers from charging more than a specified amount. Typically, the rationale for a price ceiling is an equilibrium price that is "too high." A prime example is a rent control: the poor have difficulty paying the free market rent so by legislating a lower rent, the poor will gain access to housing. The imposition of the price ceiling results predictably in a shortage of housing. Moreover, the disruption of the market lowers total economic surplus and transfers some of the producer surplus to consumers. A price subsidy is a attempt to assist low-income consumers by subsidizing the price of "essential" goods or services. The result is a level of consumption in excess of the optimal value. The reduction in total economic surplus comes from the units produced at a cost that exceeds their benefit. Another form of "price control" practiced by private firms is the first-come, first-served allocation method. Airlines in the United States used to practice this policy in handling overbooking problems. When more passengers wished to travel than the seats available, the airlines used to award the seats to those that arrived first. The current policy now seeks volunteers to give up their seat for compensation. As a result, seats are now award on the basis of value to the consumer. Generally, any first-come, first-served allocation scheme will result in an inefficient outcome, causing the total economic surplus to be smaller.

Learning Objective 3: Explain how governments should price the goods and services it provides.
Given the fact that the government has made the decision to provide a particular good, e.g., water, how should it be priced? By the price equals marginal cost rule. Suppose a city gets water from two different sources, low cost and high cost. The city will use the low-cost water first and then the high cost. Securing an extra unit of water means buying an extra unit from high cost, so the relevant cost to all consumers, independent of which source supplies their household, is the amount charged by the high-cost source.

Learning Objective 4: Analyze who pays for a per unit tax imposed on sellers.
Taxes on specific goods or services are a common form of market distortion caused by government action. Imposing a $1 per unit tax on the sellers of good acts like a $1 increase in the marginal cost of production. If the supply curve before the tax showed that the 10th unit cost $5 to produce, it will now cost $6 with the tax. Supply has been shifted up by $1 at each and every output level. The first question then is who pays how much of this $1 tax? The burden of the tax is the percentage of the tax paid by consumers and firms. Usually, the tax law levies the tax on the firms. Businesses are required to account for the tax revenue collected when they make sales. This sometimes leads to the inaccurate perception that the firms bear 100% of the tax burden. Likewise, some seem to think that firms can pass the entire amount of the tax on to consumers so the consumer's burden is 100%. For nearly all instances of taxes applied to specific goods, the burden of the tax is shared between consumers and firms. The elasticity of demand and supply determine the ultimate burden of the tax. Considering the extremes of demand, if demand were perfectly inelastic, then consumers would bear 100% of the tax burden, while if demand were perfectly elastic consumers would bear none of the tax burden.

Learning Objective 5: Define deadweight loss and illustrate the changes in consumer surplus, producer surplus, and total economic surplus when a per unit tax is imposed.
Beyond the burden of the tax is the impact of the tax on total economic surplus. As with price controls, there must be a loss in total economic surplus because the equilibrium outcome is altered. The reduction in the economic surplus is called the **deadweight loss** of the tax. It is equal to the area in the curve of the consumer surplus and producer surplus that existed before the tax but no longer occurs.

Learning Objective 6: Analyze the influence of the price elasticity of demand on the size of the deadweight loss from a per unit tax. Repeat the analysis for the price elasticity of supply. Give some examples of goods that are taxed consistent with the analysis. Understanding tax burdens and the deadweight loss of taxation is not to demonstrate that all taxes are bad and should be eliminated but to help society make wise choices when deciding what to tax. Elasticity is the critical issue. For a given supply curve, the more elastic the demand curve, the larger the resulting deadweight loss due to taxation. For a given demand curve, the more elastic the supply curve, the larger the resulting deadweight loss. Thus, goods for which either demand or supply (or, in the best case, both) is relatively inelastic are better candidates for taxes. It should not be surprising to note that alcohol, tobacco, and gasoline all have per unit taxes applied to them by more than one level of government.

III. Self-Test

Key Terms
Match the term in the right-hand column with the appropriate definitions in the left-hand column by placing the letter of the term in the blank in front of its definition. (Answers are given at the end of the chapter.)

1. _____ The reduction in total economic surplus due to the adoption of some policy, e.g., taxes.

2. _____ A situation in which no alteration is possible that will help some without harming others.

a. efficient (or Pareto-efficient)

b. deadweight loss

Multiple-Choice Questions
Circle the letter that corresponds to the best answer. (Answers are given at the end of the chapter.)

1. Which of the following is not guaranteed by the efficiency of the market equilibrium?
   A. Price represents the value of an extra unit of consumption.
   B. Rich and poor will have adequate access to the good.
   C. Price represents the cost of an extra unit of production.
   D. Neither shortage nor surplus will exist.
   E. All mutually beneficial trades will have been made.

2. Which of the following statements expresses the justification for making efficiency the first goal of economic interaction?
   A. Efficiency gives the poor an incentive to improve their economic status.
   B. Since consensus on what is a fair distribution of goods is impossible, efficiency is the next-best goal.
   C. People are not really concerned about the problems of the poor.
   D. It is too difficult to pursue more than one goal at a time.
   E. Efficiency maximizes total economics surplus and thereby allows other goals to be more fully achieved.

3. After a price ceiling is imposed, the total economic surplus in that market will
   A. rise.
   B. remain unchanged.
   C. fall.
   D. be reallocated from consumers to producers.
   E. rise or fall, depending on the price elasticity of demand.

4. Which of the following statements best characterizes the inefficiency induced by a price ceiling?
   A. Trades that would have occurred in an unregulated market aren't made.
   B. The extra benefit from the last unit consumed is less than the extra cost.
   C. The enforcement of the price ceiling is extremely costly.
   D. Producers are encouraged to produce too much.
   E. A "fair" price for any good cannot be established.

5. Compared to the first-come, first-served allocation scheme airlines used in the past, the voluntary compensation scheme now in place
   A. discriminates against the poor.
   B. improves efficiency for only the wealth.
   C. tricks the poor into unnecessarily delaying their travel.
   D. improves efficiency for all travelers.
   E. encourages passengers to show up early.

6. Which of the following policies maintains efficiency in the housing market while assisting the poor with their housing needs?
   A. A price floor.
   B. A price ceiling.
   C. A free market with subsidies to landlords.
   D. A free market with subsidies to the poor.
   E. Subsidized moving expenses for the poor.

7. In general, a $1 tax placed on each unit a producer sells will be
   A. entirely borne by the producers.
   B. split 50/50 between producers and consumers.
   C. entirely borne by the consumers.
   D. shared between producers and consumers.
   E. entirely shifted to consumers.

8. The more elastic demand is, the _____ the burden of the tax borne by _____.
   A. smaller; consumers
   B. larger; consumers
   C. smaller; consumers and producers
   D. smaller; producers
   E. larger; consumer and producers

9. The more inelastic demand is, the _____ the burden of the tax borne by _____.
   A. smaller; consumers
   B. larger; producers
   C. larger; consumers and producers
   D. smaller; consumers and producers
   E. smaller; producers

10. If a per unit tax is imposed, the more inelastic demand is, the
    A. smaller the deadweight loss.
    B. larger the deadweight loss to producers.
    C. smaller the deadweight loss to consumers.
    D. larger the deadweight loss.
    E. less likely the deadweight loss will be affected.

11. If a per unit tax is imposed, the more elastic the supply curve, the
    A. more likely the deadweight loss is to be affected.
    B. larger the deadweight loss.
    C. larger the deadweight loss to producers.
    D. smaller the deadweight loss to consumers.
    E. smaller the deadweight loss.

12. Market equilibrium is considered efficient because
    A. quantity supplied equals quantity demanded.
    B. the price consumers pay equals the amount producers receive.
    C. no more trades remain that benefit some without harming others.
    D. excess supply is zero.
    E. excess demand is zero.

13. Suppose the market for sugar is in equilibrium at $3 per pound. This means that
    A. all remaining producers will require more than $3 to produce additional sugar.
    B. too many trades have occurred.
    C. all remaining consumers value sugar at more than $3.
    D. the benefit of the last pound of sugar exceeds $3.
    E. the cost of the last pound of sugar is less than $3.

14. Deadweight loss is
    A. present in all markets.
    B. the difference between consumer surplus and producer surplus.
    C. positive in markets where equilibrium is distorted by price controls or taxes.
    D. always larger than consumer surplus.
    E. always smaller than producer surplus.

15. Suppose the market for coffee is in equilibrium at a price of $5 per pound. This means
    A. all producers who want to sell coffee are pleased.
    B. all remaining producers require less than $5 to produce coffee.
    C. all consumers who want to buy coffee are satisfied.

D. all remaining consumers value additional pounds of coffee at less than $5.

E. many trades between consumers and producers remain.

16. Suppose a local internet service provider (ISP) can support 100 simultaneous connections and has sold unlimited usage subscriptions to 400 families for $20 a piece. Access to the internet is being allocated by

A. price.

B. quality of phone line.

C. a first-come, first-served scheme.

D. quality of modem.

E. price and a first-come, first-served scheme.

17. Except in the extreme cases of perfectly inelastic or elastic demand and/or supply curves, the burden of a per unit tax imposed on sellers falls

A. equally on consumers and producers.

B. partially on consumers and partially on producers.

C. entirely on producers.

D. entirely on consumers.

E. mostly on producers.

18. The best explanation for placing taxes on tobacco products and alcohol is that

A. smoking and drinking are sinful behaviors.

B. they punish producers of tobacco and alcohol.

C. the public supports taxing these items.

D. demand for tobacco and alcohol tends to be inelastic.

E. demand for tobacco and alcohol tends to be elastic.

19. When government buys up the output for a particular industry and then resells it to consumers at a lower price,

A. no deadweight loss occurs.

B. producers will protest.

C. a deadweight loss results.

D. consumers will protest.

E. total economic surplus is expanded.

20. If government provides a private good to consumers, e.g., water, the government should set the price equal to

A. what the poorest consumer can afford.

B. the marginal cost of the least expensive source.

C. what the wealthiest consumer can afford.

D. the marginal cost of the most expensive source.

E. the average cost of all sources.

Short Answer Problems
(Answers and solutions are given at the end of the chapter.)

1. Measuring Economic Surplus
In order to fully utilize the power of the supply and demand model to understand and predict the

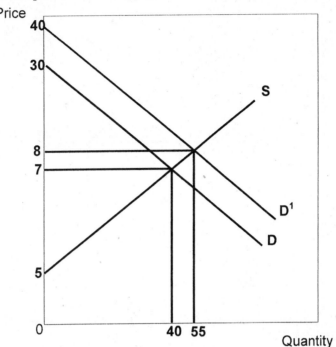

consequences of various policy alternatives, one must be able to calculate the total economic surplus with and without the proposed policy. In answering the questions posed here, you can check your understanding of the graphical and numerical interpretation of the total economic surplus.

   A. The above market is in initial equilibrium with demand and supply of D and S. The amount of consumer surplus is thus ($460/$920) _____ and the producer surplus is ($80/$40) _____. Thus, the total economic surplus is the market is ($500/$540) _____.

   B. Suppose demand increases from D to D^1. The new level of consumer surplus is ($632.50/$880) _____. The amount of producer surplus is now ($82.50/$220) _____. The total economic surplus has increased by ($462.50/$55) _____.

   C. As a result of the demand increase, consumers (are/are not) _____ better off while producers (are/are not) _____ better off.

2. Efficiency and Price Controls
The real importance of learning how to calculate the various measures of surplus in a market is so that a policy, frequently a government policy, can be analyzed. Here the effects of a price ceiling will be assessed.

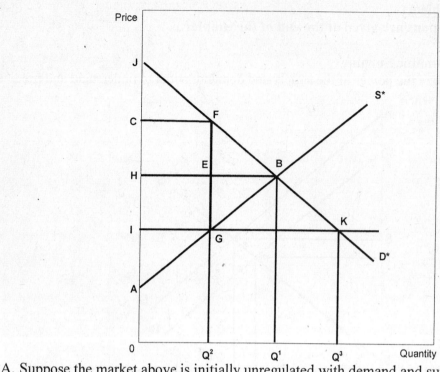

A. Suppose the market above is initially unregulated with demand and supply of D* and S*. Consumer surplus is represented by the area (0JBQ¹/HJB) _____ and producer surplus is the area (AIG/AHB) _____. The total economic surplus in the unregulated environment is (AJB/0JBQ¹) _____.

B. Suppose government imposes a price control at I, which means it is a price (ceiling/floor) _____. The effect is to create a (surplus/shortage) _____ equal to the distance (IG/GK) _____.

C. After the imposition of the price control, producer surplus is (AIG/GEB) _____ while consumer surplus becomes (CJF/IJFG) _____.

D. The deadweight loss due to the price control is the area (Q²FBQ¹/GFB) _____ and represents the value of (transactions that should have happened/production that cost more than the benefits received) _____.

3. Efficiency and Taxes

Another policy alternative to consider is taxes, which are a far more common form of government imposed market distortion. The method for analyzing the effect of a tax on total economic surplus is slightly different than for the price ceiling in Question 2: it is a numerical rather than geometric problem. Imagine that in a market the demand curve is $P = 1,000 - 3*Q$ and the supply curve is $P = 250 + 7*Q$.

A. Assume that the market is completely free of government influence. Calculate the extent of consumer surplus, producer surplus, and the total economic surplus: CS _____; PS _____; TES _____.

B. Suppose a per unit tax of $50 is imposed on sellers. The relevant demand curve is written as _____ and the supply curve is written as _____.

C. Calculate the price consumers will pay and their share of the tax, then calculate the price firms will receive and their share of the tax: P consumer _____; consumer tax burden _____; P firm _____; firm tax burden_____.

D. Calculate the extent of consumer surplus, producer surplus, and total economic surplus with the tax: CS _____; PS _____; TES _____.

E. The extent of the deadweight loss from the tax is _____.

IV. Economic Naturalist Application

Taxes on cigarettes and alcohol are frequently called "sin taxes." Presumably, the legalization of some or all illegal drugs or prostitution would also be taxed under the banner of sin taxes. Explain why cigarettes, alcohol and, if legalized, illegal drugs or prostitution are desirable items to tax independent of any moral judgment about sin. As an alternative view, consider a world where smoking, alcohol consumption, and drug taking are not thought of as "immoral." Would government still find it desirable to tax these items?

Answer:

V. Go To The Web: Graphing Exercises Using Interactive Graphs

Search the Web for estimates of the deadweight loss stemming from government action like price controls or per unit taxes. Note that a sales tax is a per unit tax: rather than assessing, say, $1 per unit, it is, in Texas, 8% of the price of one item. Do the magnitudes of the estimate surprise you?

Answer:

To review an answer to this question, and to learn more about the use of economic theory to analyze this issue (and other macroeconomic issues), please go to the Electronic Learning Session in the Student Center at the Frank/Bernanke web site: http://www.mhhe.com/economics/frankbernanke2.

VI. Self-Test Solutions

Key Terms

1. b
2. a

Multiple-Choice Questions

1. B
2. E
3. C
4. A
5. D
6. D
7. D
8. A
9. E
10. A
11. B
12. C
13. A
14. C
15. D
16. C
17. B
18. D
19. C
20. D

Short Answer Problems

1.
A. $460 [($30 - $7)×40×.5]; $40 [($7 - $5)×40×.5]; $500 ($460 + $40)
B, $880; $82.50; $462.50
C. are; are

2.
A. HJB; AHB; AJB
B. ceiling; shortage; GK
C. AIG; IJFG
D. GFB; transactions that should have happened

3.
A. $8,437.50; $19,687.50; $28,125.00
B. $P = 1,000 - 3*Q$; $P = 300 + 7*Q$
C. $790; ($15/$50) = .30; $740; ($35/$50) = .70
D. $7,350; $17,150; $24,500
E. $3,625

Chapter 8
The Quest for Profit and the Invisible Hand

I. Pretest: What Do You Really Know?

Circle the letter that corresponds to the best answer. (Answers appear immediately after the final question).

1. Which of the following is *not* an example of explicit costs?
   A. Wages paid to workers.
   B. Personal savings of the owner invested in a firm.
   C. Salaries paid to management.
   D. Fees paid for maintenance of the firm's website.
   E. Office space rent.

2. Which of the following is *not* an example of implicit costs?
   A. The return stockholders could have earned with another company.
   B. The fees the firm could have earned from leasing its computers.
   C. The revenue the firm could collect from selling its furniture.
   D. The interest the owners could have earned on their personal monies invested in the firm.
   E. The salary of the CEO.

3. To say a firm is earning normal profits means that
   A. the owners are receiving what others in the industry earn.
   B. accounting profits are large enough to cover the owners' opportunity costs.
   C. the owners are receiving more than their next best alternative.
   D. the owners are receiving more than they expected.
   E. the owners are receiving less than their next-best alternative.

4. Generally, _____ motivate firms to enter an industry while _____ motivate firms to exit an industry.
   A. economic profits; economic losses
   B. accounting profits; accounting losses
   C. accounting profits; economic losses
   D. economic profits; accounting losses
   E. normal profits; normal losses

5. If buyers and sellers were free to pursue their own selfish interests, according to the invisible hand theory, the result would be
    A. anarchy.
    B. exploitation of workers and natural resources.
    C. an equitable allocation of resources.
    D. poor consumers service.
    E. an efficient allocation of resources.

6. Which of the following would be an example of the rationing function of price?
    A. Switching from a Ph.D. in economics to finance because finance salaries are higher.
    B. Bill Gates purchasing the Mona Lisa for $5 billion.
    C. A firm attempting to lower its explicit costs.
    D. Government price controls.
    E. Choosing to skip class and hang out.

7. Suppose you are willing to work for $10 per hour and you receive an offer of $15 per hour. Your _____ is _____.
    A. economic profit; $5
    B. economic rent; $5
    C. economic rent; $15
    D. economic profit; $15
    E. economic rent; $10

8. The present value of $1000 paid a year from now is
    A. the value it will have one year from now.
    B. the value of having $1000 today instead of one year from now.
    C. the amount necessary, at the current interest rate, to be worth $1000 a year from now.
    D. more than $1000.
    E. the amount $1000 invested at the current interest rate will be worth in a year.

9. Suppose that AMD announces that yields and sales of Athlon microprocessors were much better than expected. The efficient markets hypothesis suggests that
    A. the price of a share of AMD stock will rise but very slowly.
    B. this information had already been incorporated into AMD's stock price.
    C. the price of AMD stock would rise quickly as investors try to profit.
    D. the price of Intel stock would be unchanged.
    E. the stock price of companies using Athlon in their PCs would be unchanged.

10. If economic profits are positive, then
    A. firms will be exiting the industry.
    B. accounting profits can be either negative, zero, or positive.
    C. the firm is receiving exactly a normal profit.
    D. accounting profits are either zero or positive.
    E. accounting profits must be positive.

Solutions and Feedback to Pretest

For each question you answered incorrectly, we strongly recommend taking the time to review the appropriate material before continuing. In the table below, the relevant textbook pages are listed for each question as well as the pertinent Learning Objective from the following Key Point Review.

Correct Answer	Textbook Page Numbers	Learning Objective
1. B	pp. 194-97	1
2. E	pp. 194-97	1
3. B	pp. 194-97	1
4. A	pp. 198-204	3
5. E	p. 197	2
6. B	p. 197	2
7. B	pp. 205-206	4
8. C	pp. 210-15	6
9. C	pp. 210-15	6
10. E	pp. 194-97	1

II. Key Point Review

Learning Objective 1: Define explicit and implicit costs. Discuss the three alternative measures of profit.

Explaining the forces that guide resources through the various sectors and industries of the economy requires clear definitions of a few key terms. **Explicit costs** are the payments made by the firm to the factors of production used in generating output. Common examples include wages and rent. The difference between total revenues and explicit costs equals **accounting profit**. The opportunity cost of the resources supplied by the owners of the firm defines **implicit costs**. Economists define **economic profit** as total revenues minus both explicit and implicit costs. When economic profit is less than zero, it is called an **economic loss**. Finally, **normal profit** equals the difference between accounting profit and economic profit, which, after a little algebra, equals implicit costs.

Learning Objective 2: Define the Invisible Hand Theory. Define and explain the two functions of price in a market economy.

In any free market economy, the importance of market prices cannot be overemphasized. The **rationing function of price** serves to distribute scarce goods and services to consumers who value them the most. Directing resources away from overcrowded markets and toward underserved markets is the **allocative function of price.** The rationing and allocative functions of price anchor the economic system described by Adam Smith in the late 1700s. Smith's **Invisible Hand theory** argued the actions of independent, self-interested buyers and sellers would often achieve the most efficient allocation of resources.

Learning Objective 3: Explain the role of profits and losses in motivating movement into and out of industries. Note the importance of free entry and exit and define barriers to entry.

The importance of the measures of profits and costs centers on their ability to motivate behavior. Consider a firm earning an economic profit. Applying the definition reveals that the owners of the firm are earning more than their next-best alternative. No other activity would result in a larger amount of earnings for them. Unquestionably, the owners will want to continue with their business. Earning economic profits of zero or receiving a normal profit means the owners are doing as well as their next-best alternative. Running the business allows them to recover the opportunity costs of the resources they invested in the business. By purely monetary criteria, the owners are indifferent between continuing to operate or reallocating their invested resources to their alternative use. A firm earning an economic loss fails to recover the opportunity costs of the resources the owners invested. The owners are doing worse than their next-best alternative. Now the owners should be eager to end the business and move their invested resources into their alternative use.

At the level of the industry, the presence of firms earning economic profits attracts resources from the outside. The newly arrived resources can be new-formed firms or existing firms in other industries that were earning normal profits or economic losses. In either case, firms begin to join the industry, leading to a rightward shift of the industry supply curve. For constant demand, the supply shift causes the equilibrium price and, ultimately, economic profits to fall. When economic profits are driven to zero, the market reaches the equilibrium number of firms and the process of entry ceases. The chain of reasoning applies in reverse to industries suffering economic losses. Resources are leaving, searching for a better use. As firms exit, the industry supply curve shifts to the left, cause price to rise and economic losses to lessen. When economic losses are eliminated, the process of firm exit stops. Industries with zero economic profits will experience neither entry nor exit as there is no incentive for resources to join or leave.

The freedom of resources to move between markets is critical for Smith's invisible hand to work. If new firms face obstructions to joining an industry earning economic profits, then the economic profits will not be competed to zero. **Barriers to entry** are any forces that prevents firms from entering a new market.

Learning Objective 4: Define economic rent and differentiate between economic rent and economic profit.

While economic profits are driven to zero with free entry, **economic rent**—the payment to a factor of production above the factor's reservation price—does not meet the same fate. Economic rents persist because of some unique characteristic of the factor. Michael Jordan enjoyed a considerable economic rent because his talents and skills could not be reproduced.

Learning Objective 5: Apply the Invisible Hand Theory to cost saving innovations and regulated markets.

Competitive firms, as noted in Chapter 6, cannot influence the price they receive for their output. The pursuit of economic profits then requires that they develop cost-saving innovation. If one firm in a competitive industry reduces its costs, it will start earning economic profits. Soon other firms will adopt or mimic the innovation, shifting the market supply curve to the right and lowering the equilibrium price. Eventually, the innovation will spread through the entire industry and economic profits will return to zero. But the return of zero economic profits provides an incentive for firms to discover new cost-saving innovations. The process repeats itself over and over, ensuring that production is accomplished at the lowest cost.

The invisible hand operates in regulated markets as well. When price or profits are controlled by a regulatory authority, resources will be allocated on some other basis. For example, when prices charged by airlines were regulated, prices were set to generate economic profits which the airlines were expected to use to offset losses for infrequently traveled routes. Since airlines could not compete with each other on the basis of price, they began to compete on the basis of amenities and frequency of service, leading to a less-than-efficient outcome. Similarly, programs designed to raise the price or profitability of a good to help a group of producers will only succeed in drawing more into the group, shifting the supply curve to the right and wiping out the short-term gains.

Learning Objective 6: Define the time value of money and present value. Define and explain the implication of the efficient markets hypothesis.
The invisible hand reveals itself in stock markets with incredible speed. A few terms need defining first. A share of stock in a company is a claim to a portion of the company's current and future accounting profits. The price of a share of stock is calculated as accounting profits per issued share divided by the interest rate. Since the value of the firm is based in part on future accounting profits, one must adjust for the **time value of money**: that $1 paid one month from now is less valuable than $1 paid today. Formally, one must compute the **present value** of the future profits. If the firm expects to earn M dollars of accounting profits T years from today and the interest rate is r, the present value of the future profits equals $M/(1 + r)^T$. In practice, future profits are unknown so investors must use estimates. The estimates will incorporate information about current profits, the condition of the industry the firm belongs to, the general state of the economy, and many other factors. When the available information changes, the estimates and hence the price of the stock, change as well. What is remarkable is how quickly new information affects the stock price. The **efficient markets hypothesis** claims that a company's current stock price reflects all relevant information about the company's current and future prospects. The price of tobacco stock is a particularly vivid example. In 1996, a jury awarded a lung cancer patient $750,000 in damages and within minutes the price of tobacco stock dropped 20 percent. Obviously, the stock price decline was not over the $750,000 per se, but rather represented concerns about the future viability of the tobacco industry, for this was the first case the tobacco industry had lost. The practical lesson to glean: by the time a hot stock tip appears in a stockbroker's newsletter, the opportunity to profit from it is long gone.

III. Self-Test

Key Terms
Match the term in the right-hand column with the appropriate definitions in the left-hand column by placing the letter of the term in the blank in front of its definition. (Answers are given at the end of the chapter.)

1. _i_ The opportunity cost of the resources supplied by the owners of the firm.

2. _l_ The value of M dollars which will be received T years from now with an interest rate of r.

3. _c_ Any force that prevents new firms from entering a market.

4. _h_ Payments made by the firm to its factors of production.

5. _k_ What the owners of a firm receive if their economic profits are zero.

6. _b_ That price that serves to direct resources away from overcrowded markets and toward underserved markets.

7. _e_ The difference between total revenues and the sum of explicit and implicit costs.

8. _f_ The fraction of a payment made to a factor of production that exceeds the factor of production's reservation price.

9. _n_ A dollar today is worth more than a dollar one year from today because the dollar today could be invested in an interest-bearing asset.

10. _g_ The idea that the a firm's current stock price reflects all the relevant information about its current and future earnings prospects.

11. _j_ According to Adam Smith, the actions of independent, self-interested buyers and sellers will achieve an efficient allocation of resources most of time.

12. _a_ The difference between total revenues and explicit costs.

13. _d_ When economic profits are less than zero.

14. _m_ That price that serves to distribute goods to the consumers who value them the most.

a. accounting profit

b. allocative function of price

c. barrier to entry

d. economic loss

e. economic profit

f. economic rent

g. efficient markets hypothesis

h. explicit costs

i. implicit costs

j. Invisible Hand Theory

k. normal profit

l. present value

m. rationing function of price

n. time value of money

Multiple-Choice Questions

Circle the letter that corresponds to the best answer. (Answers are given at the end of the chapter.)

1. Which of the following would *not* be included in the calculation of accounting profits?
   A. Wages of workers.
   B. The salary the owner could have earned working elsewhere.
   C. Rent.
   D. Medical insurance coverage for workers.
   E. Access to the internet.

2. It is always true that
   A. accounting profits are positive.
   B. economic profits are zero.
   C. economic profits exceed accounting profits.
   D. economic profits are positive.
   E. accounting profits exceed economic profits.

3. Normal profits occur when
   A. accounting profits are positive.
   B. economic profits are positive.
   C. accounting profits are positive and economic profits are negative.
   D. economic profits are zero.
   E. total revenues are greater than explicit and implicit costs.

4. Suppose all firms in a perfectly competitive industry are experiencing economic losses to varying degrees. One can predict that
   A. market price will fall.
   B. market supply will increases.
   C. market demand will decrease.
   D. market supply will decrease.
   E. the number of firms will remain the same.

5. Suppose all firms in a perfectly competitive industry are experiencing economic profits. One can hypothesize that
   A. market price will fall.
   B. market supply will decrease.
   C. market demand will increase.
   D. the number of firms will not change.
   E. market demand will decrease.

6. The idea of free entry and exit suggests that queues (lines) at banks should be
   A. of unequal length.
   B. segregated by type of transaction (withdrawal, deposit, etc.).
   C. of approximately equal length.
   D. segregated by type of account (checking, savings, etc.).
   E. of equal height.

7. For entry into a particular perfectly competitive industry to occur, which of the following must be true?
   A. Economic profits > Accounting profits > 0.
   B. Accounting profits > Economic profits > 0.
   C. Accounting profits > 0 > Economic profits.
   D. Accounting profits > Economic profits = 0.
   E. Accounting profits = Economic profits = 0.

8. According to the textbook, most markets in the U.S.
   A. have significant barriers to entry.
   B. possess a high degree of free entry.
   C. have minor barriers to entry.
   D. are close to monopolies.
   E. allocate resources inefficiently.

9. The reason economic profit is driven to 0 by competition but economic rent is not stems from
   A. an inability to produce more of the input earning the rent.
   B. barriers to entry.
   C. lack of antitrust legislation for input markets.
   D. a failure of the invisible hand.
   E. inefficient allocation of inputs.

10. Celine Dion earned large economic rents in the late '90s. One can predict that as a result,
    A. more amateur singers will turn professional and reduce Ms. Dion's economic rent.
    B. more amateur singers will turn professional but Ms. Dion's economic rent will be
       unaffected.
    C. few record companies will be willing to sign her.
    D. consumers will become disgusted with the size of her earnings and stop purchasing her
       records.
    E. she will make sizable contributions to Canadian charities.

11. Jose receives an offer that will pay him $1500 two years from now. If the interest rate is 7%,
    the most Jose would be willing to pay for this offer is
    A. $519.
    B. $882.
    C. $1310.
    D. $1402.
    E. $1499.

12. According to the textbook, when the Wall Street Journal compared the performance of stocks
    picked by experts to randomly picked stocks,
    A. the experts' picks performed much better.
    B. the random picks performed much better.
    C. the experts' picks performed much worse.
    D. the random picks performed much worse.
    E. the performance of the two sets of stocks were about the same.

13. The efficient markets hypothesis suggests
    A. newsletters with stock tips and recommendations are helpful to investors.
    B. a significant lag exists between new information and changes in stock price.
    C. there is little incentive for insider trading.
    D. newsletters with stock tips and recommendations are virtually useless.
    E. some stock tip newsletters are helpful, others are useless.

14. Suppose a Ph.D. mathematician from MIT discovers "the formula" for picking stocks, using
    well-known statistical models and publicly available data. One can predict that
    A. he will become the wealthiest man in the world.
    B. he will always outperform the market.
    C. other investors will ignore his behavior.
    D. as his success becomes well known, other investors will mimic his choices and thereby
       drive his return down.

E. he can sustain his success forever.

15. If all firms in a perfectly competitive industry are earning a normal profit, then
    A. more firms will be entering the industry.
    B. the number of firms is stable.
    C. firms will be exiting the industry.
    D. firms are doing better than their next best alternative.
    E. firms are doing worse than their next best alternative.

16. The enormous growth in the number of Internet-based companies in 1998 and 1999 reflects
    A. the greed among Gen-Xers.
    B. an optimism that is unwarranted.
    C. a waste of talent.
    D. the "hipness" of being in e-commerce.
    E. a movement to resources in search of economic profits.

17. In a perfectly competitive industry over the long run,
    A. economic profits tend to persist.
    B. the number of firms in an industry grows.
    C. economic losses tend to persist.
    D. the number of firms in an industry shrinks.
    E. economic profits and losses are driven toward zero by entry and exit.

18. A new production technique that reduces costs in a perfectly competitive industry will result in
    A. widespread industry adoption and a lower price to consumers.
    B. industry consolidation.
    C. sustained economic profits for the first firms that adopt the technique.
    D. a rightward shift in the demand curve.
    E. entry by new firms.

19. If the government grants grain subsidies to poor farmers, over time
    A. poor farm families are made permanently better off.
    B. as the profits of farming increase, new farmers will emerge from other sectors and drive down the recent profits to zero.
    C. as new farmers enter, government will lessen the size of the subsidy.
    D. the quality of grains will fall.
    E. the quality of grains will rise.

20. If the present value of $1000 next month is $970.87, the interest rate is
    A. impossible to calculate.
    B. 1%.
    C. 3%.
    D. 4%.
    E. 5%.

124   Chapter 8

Short Answer Problems
(Answers and solutions are given at the end of the chapter.)

1. Accounting and Economic Profits
To fully understand the factors compelling firms to leave one industry to join another, the distinction between accounting profits and economic profits must be clear. The following table shows the revenue and cost data for a firm. If you have trouble with this question, review the definition of normal profits

Output	Total Revenues	Explicit Costs	Implicit Costs
10	$70	$55	$7
20	$140	$130	$8
30	$210	$201	$9
40	$280	$280	$10
50	$350	$360	$11

A. If the firm were to produce 20 units, its accounting profits are ($10/$8) _____ and its economic profits are ($10/$2) _____.

B. When 40 units are produced, an accountant would conclude the firm is (earning a loss/breaking even) _____ while an economist would argue the firm is (earning a loss/breaking even) _____.

C. The owners of the firm are doing as well as their next-best alternative when production is (30/40) _____ units.

D. If all firms in the industry have the same revenue and cost structure as above and all are producing 40 units of output, one can predict that firms will be (entering/exiting) _____ the industry because (accounting profits are zero/economic profits are negative) _____.

E. If all firms in the industry have the same revenue and cost structure as above and all are producing 20 units of output, one can predict that firms will be (entering/exiting) _____ the industry because (accounting profits are positive/economic profits are positive) _____.

2. Stock Price Calculation and Present Value
The purpose here is to review the calculation of present value and the price of a stock. Then the two ideas will be joined to illustrate the importance of the time value of money to a stock. Suppose e-longate, an Internet company, will post accounting profits of $600,000 one year from today and $2 million two years hence. The interest rate is 7 percent, inflation will be zero for the next two years and 200,000 shares have been issued. Derrick and Evan are trying to calculate the price of a share of e-longate stock. Derrick claims that since inflation is zero and e-longate's profits are certain, the time value of money concept is irrelevant. Evan counters that the time value of money concept is still relevant because consumption today is always preferred to consumption tomorrow.

A. According to Derrick's reasoning, the present value of e-longate's accounting profit is ($2,600,000/$2,307,625) _____.

B. According to Evan's reasoning, the present value of e-longate's accounting profit is ($2,600,000/$2,307,625) _____.

C. Based on their assumptions, Derrick calculates the price of one share of e-longate stock as ($186/$13) _____ while Evan finds a value of ($11.55/$165) _____.

D. By (ignoring/including) _____ the concept of present value, (Evan/Derrick) _____ is assigning a value to the stock price of e-longate that is (too high/too low) _____.

3. No Cash on the Table

While no unexploited opportunities can exist when a market has achieved a stable equilibrium, the path to the equilibrium is littered with them. The following problem illustrates the idea in a commonplace situation: waiting in line (also known as queuing). At the local supermarket, two checkout lines are open, One and Two, and the four customers, X, Y, W, and Z, are currently checking out. Suppose that each customers take exactly 5 minutes to check out. The time is 9:59:59 a.m. Note that the time spent checking out is not counted as waiting time. It may prove useful to illustrate the positions of new customers in the table.

Line One	Line Two	Line Three
W	X	
Y	Z	

A. Suppose Carla finishes her shopping and goes to check out at 10:01. Carla should choose line (One/Two/either) _____ and will wait for (10/9) _____ minutes.

B. Manny is ready to check out at 10:04. He should pick the line (with/without) _____ Carla and will have a waiting time of (11/6) _____ minutes.

C. At 10:05, line Three opens and Carla moves into it. The reason she moves is that the new line represents (excess capacity/an unexploited opportunity) _____ to (do better than /do as well as) _____ her next-best alternative.

D. After Carla has moved to line Three, Manny finds his wait time is (5/10) _____ minutes in (line One/line Two/all three lines) _____. Apparently, the "market" of waiting time is in (equilibrium/disequilibrium) _____ because (no/a few) _____ unexploited opportunities exist.

E. Stretching the terminology a bit, Carla has experienced (accounting profit/economic profit) _____ and Manny has experienced (economic loss/normal profit) _____.

IV. Economic Naturalist Application

The textbook observes that on average, each lane on the Interstate highway will move at the same pace, owning to drivers switching lanes. Do you observe this to be true when you drive? When you pass someone driving slowly, do you find that at the next stop light they have caught up to you? How would you analyze the owning of a fast sports car when in rush hour? A poor choice? An enhanced ability to take advantage of opportunities?

Answer:

V. Go to the Web: Graphing Exercises Using Interactive Graphs

As an example colored with great irony, search the Web for information on the collapse of the Internet boom. Find some specific information on the numbers of e-commerce based firms started and ended for the years 1997 to 2002. Explain the data in terms of the entry and exit pattern discussed in the textbook. Would 2003 be a relatively good or poor time to be starting a new Internet company?

Answer:

To review an answer to this question, and to learn more about the use of economic theory to analyze this issue (and other macroeconomic issues), please go to the Electronic Learning Session in the Student Center at the Frank/Bernanke web site: http://www.mhhe.com/economics/frankbernanke2.

VI. Self-Test Solutions

Key Terms

1. i
2. l
3. c
4. h
5. k
6. b
7. e
8. f
9. n
10. g
11. j
12. a
13. d
14. m

Multiple-Choice Questions

1. B
2. E
3. D
4. D
5. A
6. C
7. B
8. B
9. A
10. B
11. C
12. E
13. D
14. D
15. B
16. E
17. E
18. A
19. B
20. C

Short Answer Problems

1.
A. $10; $2
B. breaking even; earning a loss
C. 30
D. exiting; economic profits are negative
E. entering; economic profits are positive

2.
A. $2,600,000
B. $2,307,625
C. $186; $165
D. ignoring; Derrick; too high

3.
A. either; 9
B. without; 6
C. an unexploited opportunity; do better than
D. 5; all three lines; equilibrium; no
E. economic profit; normal profit

Chapter 9
Monopoly and Other Forms of Imperfect Competition

I. Pretest: What Do You Really Know?

Circle the letter that corresponds to the best answer. (Answers appear immediately after the final question.)

1. The correct sequence of market structures from most to least competitive is
    A. pure monopoly, oligopoly, perfect competition, monopolistic competition.
    B. oligopoly, pure monopoly, perfect competition, imperfect competition.
    C. perfect competition, monopolistic competition, oligopoly, pure monopoly.
    D. perfect competition, imperfect competition, pure monopoly.
    E. perfect competition, monopolistic competition, pure monopoly, oligopoly.

2. In order to sell another unit, an imperfectly competitive firm must
    A. raise its price.
    B. increase the value of its product.
    C. lower its price.
    D. lower its quality.
    E. increase its advertising.

3. Constant returns to scale occur when a doubling of all inputs
    A. doubles the price of outputs.
    B. more than doubles output.
    C. less than doubles the price of the inputs.
    D. exactly doubles output.
    E. less than doubles output.

4. Industries with large fixed costs and small, constant marginal costs will, over time,
    A. have more and more small firms.
    B. see one or a few large firms emerge.
    C. see no change in the average size of firms.
    D. see no change in the average number of firms.
    E. see the size of their market decline.

5. The perfectly competitive firm finds that price _____ marginal revenue, while a monopolist finds that price _____ marginal revenue.
   A. equals; equals
   B. is greater than; equals
   C. equals; is greater than
   D. is less than; equals
   E. equals; is less than

6. The monopolist will maximize profits if she produces where
   A. price equals marginal costs.
   B. price equals the minimum average total cost.
   C. marginal revenue equals marginal cost.
   D. marginal revenue equals average total cost.
   E. elasticity of demand is zero.

7. The economic justification for disdaining monopoly from a social point of view is because the monopolist
   A. always earns excessive profits.
   B. can charge any price he wants.
   C. exploits the inelastic nature of demand.
   D. produces less than the socially efficient amount.
   E. can treat his consumers with complete indifference.

8. As described in the textbook, price discrimination means charging
   A. the same consumers the same price.
   B. different prices to different consumers because production costs are different.
   C. the same price to all consumers because production costs are different.
   D. different prices to different consumers when production costs are the same.
   E. higher prices to women and minorities.

9. The reason a monopolist has an incentive to price discriminate is because
   A. some consumers, who are unwilling to pay the uniform monopoly price, are willing to pay more than the marginal cost.
   B. he can always use his market power to charge a different price.
   C. his marginal costs will be lower when he price discriminates.
   D. it causes demand to become more inelastic.
   E. some consumers, who are willing to pay the uniform monopoly price, are unwilling to pay more than the marginal costs.

10. The justification for having a list price and offering a mail-in rebate coupon is to
   A. separate the market into the less price sensitive and the more price sensitive.
   B. discourage all consumers from filling out the rebate form.
   C. make the consumer wait six months for the 50-cent check.
   D. appeal to those consumers who enjoy corresponding with large corporations.
   E. appeal to those consumers who dislike corresponding with large corporations.

Solutions and Feedback to Pretest

For each question you incorrectly answered, we strongly recommend taking the time to review the appropriate material before continuing. In the table below, the relevant textbook pages are listed for each question as well as the pertinent Learning Objective from the following Key Point Review.

Correct Answer	Textbook Page Numbers	Learning Objective
1. C	pp. 222-23	1
2. C	pp. 222-23	1
3. D	pp. 224-25	3
4. B	pp. 225-28	4
5. C	pp. 222-23	1
6. C	pp. 231-33	6
7. D	pp. 233-35	7
8. D	pp. 235-42	8
9. A	pp. 235-42	8
10. A	pp. 235-42	8

II. Key Point Review

Learning Objective 1: Define an imperfectly competitive firm, and identify the three specific types. Discuss the critical difference between perfectly and imperfectly competitive firms.

The discussion of the firm up to now has focused on the competitive firm, an idealized form of market structure. Most markets vary in one way or another from the requirements of perfect competition. The analysis begins with a simple definition: a **price setter** or an **imperfectly competitive firm** is one that possesses some ability to set the price of its output. More specifically, three types have been identified. A **pure monopoly** exists when the market contains one firm producing a good or service for which there are no close substitutes. An **oligopoly** is a market with a few rival firms. A firm that is one of many producing slightly differentiated goods that are close substitutes is called a **monopolistically competitive firm**. While the three types cover a broad spectrum of circumstances, they share one important similarity: in order to sell more, they must lower their prices. Put another, but equivalent, way, all three types of firms face a downward-sloping demand curve for their output.

Learning Objective 2: Define market power. Understand how input control, patents, and government franchising confer market power.

Market power measures a firm's ability to raise the price of its output without losing all of its sales. All imperfectly competitive firms have market power of varying degrees. A cautionary remark: market power *does not* imply the firm can charge whatever price it sees fit. It can pick a price-quantity combination along its demand curve, but raising price will result in lower sales. What are the sources of market power? First, it can arise when a single firm controls an essential input in the production process of some good. Second, when a patent is issued, the inventor is granted exclusive rights to sell the invention for a specific period, thus creating market power. Copyright laws have the same sort of effect. The justification for patent law is to protect the incentives for research and development of new products; for copyrights, it is to protect intellectual contributions. Third, exclusive government licenses or franchises confer a degree of market power.

Learning Objective 3: Define constant and increasing returns to scale, economies of scale, and natural monopoly. Understand the term network economics.
Finally, and most importantly, is the nature of the cost structure. **Constant returns to scale** occur when increasing all inputs the firm uses by a given proportion results in an increase in output of the same proportion: for example, a doubling of all inputs leads to a doubling of output. If the proportional increase in all inputs leads to a greater than proportional increase in output, **increasing returns to scale** or **economies of scale** are present. Now a doubling of all inputs yields a more than doubling of output. In the presence of increasing returns to scale, the average cost of producing output falls as the scale of the firm increases. Markets with economies of scale tend to be served by a single firm. A single firm that emerges from economies of scale is termed a **natural monopoly**. The term **network economies** refers to situations where the value of a good increases as more consumers use the good. The person with the first DVD player had few movies to watch. Today, Blockbuster is about half DVD and half VHS and, in the near future, will be completely DVD. Over time, as more consumers have purchased DVD players, the more useful it becomes to own one which further stimulates sales of DVD players. With the advent of DVD recorders, the death of VHS is coming (played an 8-track tape recently?).

Learning Objective 4: Explain how fixed costs contribute to the development of natural monopolies.
A relationship exists between fixed costs and economies of scale. For some production processes, start-up costs can be substantial. Once the fixed costs are dealt with, however, the marginal cost of producing an extra unit is trivial. The production of computer software is an example. The initial costs of developing the software are large and nearly fixed, but once the program is finished, the cost of producing a single copy is quite low. The important implication: the production of more and more units will lead to lower and lower average costs, the exact requirement for economies of scale. One algebraic form of the behavior is $TC = (F + M) \times Q$. The firm's total costs are the fixed costs, F, plus M for each unit produced, meaning M is marginal cost. Calculating average costs result in $AC = F/Q + M$, suggesting that as output grows large, the ratio F/Q approaches zero and thus average costs approach marginal costs. An industry with this cost structure will reward companies that aggressively market their products or acquire rival firms.

Learning Objective 5: Define marginal revenue and explain why it is different for a monopolist as compared to a price taker.
All firms, whether perfectly or imperfectly competitive, seek the maximum amount of profit. The nature of imperfect competition introduces a new element into the process of locating maximum profit. **Marginal revenue** measures the extra revenue that the firm collects as it sells an additional unit of output. To a perfectly competitive firm, output price and marginal revenues are identical. Since the perfect competitor cannot alter the price of its output, then if the price is $5 and it sells an extra unit, the firm collects exactly $5 more in revenues. In direct contrast, all

imperfectly competitive firms must lower their price in order to sell more units. If their price is $5, then to sell an extra unit of output, the price must be lowered. The exact amount of the price reduction and the impact on total revenues depends on the underlying demand curve. However, one implication is always true: for any imperfect competitor, the price being charged is always greater than the marginal revenues from selling the last unit. For linear demand curves of the form $P = (a - b) \times Q$, the marginal revenue function is $MR = (a - 2b) \times Q$. As shown in the textbook, it is straightforward to prove that $P > MR$.

Learning Objective 6: Locate the point of profit maximization for a monopolist. Realize that a monopolist is not guaranteed an economic profit.

The imperfect competitor, like the perfect competitor and all other economic agents, should pursue an activity up to the point where the additional benefit equals the additional cost. The point of profit maximization for an imperfectly competitive firm occurs at the output level where the marginal revenues equal marginal costs. The profit-maximizing price is located on the graph by traveling up from the optimal output level until the demand curve, not the marginal revenue curve, is encountered and then moving to the left to find the optimal price on the price axis.

Learning Objective 7: Illustrate the deadweight loss due to monopoly and explain why it occurs.

The social harm of imperfect competition can now be accurately understood. It is not the consequence of freedom to charge any price nor is it because of excessive profits. The harm from monopoly stems from fewer units being produced than are socially optimal. Suppose the profit maximizing level of output for a monopolist is 10 units with marginal revenues and marginal costs of $8 and a price of $13. The socially optimal quantity would be where price (marginal benefit to the consumer) and marginal costs are identical, say, at a price –and therefore a marginal cost—of $11. But from earlier work, an $11 price to a monopolist must mean marginal revenues of less than $11, violating the Cost-Benefit Principle. The monopolist cannot maximize profits and produce the socially optimal quantity simultaneously. Some consumers who are willing to pay more than the marginal cost of production (reservation prices between $12.99 and $11) will be unwilling to make the purchase. Using the graphical techniques developed in Chapter 7, the exact amount of deadweight loss due to monopoly can be calculated.

Learning Objective 8: Define price discrimination, a perfectly discriminating monopolist, the hurdle method of price discrimination, and a perfect hurdle. Explain why the monopolist has strong incentives to price discriminate and the effect it has on the deadweight loss.

The astute reader may wonder if the deadweight loss of monopoly represents a violation of the No-Cash-on–the-Table Principle, and indeed it does. In the region of the deadweight loss, the value to the consumer exceeds the extra production cost to the monopolist. If the monopolist reduces its single, uniform price to make these sales, its marginal revenue will fall below its marginal costs. However, if the monopolist can offer discounted prices to the consumers in the deadweight loss region without affecting the price being paid by consumers already buying the good, then both parties will be better off, and output will be closer to the social optimum. **Price discrimination** is the practice of charging different buyers different prices for essentially the same good or service. Common examples of price discrimination include discounts for senior citizens and children, rebate coupons, and supersaver discounts on air travel. A **perfectly**

discriminating monopolist is one that can charge every consumer exactly his or her reservation price. In this case, output will be socially efficient because all units for which a reservation price exceeds or equals the marginal cost will be produced. However, note that consumer surplus is zero, having been transferred entirely to the monopolist. Examples of perfect price discrimination do not exist, but the incentives to discriminate are so strong that many imperfect forms do exist. The most common form of charging differential prices is the **hurdle method of price discrimination**, where a seller offers a discount to all buyers willing to overcome some obstacle. When a manufacturer offers a good for sale at $99.95 with a mail-in rebate of $9.95, the hurdle is filling out and mailing in the rebate form. Some consumers will simply pay the $99.95 and not bother with the rebate. Other consumers will find that $99.95 is above their reservation price, but that $90 is below or equal to their reservation price. They will make the purchase and "jump the hurdle," i.e., they will mail in the rebate. A **perfect hurdle** is one that separates buyers precisely according to their reservation prices and imposes no costs on those who jump the hurdle. Note that hurdle pricing need not reach the socially efficient level of output, but it does serve to move the output level closer to the social optimum.

Learning Objective 9: Discuss the various public policy approaches to natural monopolies. Natural monopolies are firms with a cost structure in which average costs always decline as output expands and exceeds marginal costs. Any monopolist will produce less than the efficient level, but a natural monopolist must earn a loss at the efficient level of output. In many countries, government has been empowered to oversee many natural monopolists. One alternative is to have state ownership of a natural monopoly, set price equal to marginal cost, and use tax revenues to cover the loss. The drawback to state ownership is a substantially reduced incentive to adopt cost saving innovations. In the United States, the most popular method for controlling natural monopolies has been direct regulation. Under **Cost-plus regulation**, under which a monopolist is permitted to charge a price that covers his explicit costs plus a markup to cover the opportunity costs of the owners. The problem with the approach is twofold. First, much time and effort is wasted on arguing about which costs should be counted in the rate base.

Second, the incentive to reduce costs, while stronger than with state ownership, is still weaker than with an unregulated private firm. Another alternative is for government to solicit bids from private firms for the rights to the natural monopoly market. The appeal of exclusive contracting is that it retains all the private incentives to seek and adopt cost-saving measures. Municipal fire protection, garbage collection, and cable television are excellent examples of how well contracting can work. However, it is unlikely to work well when the service to be provided is complex or requires large fixed investments. Enforcement of existing antitrust legislation is yet another possibility, but the record of past lawsuits is far from encouraging. In fact, it seems highly reasonable to suspect that some firms have failed to reach as much economy of scale as feasible because mergers have been prevented by the U.S. Justice Department. The final possibility is to simply ignore the problem of natural monopoly. The rationale is (1) since monopolists practice a good deal of discount pricing, most of the monopoly profits come from people voluntarily paying the list price, (2) average costs are lower because of economies of scale, and (3) upward of two-thirds of the monopoly profit is collected in tax revenue.

III. Self-Test

Key Terms
Match the term in the right-hand column with the appropriate definitions in the left-hand column by placing the letter of the term in the blank in front of its definition. (Answers are given at the end of the chapter.)

1. _g_ The extra revenue the firm collects when it sells an extra unit.

2. _l_ A threshold that completely separates buyers whose reservation price lie above it from those whose reservation price is below it.

3. _i_ A market with a relatively large number of sellers selling the same product with slight differentiation.

4. _h_ The ability to raise price without losing all sales.

5. _f_ When a proportional increase in all factors of production results in a greater than proportional increase in output.

6. _n_ The practice of charging different prices to different consumers for the same good or service.

7. _b_ When a natural monopoly is allowed to charge a price equal to its explicit costs plus a markup to cover the owners' opportunity costs.

8. _p_ A market with a single seller of a unique product.

9. _j_ A monopoly that results from the existence of economies of scale.

10. _m_ A monopolist who charges every consumer his reservation price.

11. _c_ The other term for situations where a proportional increase in all factors of production results in a greater than proportional increase in output.

12. _a_ When a proportional increase in all factors of production results in an increase in output of the same proportion.

13. _d_ When the seller offers a discount to all buyers who overcome some obstacle.

14. _k_ A market with a few sellers of a given product.

15. _e_ A firm with some latitude to set the price of its output.

16. _o_ Another term for a price setter.

a. constant returns to scale

b. cost-plus regulation

c. economies of scale

d. hurdle method of discrimination

e. imperfectly competitive firm

f. increasing returns to scale

g. marginal revenue

h. market power

i. monopolistically competitive firm

j. natural monopoly

k. oligopoly

l. perfect hurdle

m. perfectly discriminating monopolist

n. price discrimination

o. price setter

p. pure monopoly

Multiple-Choice Questions
Circle the letter that corresponds to the best answer. (Answers are given at the end of the chapter.)

1. Suppose a firm collects $100 in total revenues when it sells 10 units, and it receives $99 in total revenues when it sells 11 units. The firm is a(n)
   A. pure monopolist.
   B. oligopolist.
   C. perfect competitor.
   D. imperfect competitor.
   E. monopolistic competitor.

2. De Beer's accounts for approximately 80% of diamond sales worldwide. The source of its market is
   A. exclusive ownership of South African diamond mines.
   B. its patent on diamond production.
   C. the perfectly inelastic demand for diamonds.
   D. the perfectly elastic demand for diamonds.
   E. Western engagement customs.

3. Increasing returns to scale occur when a 50% increase in all inputs
   A. increases output by 50%.
   B. increases output by more than 50%.
   C. increases input prices by more than 50%.
   D. increases output by less than 50%.
   E. decreases output by more than 50%.

4. Industries where economies of scale exist will tend to be
   A. dominated by either a single firm or a few firms.
   B. resistant to cutting price.
   C. comprised of many equal sized firms.
   D. less concerned with expanding output.
   E. highly profitable.

5. Given the total cost function, TC = 100 + 7*Q, fixed costs are
   A. $100.
   B. $100/Q.
   C. $7.
   D. $7/Q.
   E. $107.

6. Given the total cost function TC = a + b*Q with (a,b) > 0, average costs will
   A. be approximately constant over most of the output range.
   B. fall at first and then rise as output rises.
   C. fall over the entire range of output.
   D. rise at first and then fall as output rises.

E. rise over the entire range of output.

7. Suppose a monopolist is charging $12 for output. One can infer that
    A. marginal revenues are greater than $12.
    B. average revenues are less than $12.
    C. marginal revenues are $12.
    D. marginal revenues are less than $12.
    E. There is insufficient information.

8. If the monopolist's demand curve is P = 30 - 5*Q, then her marginal revenue is
    A. 30 - 5*Q.
    B. 60 - 10*Q.
    C. 60 - 5*Q.
    D. -5*Q.
    E. 30 - 10*Q.

9. The profit maximizing rule, P = MC, applies to
    A. all firms.
    B. monopolists only.
    C. monopolists and perfect competitors.
    D. perfect competitors only.
    E. monopolistic competitors only.

10. A monopolist calculates her marginal revenues to be $15 and her marginal costs to be $16 at her current output level. One can infer that she
    A. is loss minimizing.
    B. should expand output.
    C. is profit maximizing.
    D. should contract output.
    E. should raise her price.

11. Perfect competition is efficient and monopoly is not because in perfect competition
    _____, while in monopoly _____.
    A. P = MC; P > MC
    B. P < MR; P = MR
    C. P = MR; P < MR
    D. P = MC; P < MC
    E. P = MR; P = MC

12. Suppose monopolist M charges a uniform price of $10 based on profit maximization and has constant marginal costs of $3. Beth is willing to pay $6 for the monopolist's output. Therefore,
    A. the monopolist should lower his price to $6 for all consumers.
    B. the monopolist should ignore Beth's want; he is already profit maximizing.
    C. if resale of the output is impossible, the monopolist should lower his price to $6 just for Beth.

D. if resale of the output is possible, he should lower his price to $6 for Beth.

E. the monopolist will not be better off if he lowers his price to $6 just for Beth.

13. Suppose monopolist N produces good X. He sells one version of X to consumers and another version to businesses. The marginal cost of the consumer version is $5 per unit while the business version has marginal costs of $5.75. One can infer that

A. the monopolist will charge two different prices and is not practicing price discrimination.

B. the monopolist will charge one uniform price to both consumers and businesses.

C. the monopolist will charge two different prices and is perfectly price discriminating.

D. the monopolist will charge two different prices and is imperfectly price discriminating.

E. businesses will try to sell their units to consumers for a profit.

14. Suppose a monopolist is considering two different pricing schemes: offering the good $100 per unit with a $10 rebate coupon or just charging a flat $90. His economic consultant would advise him to

A. charge the $90 price.

B. charge the $100 price and "misplace" most of the rebate coupons.

C. charge the $100 price because less than 100% of the buyers will mail in the rebate.

D. do either; the impact will be the same.

E. charge the $90 price because most consumers ignore rebate offers.

15. A consumer goes to purchase a TV advertised for $300. As he is checking out, the clerk informs him of a $20 rebate offer for the TV, which he fills out and receives in 3 months. One can infer that the consumer had

A. a reservation price of at least $300, but jumped the hurdle anyway.

B. a reservation price of at most $280.

C. a reservation price of exactly $300.

D. a reservation price of at least $280.

E. obviously not done enough research on the price of the TV.

16. A monopolist sets his or her price at $100 and offers a 10% rebate. For this to be a perfect hurdle, it must be the case that

A. everyone takes advantage of the rebate.

B. those with a reservation price of $90 don't make a purchase.

C. no one takes advantage of the rebate.

D. those with a reservation price of $100 make the purchase and claim the rebate.

E. those with a reservation price of $100 or more purchase and ignore the rebate, while those with a reservation price between $99 and $90 purchase and use the rebate.

17. A price taker _____, and a price setter _____.

A. equates price to marginal revenues; equates price to marginal costs.

B. seeks to maximize revenues; seeks to maximize profits.

C. never earns a profit; always earns a profit.

D. must accept the market price; may charge any price he wants.

E. equates price to marginal revenues; finds that price is greater than marginal revenue.

18. The term natural monopoly refers to
    A. government ownership of parks.
    B. industries with constant returns to scale.
    C. industries with small fixed costs.
    D. industries with economies of scale.
    E. the desire of all firms to be monopolists.

19. If a monopolist knows that, at his current output level, marginal revenues are $8 and marginal costs are $8, then he
    A. must be earning a profit.
    B. is profit maximizing.
    C. must be earning a loss.
    D. needs to raise price.
    E. needs to reduce output.

20. Discounts extended to children and senior citizens by movie theaters are an example of
    A. perfect price discrimination.
    B. uniform pricing.
    C. discrimination.
    D. imperfect price discrimination.
    E. fair and reasonable pricing policies.

Short Answer Problems
(Answers and solutions are given at the end of the chapter.)

1. Profit Maximization for a Monopoly

This question reviews many different concepts and calculations: total revenue and marginal revenue, marginal costs, and profit maximization. All the major numerical calculations for monopoly are covered here.

Output	Price	Total Revenues	Marginal Revenues	Total Costs	Marginal Costs
10	$9.00		NA	$100.00	NA
15	$8.50			$105.00	
20	$8.00			$115.00	
25	$7.50			$135.00	
30	$7.00			$157.50	
35	$6.50			$185.00	

A. Fill in the missing data for total revenues, marginal revenues, and marginal costs.
B. The monopolist (should/should not) _____ produce 20 units of output because (marginal revenues/marginal costs) _____ exceed (marginal revenues/marginal costs) _____.
C. The monopolist (should/should not) _____ produce 35 units of output because (marginal revenues/marginal costs) _____ exceed (marginal revenues/marginal costs) _____.
D. The profit maximizing level of output is (25/30) _____ units.

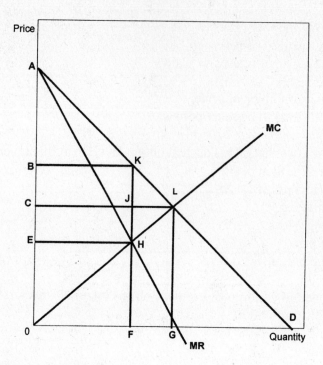

2. Deadweight Loss and Monopoly

The proper justification for disapproving of monopolies is not because they can charge whatever unreasonable price they wish, but the deadweight loss they impose on society. The graph above will review the monopolist's point of profit maximization, the perfectly competitive outcome, and the deadweight loss.

    A. The profit maximizing price and output for the monopolist are represented by the distances (0E/0B) _____ and (0F/0G) _____, respectively.

    B. The area of total revenues is equal to (0EHF/0BKF) _____.

    C. The area BAK represents the (deadweight loss/consumer surplus) _____ in the monopoly market.

    D. If this market were perfectly competitive, i.e., the curve MC becomes the industry supply curve, the equilibrium price and output would be equal to the distances (0C/0B) _____ and (0F/0G) _____, respectively.

    E. The deadweight loss due to monopoly is the area (JKL/HKL) _____ and shows the (extent of excess monopoly profits/transactions that should but do not occur)

    _____.

3. Natural Monopoly

One of the two important subtopics under the heading of monopoly is that of the natural monopoly. Many of the instances of monopoly that consumers encounter are natural monopolies. This question will review the concept of natural monopoly in a graphical setting.

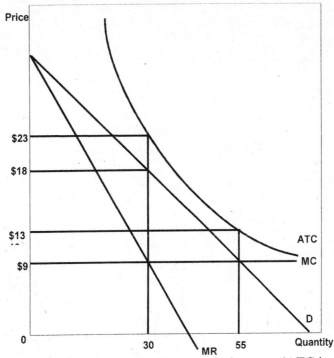

A. The graph suggests the firm is a natural monopoly because (ATC is always above the demand curve/ATC is always above MC) _____.

B. The monopolist will produce (30/55) _____ units and charge a price of ($13/$18) _____.

C. As a result, the monopolist will have total revenues of ($540/$690) _____ and total costs of ($690/$660) _____, leading to a (profit/loss) _____ of ($150/$165) _____.

D. If the monopolist produced at the efficient solution, i.e., where P = MC, then it would collect revenues of ($540/$495) _____, have total costs of ($690/$715) _____ and a (profit/loss) _____ of ($150/$220) _____.

4. Price Discrimination

The other important subtopic in monopoly is price discrimination. The deadweight loss of monopoly is not the result of an evil corporation wishing to deny sales to needy consumers. Rather, it is the recognition that producing all units for which the marginal benefit exceeds the marginal cost will result in lower profits. If a firm can locate a way to charge different prices to different consumers, then the deadweight loss is lessened.

Quantity	Price	Marginal Costs	Total Costs
0	$20		$1.00
1	$17	$2.00	$3.00
2	$14	$2.00	$5.00
3	$11	$2.00	$7.00
4	$8	$2.00	$9.00
5	$5	$2.00	$11.00
6	$2	$2.00	$13.00

A. Suppose the monopolist is initially unable to practice any form of price discrimination. In order to profit maximize, he will charge ($5/$11) _____ and produce (3/5) _____ units.

B. Thus, without price discrimination, the monopolist earns a profit of ($26/$14) _____. The deadweight loss is due to the fact that the value to consumers of units 4, 5, and 6 exceeds the (average cost/marginal cost) _____ of producing them.

C. Now suppose the monopolist can perfectly price discriminate. He will produce (5/6) ____ units and charge (5/6) _____ different prices.

D. Under perfect price discrimination, total revenues are ($12/$57) _____, and profits are ($44/$34) _____. The ability to practice perfect price discrimination has increased the monopolist's profitability by ($18/$8) _____.

IV. Economic Naturalist Application

As you make purchases during the next month, note how often you are subjected to price discrimination. It is obvious at some firms: the movie theater and university sponsored events. But less obvious examples abound based on the hurdle method: the large electronics chains frequently offer rebates as do the manufacturers of electronics. Also note how often the hurdle affects your purchasing decision. Do you frequently obtain and complete the rebate offer (jump the hurdle)? Would you have not made the purchase otherwise?

Answer:

V. Go to the Web: Graphing Exercises Using Interactive Graphs

A common example of natural monopoly and price discrimination is the electric utility. The marginal cost of an extra kilowatt hour [KWH] is relatively low but a substantial investment in the plant and capital equipment (fixed costs) is required. Residential, commercial, and industrial users are charged different prices. However, other regulatory environments for electric utilities are changing. At least 24 states have adopted deregulation plans for electricity. After you search the Web for relevant information, analyze the impacts of movements to deregulation.

Answer:

To review an answer to this question, and to learn more about the use of economic theory to analyze this issue (and other microeconomic issues), please go to the Electronic Learning Session in the Student Center at the Frank/Bernanke web site:
http://www.mhhe.com/economics/frankbernanke2.

VI. Self-Test Solutions

Key Terms

1. g
2. l
3. i
4. h
5. f
6. n
7. b
8. p
9. j
10. m
11. c
12. a
13. d
14. k
15. o
16. e

Multiple-Choice Questions

1. D
2. A
3. B
4. A
5. A
6. C
7. D
8. E
9. D
10. D
11. A
12. C
13. A
14. C
15. A
16. E
17. E
18. D
19. B
20. D

Short Answer Problems

1.

Output	Price	Total Revenues	Marginal Revenues	Total Costs	Marginal Costs
10	$9.00	$90.00	NA	$100.00	NA
15	$8.50	$127.50	$7.50	$105.00	$1.00
20	$8.00	$160.00	$6.50	$115.00	$2.00
25	$7.50	$187.50	$5.50	$135.00	$4.00
30	$7.00	$210.00	$4.50	$157.50	$4.50
35	$6.50	$227.50	$3.50	$185.00	$5.50

A. See table above.

B. should not; marginal revenues; marginal costs

C. should not; marginal costs; marginal revenues

D. 30

2.

A. 0B; 0F

B. 0BKF

C. consumer surplus

D. 0C; 0G

E. HKL; transactions that should but do not occur

3.

A. ATC is always above MC

B. 30; $18

C. $540; $690; loss; $150

D. $495; $715; loss; $220

4.

A. $11; 3

B. $26; marginal cost

C. 6; 6

D. $57 (sum the 6 prices); $44; $18

Chapter 10
Thinking Strategically

I. Pretest: What Do You Really Know?
Circle the letter that corresponds to the best answer. (Answers appear immediately after the final question.)

1. Game theory is important in understanding
   A. how perfectly competitive firms behave.
   B. production decisions by firms.
   C. consumer demand.
   D. interdependency and choice.
   E. the behavior of a pure monopolist.

2. The prisoner's dilemma refers to games where
   A. neither player has a dominant strategy.
   B. one player has a dominant strategy and the other does not.
   C. each player has a dominant strategy.
   D. each player has a dominant strategy that results in the largest possible payoff.
   E. each player has a dominant strategy that results in a lower payoff than his or her dominated strategies.

3. Cheating by firms that belong to a cartel is an example of
   A. profit maximization.
   B. need for stronger antitrust legislation.
   C. perfect competition.
   D. the prisoner's dilemma.
   E. the "smart for all, dumb for one" principle.

4. A commitment problem exists when
   A. players cannot make credible threats or promises.
   B. players cannot make threats.
   C. players decide whether to play the game.
   D. players cannot make promises.
   E. players are playing games where timing does not matter.

5. According to the textbook, the assumption of self-interested players in game theory is
   A. rarely found in practice.
   B. the only motivation for daily behavior.
   C. violated infrequently.
   D. extremely accurate.
   E. inconsistent with some choices individuals make.

6. Which of the following is not a requirement of a game?
   A. Players.
   B. Payoffs.
   C. Dominant strategies.
   D. Strategies.
   E. Knowledge of the payoffs.

7. According to the textbook, standing at a concert and talking loudly at parties are examples of
   A. rude behavior.
   B. unpleasant but frequent behaviors.
   C. undesirable outcomes stemming from a prisoner's dilemma.
   D. psychological solutions to a commitment problem.
   E. material solutions to a commitment problem.

8. The use of psychological incentives to solve commitment problems would be least effective in games played
   A. repeatedly between strangers.
   B. once between family members.
   C. repeatedly between family members.
   D. once between strangers.
   E. repeatedly between friends.

9. If both players of a game choose the best strategy available given the other player's strategies, the game is a(n)
   A. dominant strategy.
   B. dominated strategy.
   C. Nash equilibrium.
   D. ultimatum equilibrium.
   E. Rambler equilibrium.

10. The essential characteristic of a credible threat is
    A. there must be a very serious penalty.
    B. that the threatener may or may not carry out the threat.
    C. that the threatener and the threatenee must know each other well.
    D. that it is in the threatener's interest to act on the threat.
    E. that it is legally enforceable.

Solutions and Feedback to Pretest
For each question you answered incorrectly, we strongly recommend taking the time to review the appropriate material before continuing. In the table below, the relevant textbook pages are listed for each question, as well as the pertinent Learning Objective from the following Key Point Review.

Correct Answer	Textbook Page Numbers	Learning Objective
1. D	pp. 252-55	1
2. E	pp. 255-59	2
3. D	pp. 259-61	3
4. A	pp. 264-68	5
5. E	pp. 268-71	6
6. C	pp. 252-55	1
7. C	pp. 259-61	3
8. D	pp. 268-71	6
9. C	pp. 252-55	1
10. D	pp. 264-68	5

II. Key Point Review

Learning Objective 1: Define the basic elements of a game, a payoff matrix, a dominant strategy, a dominated strategy, and a Nash equilibrium.
Up to now, the discussion of decision making has not considered the potential for interactions among the economic agents. The perfectly competitive firm is so small that interaction is useless, while the monopolist, who is the sole supplier, has no one to interact with. Relaxing the assumption of independence allows for introducing a new model: game theory. The **basic elements of a game** are the players, the strategies available to the players, and the payoffs each player receives for each possible combination of strategies. Typically, one constructs a **payoff matrix**, a table that describes the payoffs in a game for each possible combination of strategies. When one player has a strategy that yields a higher payoff no matter what strategy the other player chooses, that player has a **dominant strategy**. A **dominated strategy** is one that leads to a lower payoff than an alternative choice, regardless of the other player's choice. The situation in which each player's strategy is the best he or she can choose given the other player's strategies is called a **Nash equilibrium**. If both players in a given game have dominant strategies, then an equilibrium must occur. But equilibrium can be reached in games where not all players have dominant strategies.

Learning Objective 2: Define and explain the classic prisoner's dilemma game.
A very important subclass of games deserves special consideration. A game in which each player has a dominant strategy, and when it is played the resulting payoffs are smaller than if the players had played their dominated strategy, is called the **prisoner's dilemma**. The basic result of the prisoner's dilemma is to highlight the conflict between the narrow self-interests of the individuals and the broader interests of a larger group.

Learning Objective 3: Define a cartel. Apply the prisoner's dilemma game to imperfectly competitive firms and to everyday life. Explain the tit-for-tat strategy and define a repeated prisoner's dilemma.

The common example of the prisoner's dilemma applied to firm behavior involves collusive agreements among firms. A **cartel** is a coalition of firms agreeing to restrict output in order to earn economic profits. The strategies available to the firms in a cartel are to cheat or abide by the agreement. If all firms abide, then output is restricted and economic profits are earned. However, if one firm cheats while the other firms abide, the cheating firm can stand to earn enormous profits. Unfortunately, all firms find the strategy of cheating increases their profits so all firms choose to cheat and the cartel is rendered useless. There are many noneconomic examples of the prisoner's dilemma, including the everyday observation that everyone stands up at a concert and shouts at a party. In many situations, including cartel behavior, the game is played over and over. A member country in OPEC must decide today whether to cheat on the agreement. The country will confront the same question tomorrow, the day after tomorrow, the day after that, and so on. A **repeated prisoner's dilemma** is a standard prisoner's dilemma that is played repeatedly. A surprisingly simple but highly effective strategy exists for policing cheating in a repeated prisoner's dilemma game. The **tit-for-tat** strategy involves the players cooperating the first time the game is played and then mimicking their partner's last move on each successive move. The players are adopting a position of, "If you cheat today, I will cheat tomorrow. If you don't cheat today, I will not cheat tomorrow."

Learning Objective 4: Define a decision tree and the ultimatum bargaining game. Understand the circumstances under which it is correct to employ a decision tree.

The next important modification involves adding a timing element to the playing of the game. In the basic games, choices occur simultaneously. Now the players will make choices in a particular order. To successfully model games in which timing matters requires some new machinery. A **decision tree** or **game tree** is a diagram that describes the possible moves in a game, in sequence, and lists the payoffs corresponding to each possible combination of moves. Games in which the first player has the power to confront the second player with a take-it-or-leave-it offer are called **ultimatum bargaining games**.

Learning Objective 5: Define a credible threat, a credible promise, the commitment problem, and a commitment device. Explain how the commitment problem interferes with reaching equilibrium.

A **credible threat** is an action that is in the interest of the threatener to carry out, while a **credible promise** is an action that is in the interest of the promiser to keep. In the kidnapper game, the kidnapper must kill the victim, even if the victim promises not to reveal the kidnapper's identity, because the promise is not credible. Both the prisoner's dilemma and the kidnapper game suffer from the same defect. The **commitment problem** is a situation in which individuals cannot achieve their goals because of an inability to make credible threats or promises. However, it might be possible to change the incentives so as to make an otherwise empty threat or promise credible. Such a change is known as a **commitment device**. For example, in the kidnapping game, the victim could commit a serious crime in the presence of the kidnapper and allow him or her to make a record of it. Now the victim has an incentive not to tell the authorities, less the victim's crime be disclosed. More mundanely, the practice of paying waiters' low wages and letting the customer reward the waiter with a tip is an attempt to solve a common commitment problem.

Learning Objective 6: Discuss the role of preferences in solving the commitment problem.
The standard assumption of most game theory models is that the players are motivated by narrowly-defined self-interests. Many behavioral choices, e.g., leaving a tip in an out-of-town restaurant, appear inconsistent with this assumption. The observation that people are motivated by more than self-interest does make prediction more difficult, but at the same time it extends the ways in which the commitment problem can be solved. Psychological incentives can be developed to serve as commitment devices when it is impractical to change the material incentives.

III. Self-Test

Key Terms
Match the term in the right-hand column with the appropriate definitions in the left-hand column by placing the letter of the term in the blank in front of its' definition. (Answers are given at the end of the chapter.)

1. ____ Situations where players cannot achieve their goals because of an inability to make credible threats or promises.
2. ____ A game in which each player has a dominant strategy.
3. ____ When the first player has the power to confront the second player with a take-it-or-leave-it offer.
4. ____ Any combination of strategies in which each player's strategy is the best, given the other player's strategies.
5. ____ The description of the payoffs in a game for each possible combination of strategies, usually presented in a table.
6. ____ A strategy for the repeated prisoner's dilemma game in which the players cooperate on the first move and then mimic their partner's last move on each successive move.
7. ____ A promise to take an action that is in the promiser's interest to keep.
8. ____ Something that changes the incentives such that otherwise empty threats and promises become credible.
9. ____ The players, the strategies available to each player, and the payoffs each player receives for each possible combination of strategies.
10. ____ A coalition of firms that agree to restrict output for the purpose of earning an economic profit.
11. ____ When a prisoner's dilemma confronts the same players again and again.
12. ____ A diagram that describes the possible moves in a game in sequence and lists the payoffs that correspond to each possible combination of moves.
13. ____ A threat to take an action that is in the threatener's interest

a. basic elements of a game
b. cartel
c. commitment device
d. commitment problem
e. credible promise
f. credible threat
g. decision tree
h. dominant strategy
i. dominated strategy
j. game tree
k. Nash equilibrium
l. payoff matrix
m. prisoner's dilemma

to carry out.

14. ___ Any other strategy available to a player with a dominant strategy.

15. ___ A synonym for decision tree.

16. ___ A strategy that yields a higher payoff no matter what the other players choose.

n. repeated prisoners dilemma

o. tit-for-tat

p. ultimatum bargaining game

Multiple-Choice Questions

Circle the letter that corresponds to the best answer. (Answers are given at the end of the chapter.)

1. Which of the following circumstances does not involve game theory?
    A. A local gas station owner wondering how his competition across the street will react to his decision to lower prices.
    B. Buying a can of beef stew at the grocery store.
    C. Negotiating a salary when two firms have made offers.
    D. Deciding whether to have an extramarital affair.
    E. Playing poker.

2. Which of the following is not true of Nash equilibrium in a game involving players A and B?
    A. Given the strategies of player B, player A has chosen the highest payoff strategy.
    B. Neither player A nor B wants to choose a different strategy.
    C. Both players are content with their choices.
    D. Both players must have dominant strategies.
    E. Given the strategies of player A, player B has chosen the highest payoff strategy.

3. A Nash equilibrium must result in
    A. both players being made better off.
    B. both players being made worse off.
    C. one player being worse off and one being better off.
    D. dominate strategies for both players.
    E. neither player wishing to change his or her strategy.

4. For a game involving players A and B with strategies X and Z, which of the following is not a requirement for a prisoner's dilemma?
    A. Player A must have a dominant strategy.
    B. Player B must have a dominant strategy.
    C. The payoff to playing their dominated strategies must be more than the payoff to their dominant strategies.
    D. The payoff to playing their dominant strategies must be more than the payoff to their dominated strategies.
    E. A Nash equilibrium must exist.

5. The reason most cartels end or cease to be effective is because
    A. of enforcement of antitrust legislation.
    B. of the development of substitutes.

C. one of the member firms absorbs the other firms.

D. consumers discover the agreement and buy from other firms.

E. of the incentives to cheat on the agreement.

6. According to the textbook, cigarette manufacturers
   A. supported the ban on cigarette advertising on TV because of their concern over health effects of smoking.
   B. would have been better off without the ban on TV advertising.
   C. were made worse off by the ban on TV advertising.
   D. had their prisoner's dilemma solved by the ban on TV advertising.
   E. saw their profits fall after the ban on TV advertising.

7. As described in the textbook, which of the following is not characteristic of an ultimatum bargaining game?
   A. The first player establishes the terms.
   B. The second player either accepts or rejects the terms.
   C. The offer is a take-it-or-leave-it offer.
   D. The second player may accept the terms.
   E. The second player will always reject the terms.

8. According to the textbook, one possible way of solving the commitment problem in the kidnapping game is for the victim to
   A. give the kidnapper a blank check.
   B. promise never to reveal the kidnapper's identity.
   C. offer to cut off one finger to show his sincerity.
   D. give the kidnapper a credit card.
   E. do something illegal and allow the kidnapper to record it.

9. According to the textbook, owners of restaurants have solved the commitment problem with their wait staff by
   A. paying very high wages.
   B. asking for comments from customers.
   C. paying low wages.
   D. scheduling frequent motivational seminars.
   E. paying low wages and encouraging tipping by customers.

10. The solution to a commitment problem
    A. must be a change in the material incentives.
    B. is never a change in the psychological incentives.
    C. must be a change in the psychological incentives.
    D. can be a change in the material incentives, the psychological incentives, or both.
    E. is either a change in the material incentives or the psychological incentives, but never both.

11. Psychological incentives to commitment problems would work best
    A. with complete strangers.
    B. when the game is played once and never again.

C. when the game is played once and maybe again.
D. with coworkers.
E. with immediate family members playing the game everyday.

12. If someone informs the clerk that he was given $20 of change when he was only owed $10, one can conclude that
    A. the individual is irrational.
    B. preferences to be perceived as being honest altered his motivation and choice.
    C. the individual is wealthy.
    D. somebody else must have witnessed the error.
    E. the clerk seemed dishonest.

13. For honesty to work as a solution to a commitment problem between players A and B,
    A. the entire world must be honest.
    B. A and B must be honest.
    C. only A need be honest.
    D. only B need be honest.
    E. A and B must be honest, and they must perceive the other as being honest.

14. Game theory is not useful in understanding perfect competition because
    A. by assumption, the firms too small to influence price and thus are not interdependent.
    B. perfectly competitive firms are honest.
    C. the players can't be identified.
    D. the payoffs to their choices are unknown.
    E. their strategies can't be discerned.

15. The statement, "I'll work harder this semester to improve my GPA" is
    A. a credible threat.
    B. an empty promise.
    C. an empty threat.
    D. a credible promise.
    E. a possible credible promise.

16. According to the textbook, in the game where player A divides a sum of money and then player B accepts or rejects the division, the most common distribution for A to propose is
    A. 99% for A and 1% for B.
    B. 1% for A and 99% for B.
    C. 50% for A and 50% for B.
    D. 60% for A and 40% for B.
    E. 80% for A and 20% for B.

17. All but one of the following behaviors are inconsistent with the assumption of narrowly self-interested individuals. Which one?
    A. Leaving a tip at an out-of-town restaurant.
    B. Negotiating a new car price that is 10% less than the wholesale price.
    C. Taking only one newspaper out of the machine.

D. Returning a lost wallet full of cash to the owner.
E. Suing someone over a $50 dispute.

18. Juan needs to hire an honest manager to run his new store. Jesus is an honest person and wants the job. To convince Juan of his honesty, Jesus should
   A. repeatedly claim his honest nature.
   B. point out others' dishonesty.
   C. decry the dishonesty of politicians.
   D. behave honestly.
   E. associate with dishonest people in order to stand out.

19. During the Iran-Iraq war, both countries needed revenues to fund their war efforts. They accomplished this by
   A. asking the other members of OPEC to lend them money.
   B. requesting that OPEC raise the official price of crude oil.
   C. overproducing crude oil and selling it below the official price, i.e., cheating.
   D. increasing their exports of sand.
   E. asking the World Bank for additional loans.

20. In the Scarlet Letter, the punishment for adultery was to always wear a large, red letter "A". This was an example of
   A. unenlightened punishment.
   B. using public ridicule to solve the commitment problem in marriage.
   C. overbearing control by the church.
   D. using material incentive to solve the commitment problem in marriage.
   E. narrow self-interest.

Short Answer Problems
(Answers and solutions are given at the end of the chapter.)

1. Constructing a Payoff Matrix

At least half the battle in game theory is to become comfortable with constructing and reading the payoff matrix. With some practice, it will begin to make more sense. The purpose here is to properly place the information in the question into the payoff matrix. Suppose two players, X and Z, are going to play a game with two strategies: M and N. The payoffs for player X to choose strategies M and N are $50 and $75 when player Z chooses strategy M, and $100 and $125 when player Z chooses strategy N. The payoffs for player Z to choose strategies M and N are $50 and $80 when player X chooses strategy M, and $100 and $90 when player X chooses strategy N.

A. Fill in the payoff matrix. Start by placing Player *X* in the uppermost cell and, in the two cells below, place the strategies, with *M* first. Put Player *Z* in the leftmost cell and, in the two cells beside, place the strategies, with *M* on top. In the cells that contain the payoffs (the four innermost cells), put the outcome for *X* above the outcome for *Z*.

B. For Player *X*, given that Player *Z* picks strategy *M*, his or her best choice is strategy (*M/N*) _____ because ($50/$75) _____ exceeds ($50/$80) _____. For Player *X*, given that Player *Z* picks strategy *N*, his or her best choice is strategy (*M/N*) _____ because ($125/$80) _____ exceeds ($90/$100) _____.

C. For Player *Z*, given that Player *X* picks strategy *M*, his or her best choice is strategy (*M/N*) _____ because ($80/$100) _____ exceeds ($50/$75) _____. For Player *Z*, given that Player *X* picks strategy *N*, his or her best choice is strategy (*M/N*) _____ because ($100/$125) _____ exceeds ($90/$100) _____.

D. Therefore, Player *X* will pick strategy (*M/N*) _____, and Player *Z* will pick strategy (*M/N*) _____.

2. Dominant Strategies and Nash Equilibrium

The point of this question is to approach the payoff matrix from the other view: the matrix is already constructed so that the correct meaning of the values will be reviewed as well as the type of strategies involved and whether an equilibrium exists.

		Firm A	
		Invest	Not Invest
Firm B	Invest	$20 A $20 B	$5 A $70 B
	Not Invest	$70 A $5 B	$10 A $10 B

A. If firm B does not invest but firm A does, then firm B receives ($5/$20) _____ and firm A receives ($20/$70) _____.

B. Firm A concludes that investing is a (dominant/dominated) _____ strategy and that not investing is a (dominant/dominated) _____ strategy.

C. Firm B concludes that investing is a (dominant/dominated) _____ strategy and that not investing is a (dominant/dominated) _____ strategy.

D. Thus, one can predict firm A and firm B will (both invest/both not invest) _____, which (does/does not) _____ represent a Nash equilibrium.

3. Prisoner's Dilemma

The following table shows the gain or loss from running negative political ads by the two presidential candidates.

		Bush	
		Negative Ads	Clean Ads
Gore	Negative Ads	-2% Bush -2% Gore	-6% Bush +6% Gore
	Clean Ads	+5% Bush -5% Gore	+1% Bush +1% Gore

A. The best strategy for candidate Bush is (negative ads/clean ads) _____, while the best strategy for candidate Gore is (negative ads/clean ads) _____.

B. As a result, the equilibrium outcome is that (neither/both) _____ will run negative ads. This (is/is not) _____ a prisoner's dilemma because both candidates (choose to run negative ads/would be better off not running negative ads) _____.

C. The results from the discussion of cartel agreements would suggest that if both candidates agreed to not run negative ads at the beginning of the campaign, the agreement (would/would not) _____ be upheld, particularly if the election were going to be close.

4. Timing Games

The final exercise takes up the problem of games in which timing matters, i.e., one player makes a choice and then the other player makes a choice.

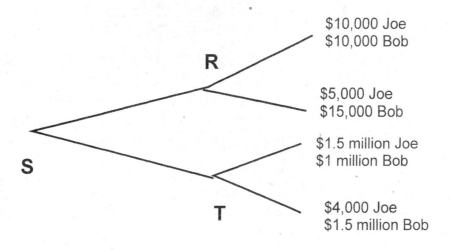

A. Joe and Bob are playing a game where Joe goes first at point S, choosing either R or T, and then Bob picks either the upper or lower branch. Clearly, Bob will always pick the (upper/lower) _____ branch of either R or T.

B. Knowing how Bob will choose causes Joe to pick the (upper/lower) _____ branch at point S.

C. The outcome of this game is that Joe will get ($10,000/$5,000) _____ and Bob will get ($15,000/$10,000) _____.

D. Suppose Bob tells Joe that, if he will pick the lower branch at S, then Bob will pick the upper branch at T. This would be viewed as (an empty/a credible) _____ promise.

E. Suppose Bob makes the same promise, but includes the statement that he will pay Joe $600,000 if he fails to select the upper branch. The promise is (still an empty one/now credible) _____.

IV. Economic Naturalist Application

Many behaviors that were difficult to model can now be easily framed in the context of
game theory. For example, try modeling the decision to cheat or remain faithful in a
marriage. Identify the players and their strategies. How often do they play the game?
Would the tit-for-tat strategy seem to work as a solution? How does the lessening of the
social stigma of divorce affect the game?
Answer:

V. Go to the Web: Graphing Exercises Using Interactive Graphs

Search the web for data on the actual world price of crude oil, the official OPEC price,
and the production values for the individual OPEC countries from 1973 to 1993.
Characterize the strength of the OPEC cartel over the two decades. Does cheating
appear to have existed? By which countries? Did any of the OPEC members' contract
production help to stabilize the price?
Answer:

To review an answer to this question, and to learn more about the use of economic theory to
analyze this issue (and other microeconomic issues), please go to the Electronic Learning
Session in the Student Center at the Frank/Bernanke web site:
http://www.mhhe.com/economics/frankbernanke2.

VI. Self-Test Solutions

Key Terms

1. d
2. m
3. p
4. k
5. l
6. o
7. e
8. c
9. a
10. b
11. n
12. g
13. f
14. i
15. j
16. h

Multiple-Choice Questions

1. B
2. D
3. E
4. D
5. E
6. D
7. E
8. E
9. E
10. D
11. E
12. B
13. E
14. A
15. E
16. C
17. B
18. D
19. C
20. B

Short Answer Problems

1.

		Player X	
		M	N
Player Z	M	$50 X $50 Z	$75 X $100 Z
	N	$100 X $80 Z	$125 X $90 Z

A. See table above.
B. N; $75; $50; N; $125; $100
C. N; $80; $50; M; $100; $90
D. N; M

2.
A. $5; $70
B. dominant; dominated
C. dominant; dominated
D. both invest; does

3.
A. negative ads; negative ads
B. both; is; would be better off not running negative ads
C. would not

4.
A. lower
B. upper
C. $5,000; $15,000
D. an empty
E. now credible

Chapter 11
Externalities and Property Rights

I. Pretest: What Do You Really Know?

Circle the letter that corresponds to the best answer. (Answers appear immediately after the final question).

1. An external cost of an activity is one that is
   A. borne by those not directly involved.
   B. borne only by those directly involved.
   C. included in the private marginal cost curve.
   D. present only if the activity yields pollution.
   E. transferred from producers to consumers.

2. Which of the following is *not* an example of an activity with external benefits?
   A. Eating a sandwich.
   B. Planting flowers in the front yard.
   C. Getting a haircut.
   D. Washing and waxing the car.
   E. Practicing safe sex.

3. The existence of externalities results in
   A. harm to those directly involved.
   B. a misallocation of resources.
   C. a greater-than-optional level of production.
   D. a less-than-optimal level of production.
   E. harm to those indirectly involved.

4. The major implication of the Coase Theorem is that
   A. government regulation is necessary to solve externalities.
   B. competitive pressures will eliminate externalities.
   C. resolving externalities is more costly than allowing them.
   D. individuals can solve many externalities if they can buy and sell the right to "commit" the externality.
   E. governmental solutions to externalities can only fail.

5. It is always the case that
   A. pollution should be reduced as much as technically feasible.
   B. the marginal benefit of reduced pollution is nearly zero.
   C. the optimal amount of any negative externality is close to zero.
   D. negative externalities always require a legislative solution.
   E. the optimal amount of any negative externality is greater than zero.

6. The tragedy of the commons refers to the
   A. overuse of resources that have no price.
   B. plight of the common man.
   C. first, little-known play by William Shakespeare.
   D. tendency for cattle to eat too much.
   E. overuse of resources that have no cost.

7. The reason public restrooms on the Interstate are generally less clean than restrooms at gas
   stations along the Interstate is because
   A. gas stations only allow paying customers to use restrooms.
   B. state employees don't work as hard as private sector employees.
   C. public restrooms lack clear ownership.
   D. people just don't care as much as they once did.
   E. gas station restrooms lack clear ownership.

8. When a player's performance is judged relative to others' performance and not by an absolute
   standard,
   A. players will over invest in performance enhancements.
   B. players will under invest in performance enhancements.
   C. the incentive to sabotage other players is lessened.
   D. a positional externality is not possible.
   E. the incentive to "play fair" is maximized.

9. According to the textbook, social norms can be viewed as
   A. a way to lessen the question of "Who am I?"
   B. a tool of the government.
   C. an informal solution to a positional arms race.
   D. a useful way to organize marketing campaigns.
   E. irrelevant to positional externalities.

10. Which of the following is *not* an example of a positional arms race?
    A. Strength training by NBA players.
    B. Plastic surgery by movie stars.
    C. Nuclear weapons stockpiling by nations.
    D. Vocabulary training of children by parents.
    E. Grocery shopping by families.

Solutions and Feedback to Pretest

For each question you answered incorrectly, we strongly recommend taking the time to review the appropriate material before continuing. In the table below, the relevant textbook pages are listed for each question as well as the pertinent Learning Objective from the following Key Point Review.

Correct Answer	Textbook Page Numbers	Learning Objective
1.	pp. 277-80	1
2.	pp. 277-80	1
3.	pp. 277-80	1
4.	pp. 280-86	2
5.	pp. 280-86	2
6.	pp. 287-91	3
7.	pp. 287-91	3
8.	pp. 291-95	4
9.	pp. 295-97	5
10.	pp. 291-95	4

II. Key Point Review

Learning Objective 1: Define external costs, external benefits, and externalities. Discuss the effect of externalities on the efficiency of resource allocation.

Chapter 11 examines several different circumstances in which the market system fails to achieve the efficient outcome. Frequently, when a group pursues some activity, the activity produces unintended effects that have an impact on people not directly engaged in the activity. The effect is called an **external benefit** or **positive externality** when it serves to benefit those not directly involved. It is termed an **external cost** or **negative externality** when it imposes a cost on those not directly involved. To simplify the terminology, when either an external cost or benefit is present, an **externality** exists. The difficulty externalities present stems from an assumption made by the theory of the invisible hand in Chapter 8 that all costs and benefits are contained in the private supply and demand curves. When a cost or benefit is missing, as will be the case with externalities, the equilibrium outcome will not be efficient. In graphical terms, when the market for a good or service has an external cost, say of $5, the private supply curve might indicate that the marginal cost of producing the 10th unit is $20 but the social marginal cost is actually $25. For every level of output, the private marginal cost is less than the social marginal cost. With a given demand curve, the equilibrium outcome based on the private supply curve results in an equilibrium price that is less than the efficient price and an equilibrium quantity that is greater than the efficient quantity. For an external benefit, the private demand curve understates the marginal benefit of an additional unit. If the external benefit is, say $7, and the private marginal benefit of the 11th unit is $12, then the social marginal benefit of the 11th unit is actually $19. For every level of output, the private marginal benefit is less than the social marginal benefit. The equilibrium outcome based on private demand will thus produce an equilibrium price less than the efficient price and an equilibrium quantity less than the efficient quantity.

Learning Objective 2: Define and explain the Coase Theorem. List and discuss common legal remedies for externalities. Defend the claim that the optimal amount of a negative externality is never zero.

The fact that externalities lead to inefficient outcomes means that a reallocation exists such that some individuals would be better off without making others worse off. Ronald Coase, a professor at the University of Chicago Law School, noted that the possibility of reallocation means individuals can reach private solutions to externalities. The **Coase theorem** indicates that if people can negotiate without cost the purchase and sale of the right to cause an externality, they can always arrive at the socially efficient solution. Of course, many examples of externalities exist where negotiations between all affected parties would either be quite costly or simply impractical. Thus, the burden of solving costly externalities is placed on government. Indeed, most legislation is an attempt to correct some sort of externality. Examples include speed limits, zoning laws, pollution controls, and free speech. Finally, the point must be emphasized that the optimal outcome of *any* negative externality is *not* zero. Even for externalities that cause serious damage to health, the benefits of further reductions in the amount of pollution must be balanced against the costs of the further reduction. Unless the marginal cost of reducing the externality is zero, it will never be efficient to completely eliminate the external cost.

Learning Objective 3: Define the tragedy of the commons and understand the basics of the problem. Explain why private ownership can, in some cases, solve the problem. Note situations when private ownership will not succeed.

The next problem that can prevent the market system from reaching the efficient outcome concerns property rights. If Joe Average owns a car, then he possesses a private property right to the car. He can sell it, lovingly care for it, or give it away. If it is stolen, and law enforcement finds it, it will be returned to him. Not all resources have such clear ownership. For example, no one person, firm, or country owns the fish in the sea. As a result, the fish in the sea are treated as if they have a price of zero. The **tragedy of the commons** refers to the tendency for resources that have no price to be used until the marginal benefit is driven to zero. The solution seems to be a simple matter of assigning the property rights to someone and in some cases this is what is done. Sometimes assigning the property rights is too costly or completely impractical. The problem of harvesting whales is an excellent example. Monitoring would be very costly and no institutional framework exists for resolving disputes. On the other hand, some success has been had with assigning the property rights of elephants to tribes in Africa.

Learning Objective 4: Understand the difference between relative and absolute performance. Define a positional externality, a positional arms race, and a positional arms control agreement.

The final circumstance that results in a failure to achieve an efficient outcome involves rewarding relative performance. Although professional sports represents the most common example of relative reward, it is by no means the only one. Rewards based on relative performance are only concerned with a players rank. The low score at the Master's Golf Tournament wins whether the low score is –15 or -1. Suppose that a $50,000 medical procedure was guaranteed to cut 3 strokes from a professional golfer's game. The first player to have the procedure would move up in the rankings. A **positional externality** occurs when an increase in one person's performance reduces the expected reward of another's in situations where rewards are based on relative performance. The player who first had the procedure done caused a positional externality. Predictably, other golfers will notice the improvement in the score of the player who had the procedure. Other golfers will now have the $50,000 procedure. After all the golfers have had the procedure, the average scores will be 3 strokes lower but the rankings will be the same as before. Golf has experienced a **positional arms race**—a series of mutually offsetting investments in performance enhancement caused by a positional externality. The inefficiency is the spending on the procedure without any change in the outcome because relative performance is the standard for reward. Since a positional arms race imposes costs without altering the ultimate outcome, players have an incentive to discourage or prohibit the arms race. A **positional arms control agreement** restricts the players from making mutually offsetting performance-enhancing investments. Campaign spending limits in politics and roster limits in professional sports appear to be arms control agreements.

Learning Objective 5: Explain how social norms can serve as optional arms control agreements.
Positional arms control agreements need not always be written as laws or regulations. Social norms can also serve to limit a positional arms race. Currently, body piercings and tattoos are very fashionable. As the number and placement of piercings becomes more and more extreme, a social backlash will develop against piercings and some new fashion that makes a radical statement will replace it. The length of a man's hair is another good example of social norms and a positional arms race.

III. Self-Test

Key Terms
Match the term in the right-hand column with the appropriate definitions in the left-hand column by placing the letter of the term in the blank in front of its definition. (Answers are given at the end of the chapter.)

1. ____ The tendency for a resource with no price to be used up to the point where it's the marginal benefit.

a. Coase theorem

2. ____ A series of mutually offsetting investments in performance enhancement that is stimulated by a positional externality.

b. external benefit

3. ____ When the benefits of an activity are received by people other than those who are directly pursuing the activity.

c. external cost

4. ____ A synonym for external benefit.

d. externality

5. ____ An agreement to limit the contestants' mutually offsetting investments in performance enhancements.

e. negative externality

6. ____ If individuals can negotiate the purchase and sale of the right to produce an externality at no cost, an efficient solution will emerge.

f. positional arms control agreement

7. ____ An activity with an external cost or benefit.

g. positional arms race

8. ____ When an increase in one person's performance reduces the expected reward of another person in situations where rewards depend on relative performance.

h. positional externality

9. ____ When the costs of an activity are borne by people other than those who are directly pursuing the activity.

i. positive externality

10. ___ A synonym for external cost.

j. tragedy of the commons

Multiple-Choice Questions
Circle the letter that corresponds to the best answer. (Answers are given at the end of the chapter.)

1. Which of the following is not an example of an activity with an external cost?
    A. Noise pollution from a steel mill.
    B. Keeping junk in the front yard.
    C. A car burning oil.
    D. Having to buy batteries for the new remote that came with the new TV.
    E. Speeding on the Interstate.

2. When collective action is taken, e.g., the passing of a new law, it is frequently an attempt to
    A. eliminate a negative externality.
    B. encourage a positive externality.
    C. increase the income of lawyers.
    D. correct a resource misallocations due to an externality.
    E. further burden the operation of the economy.

3. If an unregulated activity produces a negative externality, one can infer that
    A. the equilibrium price is greater than the socially optimal price.
    B. demand for the activity is greater than the socially optimal demand.
    C. the equilibrium quantity is greater than the socially optimal quantity.
    D. the equilibrium quantity is less than the socially optimal quantity.
    E. supply of the activity is less than the socially optimal supply.

4. In the case of either a positive or negative externality, it will always be true that, relative to the social optimum,
    A. the price will be too low.
    B. the price will be too high.
    C. the quantity will be too large.
    D. demand will be too small.
    E. supply will be too great.

5. The motivation for private solutions to externalities is that
    A. resources are misallocated and thus unexploited opportunities exist.
    B. individuals are today more concerned about pollution.
    C. of profit maximization.
    D. of utility maximization.
    E. Of individuals for governmental solutions.

6. All but *one* of the following factors would lessen the ability of the Coase Theorem to solve an externality. Which one?
   A. Negotiating requires lawyers and legal documents.
   B. Many individuals bear the external cost.
   C. The externality is an external benefit.
   D. Many individuals generate the external cost.
   E. The parties involved distrust and dislike each other.

7. Which of the following would *not* be subject to the tragedy of the commons?
   A. Whales in the ocean.
   B. Timber on public lands.
   C. Cattle on a ranch.
   D. Buffalo roaming free in the West.
   E. The atmosphere.

8. Since the cost of obtaining more of any resource is _____, viewing any resource's price as zero leads to _____.
   A. positive; under utilization
   B. negative; over utilization
   C. zero; an efficient allocation
   D. positive; over utilization
   E. positive; a surplus

9. Viewed from the perspective of a common property rights problem, reductions in the poaching of elephants for their ivory could be accomplished by
   A. assigning the property rights of the elephant herds to specific tribes.
   B. increasing enforcement efforts against poachers.
   C. lessening the demand for ivory.
   D. taxing ivory products.
   E. banning the importation of ivory.

10. Which of the following is *not* a characteristic of a positional arms race?
   A. The benefit of the performance-enhancing investments is offset.
   B. The investments are costly.
   C. The rank ordering (1st place, 2nd place, etc.) before and after the investment is the same.
   D. Efficiency is necessarily improved.
   E. In theory, the race will continue forever.

11. Dustin owns a very powerful stereo system. Dustin's private property rights allow him to do all of the following except
   A. sell it for a price he finds reasonable.
   B. choosing not to play it.
   C. playing whatever type of music he likes.
   D. open his windows at 3:00 am and turn the volume to its maximum.
   E. give it to a friend.

12. If one major league pitcher were to develop a new, highly effective pitch called the "slipper," this would be
    A. a positional externality.
    B. a positive externality.
    C. efficient.
    D. an asset to the game.
    E. an example of the Coase Theorem.

13. If all major league pitchers were to learn a new, highly effective pitch called the "slipper," this would
    A. leave the earned run average of pitchers unchanged but alter the rankings.
    B. raise batting averages.
    C. increase fan attendance.
    D. lower the earned run average of pitchers but leave the rankings unchanged.
    E. increase the number of home runs.

14. Both Presidents Roosevelt and Kennedy had extramarital affairs that the press was aware of but did not report when they were in office. President Clinton's sexual relationships have been well documented and publicized. The difference can be understood as
    A. a greater need for the public today to know about the sexual behavior of the president.
    B. less tolerance today for marital affairs.
    C. a positional arms race by the media.
    D. the general decay of the moral fabric of the U.S.
    E. an apparent characteristic of Democratic presidents.

15. From the individual's standpoint, a positional arms race is _____ , while from society's point of view it is _____ .
    A. efficient; efficient
    B. inefficient; inefficient
    C. inefficient; efficient
    D. efficient; inefficient
    E. necessary; efficient

16. Assume that to be labeled a nerd (someone who studies daily and has a high GPA) in high school or college is a social negative. According to the textbook,
    A. this is a cruel and unfair stereotype.
    B. those who study hard would be better off if this negative stereotype was eliminated.
    C. the negative stereotype serves to discourage many from studying hard thus increasing the payoff to those who do.
    D. the negative stereotype serves to comfort those who don't study and make poor grades.
    E. being labeled a nerd has no impact on studying or GPA.

17. Unkind jokes and sarcastic remarks about whether someone has had their fanny lifted or nose straightened are a(n)
    A. sign of immaturity.
    B. sign of jealousy.

C. attempt to limit the amount of plastic surgery by social norms.
D. example of a positional arms race.
E. externality.

18. In the case of either an external cost or an external benefit, the invisible hand fails to generate the efficient outcome because
A. the model is not capable of incorporating externalities.
B. buyers and sellers only take their self-interests into account.
C. too much is produced.
D. too little is produced.
E. the environment is treated as a common property.

19. If, after an externality is corrected, the equilibrium price rises and the equilibrium quantity falls, the externality must have been a(n)
A. external benefit.
B. internal cost.
C. external cost.
D. positive externality.
E. positional externality.

20. Which of the following is an example of a governmental solution to an external benefit?
A. Requiring autos to meet minimum emissions regulation.
B. Building safety requirements for office buildings.
C. Regulations of food additives.
D. Public service ads encouraging safe sex practices.
E. Public service ads discouraging smoking.

Short Answer Problems
(Answers and solutions are given at the end of the chapter.)

1. Externalities and Efficiency
Public debate on pollution frequently become quite heated with both sides entrenched in their own rhetoric. By phrasing the question as an economic one, the Cost-Benefit Principle can guide the discussion to a solution that is efficient and hence allows for the greatest economic good for society. The following question examines the issue of reducing air pollution by requiring various devices on automobiles in a graphical setting.

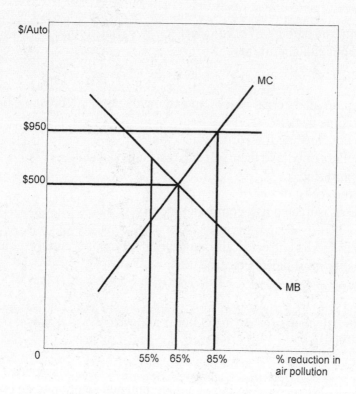

A. A (55/85) _____ percent reduction in air pollution would be justified because the (marginal benefits/marginal costs) _____ exceed the (marginal benefits/marginal costs) _____.

B. The marginal benefit of a 65 percent reduction in air pollution has a value of ($500/$950) _____.

C. The socially optimal or efficient solution is a (65/85) _____ percent reduction because the (marginal benefits/marginal costs) _____ equal the (marginal benefits/marginal costs) _____.

D. Suppose the EPA proposes a device for autos that would cost $950 per car and reduce air pollution by 85 percent. This regulation (would/would not) _____ pass the Cost-Benefit Principle because the (marginal benefits/marginal costs) _____ exceed the (marginal benefits/marginal costs) _____.

2. Positional Externalities and Relative Performance

The following question reviews the concept of positional externalities and the resulting positional arms race. It also shows how different reward systems cause different outcomes and how positional externalities are similar to the prisoner's dilemma discussed in Chapter 10. Sally and Johanna are the only players in a local golf tournament. They can either practice for 5 hours or not practice at all. Practice has both direct monetary costs and opportunity costs. Their scores for an 18-hole round of golf with and without practice are shown in the following table. Total prize money is $10,000. Two possible reward structures exist. Plan X, in which low score wins $9,000, second place wins $1,000 and a tie results in $5,000 each. Plan Z requires a player to score 71 or less for first place, and 72 to 80 for second place. The $9,000 will be split between those with a 71 or lower score with a guaranteed minimum of $1,000. The $1,000 for second place will be split between those with a score between 72 and 80. Assume that narrowly defined self-interest motivates both players.

		Sally	
		No Practice	5 Hours
Johanna	No Practice	78 Sally 78 Johanna	72 Sally 78 Johanna
	5 Hours	78 Sally 72 Johanna	72 Sally 78 Johanna

A. Plan X rewards (absolute/relative) _____ performance while plan Z rewards (absolute/relative) _____ performance.

B. Assume the tournament adopts plan X. Sally finds her best strategy is to (practice/not practice) _____ while Johanna finds her best strategy is to (practice/not practice) _____.

C. Under plan X (both/neither) _____ player will practice and the ultimate winner is (changed/unchanged) _____. Thus, practicing (is/is not) _____ a positional arms race.

D. Under plan Z, the best strategy for Sally is to (practice/not practice) _____ and for Johanna the best strategy is to (practice/not practice) _____.

E. A positional arms race (does/does not) _____ develop under plan Z because (neither player can reach a 71/practice is banned) _____.

3. Common Property Rights

Another important social issue that generates public controversy is the treatment of resources with common property rights. The question here shows how even in the presence of private property rights, problems with the proper usage of a resource may still arise. Suppose four land owners M, N, O, and P own adjacent lots. Recently, a pool of natural gas was discovered under all four lots but does not extend beyond the four lots. Below is data on the relationship between number of gas wells, output per well, and revenues per well. It is an engineering reality that the more quickly a pool is depleted, the smaller the total amount of gas extracted.

Total number of wells on the entire pool	Average cubic feet of gas produced per day	Revenue per well per day
4	100	$100
8	95	$95
12	93	$93
16	75	$75
20	67	$67
24	51	$51
28	40	$40
32	37	$37

A. Suppose the marginal cost of a gas well is $94. As a result, the optimal number of wells to drill on the pool is (12/8) _____. If each owner sets marginal cost equal to revenues, then a total of (8/32) _____ wells will be drilled.

B. As a result, each owner will produce (95/37) _____ cubic feet of natural gas and receive ($95/$37) _____ in revenues for a (profit/loss) _____ of ($1/$57) _____.

C. Suppose that instead of four owners, the pool of natural gas was owned by a single person. If the marginal cost of a well is $94, the single owner would drill (32/8) _____ wells, which is (greater than/equal to) _____ the socially optimal number of wells.

D. The difference between the single-owner outcome and the multiple-owner outcome is that the multiple owners see the pool as (private property/common property) _____ while the single owner sees it as (private property/common property) _____.

4. Coase Theorem

The final question applies the Coase theorem to locate a solution to a neighborhood problem. Jennifer is considering whether to paint her house and if so, what color to choose. She settles on three options: leave it "as is," paint it beige, or paint it neon yellow. Jennifer's neighbors are able to easily see her house. The following table shows the monetary values of utility for Jennifer and her neighbors under the three possibilities.

	Leave as is	Beige paint	Neon Yellow paint
Jennifer	-1	5	20
Neighbors	1	4	-10

A. The largest economic surplus occurs when Jennifer paints her house (neon yellow/beige) _____ and the lowest economic surplus occurs when Jennifer (paints her house beige/leaves it as is) _____.

B. Suppose Jennifer decides to paint her house neon yellow. A Coase theorem styled solution would be for Jennifer to pay her neighbors ($20/$10) _____. Alternatively, Jennifer's neighbors could pay her ($20/$10) _____ to agree not to paint the house neon yellow.

C. Suppose that Jennifer's neighbors are unfamiliar with the Coase theorem and instead decide to pass an ordinance banning all neon colors on homes. The action reduces the maximum increase in utility Jennifer could experience by ($15/$20) _____.

IV. Economic Naturalist Application

Analyze the Internet with respect to externalities. Does the Internet (and having access to it) impose external costs? Does the Internet provide external benefits? Give examples of both and solutions to discourage the external costs and encourage the external benefits.
Answer:

V. Go to the Web: Graphing Exercises Using Interactive Graphs

Search the web for information on endangered species. Specifically, examine the writings of environmental activists. What kinds of proposals do they favor for protecting species near extinction? Do you find any mention of a lack of private property rights? How would you analyze using popular Hollywood actors to discourage the wearing of fur or ivory products.
Answer:

To review an answer to this question, and to learn more about the use of economic theory to analyze this issue (and other microeconomic issues), please go to the Electronic Learning Session in the Student Center at the Frank/Bernanke web site:
http://www.mhhe.com/economics/frankbernanke2.

VI. Self -Test Solutions

Key Terms

1. j
2. g
3. b

4. i
5. f
6. a
7. d
8. h
9. c
10. e

Multiple-Choice Questions

1. D
2. D
3. C
4. A
5. A
6. C
7. C
8. D
9. A
10. D
11. D
12. A
13. D
14. C
15. D
16. C
17. C
18. B
19. C
20. D

Short Answer Problems

1.
A. 55: marginal benefits; marginal costs
B. $500
C. 65; marginal benefits; marginal costs
D. would not; marginal costs; marginal benefits

2.
A. relative; absolute
B. practice; practice
C. both; unchanged; is
D. not practice; not practice
E. does not; neither player can reach a 71

3.
A. 8; 32
B. 37; $37; loss; $57
C. 8; equal to
D. common property; private property

4.
A. neon yellow; leaves it as is
B. $10; $10
C. $15

Chapter 12
The Economics of Information

I. Pretest: What Do You Really Know?

Circle the letter that corresponds to the best answer. (Answers appear immediately after the final question).

1. According to the textbook, middlemen
   A. add no value to economic activity.
   B. only add value if the consumer gets a good deal.
   C. only add value to themselves.
   D. provide value through information and coordination.
   E. exist for no reason.

2. The optimal amount of information to acquire before making a purchase is
   A. zero.
   B. as much as technically possible.
   C. the amount where the total cost of acquiring information equals the total benefit.
   D. independent of the expenditure to be made.
   E. the amount where the marginal cost of acquiring information equals the marginal benefit.

3. The equilibrium allocation of any good in the presence of free riders will be
   A. more than optimal.
   B. Optimal, but not all revenue will be collected.
   C. optimal.
   D. less than optimal.
   E. indeterminate.

4. Seka and Jill mover to LA at the same time and both wish to find apartments to rent. Seka is staying with her Aunt while Jill is at the Best Western motel. One can predict that
   A. Seka and Jill will spend the same amount of time searching.
   B. Jill will search more than Seka.
   C. Seka will search more than Jill.
   D. Jill will have better information.
   E. the magnitude of their search times is indeterminate.

5. Terri decides to play the lottery. She has a 1% probability of winning $1,000 and a 99% probability of winning zero. The expected value of her decision to play is
   A. $1,000.
   B. $100.
   C. $10.
   D. $1.
   E. zero.

6. If the expected value of the next apartment in a search is zero, then
   A. all persons will consider seeing the next apartment.
   B. only risk-adverse persons will consider seeing the next apartment.
   C. only risk-neutral persons will consider seeing the next apartment.
   D. no one will consider seeing the next apartment.
   E. only risk-loving persons will consider seeing the next apartment.

7. The lemons model is used to explain
   A. the market for citrus products.
   B. markets with asymmetric information.
   C. just the market for used cars.
   D. how not to buy a lemon in the first place.
   E. markets with symmetric information.

8. The costly-to-fake principle indicates that
   A. counterfeiting art objects is difficult.
   B. for a seller to have credibility, he must overstate a lot.
   C. for a buyer to have credibility, he must offer a price that is difficult to fake.
   D. for information to be seen as credible, it must be costly to fake.
   E. faking is a costly strategy.

9. Which of the following behaviors is not based on statistical discrimination?
   A. A 60-year-old paying more for life insurance than a 30-year-old.
   B. Taking a cab home at night rather than walking.
   C. A 45-year-old married female paying less for auto insurance than an 18-year-old male.
   D. A BMW having a higher price than a Buick.
   E. A coach designing a play for his best 3-point shooter when the team is down by 3 points.

10. In the absence of legal requirements, insurance is most attractive to
   A. the wealthy.
   B. those with lowest likelihood of filing a claim.
   C. the poor.
   D. those with the highest likelihood of filing a claim.
   E. those with an average likelihood of filing a claim.

Solutions and Feedback to Pretest
For each question you answered incorrectly, we strongly recommend taking the time to review the appropriate material before continuing. In the table below, the relevant textbook pages are listed for each question as well as the pertinent Learning Objective from the following Key Point Review.

Correct Answer	Textbook Page Numbers	Learning Objective
1. D	pp. 302-07	1
2. E	pp. 302-07	1
3. D	pp. 302-07	1
4. C	pp. 307-08	2
5. C	pp. 307-08	2
6. C	pp. 307-08	2
7. B	pp. 309-14	4
8. D	pp. 309-14	4
9. D	pp. 314-16	5
10. D	pp. 316-17	6

II. Key Point Review

Learning Objective 1: Describe the optimal amount of information to obtain about goods and services. Define the free rider problem. Cite two generalizations about factors affecting the amount of searching.
Information is as scarce and valuable a resource as water. The exchange of information, in contrast to water, is often conducted in informal settings without explicit prices, but the principles guiding market decisions about water also guide the decisions about information. Sales agents and other middlemen provide genuine economic value by guiding goods and services to the consumers who value them the most. Internet sites like eBay serve to increase the economic surplus by coordinating exchanges that would not have occurred 10 years ago.
The rule for locating the optimal amount of information is the familiar Cost-Benefit Principle. Individuals should continue to acquire information as long as the marginal benefit exceeds the marginal cost. The question can also be taken as, "What is the optimal amount of ignorance?"

The optimal amount of information and advice may not be realized. Suppose John has questions about the features of a new stereo system and goes to the local electronics store where the salesman spends an hour demonstrating equipment. John may then go home and purchase the stereo system on the Internet for 25% less than the price at the local store. The implication is the local stereo shop may provide too little information precisely because they expect to lose the sale to an Internet or mail order company. The **free-rider problem** exists when too little of a good is produced because nonpayers cannot be excluded from using the good. Finally, two guidelines for the amount of searching to engage in can be identified. First, the more expensive the item is, the greater the optimal amount of searching there will be. By extension, items with large price variations will induce more searching than items with a narrow range of price variation. Second, the more costly it is to search, the smaller the optimal amount of searching. Households with Internet access should search more than households without Internet access.

Learning Objective 2: Define the following: the expected value of a gamble, a fair gamble, a better-than-fair gamble, a risk-neutral person, and a risk-averse person. Explain how the concept of a gamble relates to searching.

To some extent, all searching entails an element of risk. Deciding whether it is worthwhile to visit another Internet site in hopes of getting a lower price is a gamble with, only a small cost if one loses. Deciding whether it is worthwhile to drive halfway across Houston in rush hour traffic and then wait an hour until the manager can show a vacant apartment that might rent for less than one's current choice is a gamble with a much higher cost if one loses. The **expected value of a gamble** is the sum of the possible outcomes of the gamble multiplied by their respective probabilities. The expected value is the average amount one would win or lose by playing the gamble an infinite number of times. For example, a gamble with a 75% probability of winning $50 and a 25% probability of losing $5 has an expected value of [(.75×$50) + (.25×-$5)] or $36.25. A **fair gamble** is one with an expected value of zero and a **better-than-fair gamble** is one with an expected value greater than zero. An individual is classified as **risk neutral** if he or she is willing to accept a fair gamble and **risk averse** if he or she only accepts better-than-fair gambles.

Learning Objective 3: Discuss the commitment problem present in searching. List examples of devices to lessen the commitment problem.

Similar to the difficulties players experienced in the prisoner's dilemma and decision tree games in Chapter 10, commitment problems arise when a search is costly. No one can or would examine all possible alternatives, for example, looking at every possible vacant apartment. But suppose a week after Stanley decided on an apartment to rent, he found an identical one for $100 less per month. Or what if a week after Stanley decided on an apartment, someone else offered $100 more per month to Stanley's landlord for the apartment. Lease agreements exist partially to protect both tenant and landlord from the commitment problem. The legal convention of marriage serves an analogous purpose for relationships.

Learning Objective 4: Define asymmetric information. Define and explain the Lemons model. Discuss the role of credibility and define the costly-to-fake principle.

In many cases, buyers and sellers find they have unequal amounts of information about the good or service they wish to exchange. A buyer knows very little about the actual history of a used car and an employer can only crudely gauge an applicant's motivation. **Asymmetric information** exists when buyers and sellers are not equally well informed about the characteristics of the good or service they wish to exchange. George Akerlof developed a model of how asymmetric information influences the market outcome. The **Lemons model** predicts that in the presence of asymmetric information, the average quality of goods offered for sale will be reduced. Using the market for used cars, the presence of lower-than-average quality cars will drive the higher-than-average quality cars out of the market. The buyer cannot reliably evaluate the seller's claims about the quality of the car, and thus the sellers of higher-than-average quality cars cannot get a reasonable price. However, the Lemons model's effects can be lessened if the seller can supply a signal to the buyer that the car is of higher-than-average quality. The **costly-to-fake principle** indicates that for a signal to communicate credible information, it must be costly or difficult to fake. The salesman's word is not costly to fake and is not credible. A 5,000-mile warrantee is costly and is credible. The cost-to-fake principle also helps to explain why many self-employed professionals, (e.g., lawyers) drive expensive cars, wear expensive suits, and live in the best neighborhoods. Conspicuous consumption may serve as a signal of ability. If a lawyer wears $5,000 suits, he must have higher earnings, which must mean he is a successful lawyer.

Learning Objective 5: Define statistical discrimination and give examples of its existence.
Not all circumstances of asymmetric information favor the seller over the buyer. With insurance, the firm issuing a policy knows very little about the potential for the client to file a claim. The missing information is of definite value to the firm, so they have an incentive to develop methods of filling in the missing data even if the methods are imprecise. Consider, while not all 17-year-old males are reckless drivers, as a group they generate a larger number of auto accident claims. And while not all 40-year-old females are cautious drivers, as a group they generate a smaller number of accident claims. As a result, all 17-year-old males pay more for auto insurance and most 40-year-old females tend to pay much less. **Statistical discrimination** is the practice of making judgments about some attribute of individuals, goods, or services based on the value of the attribute for the groups to which they belong. The use of statistical discrimination is widespread when it is costly or impossible to obtain information on the individual. An excellent score on the SATs does not guarantee success in college, but on average those who score well do well in college. One's college GPA does not entirely describe one's potential as an employee, but generally speaking, a higher GPA and workplace performance are positively correlated. Note that statistical discrimination is the result of observable differences in behavior, not the cause of the differences. For example, even as insurance companies practice statistical discrimination, within the broad groupings, everyone pays the same rate.

Learning Objective 6: Define adverse selection and moral hazard and analyze their effects on resource allocation.
Within groups people still vary greatly with respect to filing claims. **Adverse selection** refers to the tendency for insurance policies to be purchased disproportionately by those who are more costly to insure. Jon believes he will not get seriously ill in the next five years and does not purchase health insurance. Sally believes a serious illness is a real possibility in the next five years and makes the purchase. If Sally does get ill, the claim will exceed her premium payments and the following year's rates will have to rise. The increase in the premium made Jon even less interested in buying health insurance, while Sally's illness may foreshadow more illness so she continues buying the insurance. The pool of insured people becomes "sicker" and the cost of paying claims, and hence premiums, rises. **Moral hazard** is the tendency to exercise less effort and caution toward items that are insured against theft or damage.

Leaning Objective 7: Define the concept of the disappearing political discourse.
The final idea presented is an explanation of why political debate on controversial issues falls over time. **Disappearing political discourse** is the notion that people who support a position may remain silent because speaking out entails a risk of being misunderstood. The economic arguments for legalizing drug consumption are quite convincing: organized crime would lose a large source of revenue, the drugs could be standardized to prevent overdoses and poisoning, taxes could be imposed, and law enforcement resources could be reallocated to other crimes. However, the only people who voice their support for legalization tend to be drug users. This is precisely why politicians who support or might support legalization remain silent, so as not to be

thought a drug user. By remaining silent, the politician ensures he or she will not be misunderstood.

III. Self-Test

Key Terms
Match the term in the right-hand column with the appropriate definitions in the left-hand column by placing the letter of the term in the blank in front of its definition. (Answers are given at the end of the chapter.)

1. _____ Someone who accepts any fair or better-than-fair gamble.
2. _____ A model of how asymmetric information tends to reduce the average quality of goods offered for sale.
3. _____ The pattern in which insurance tends to be purchased disproportionately by those most costly to insure.
4. _____ The tendency for people who support a position to remain silent for fear of being misunderstood.
5. _____ An incentive problem in which too little of a good or service is provided because nonpayers cannot be excluded from using it.
6. _____ The sum of the possible outcomes of a gamble times their respective probabilities.
7. _____ Someone who rejects all fair gambles.
8. _____ When buyers and sellers are not equally informed about the characteristics of the goods for sale.
9. _____ The tendency to expend less effort protecting those goods that are insured against theft or damage.
10. ___ The practice of making judgments about the quality of people or goods based on the average characteristics of the groups to which they belong.
11. ___ To substantiate the credibility of a claim, the claim must be costly or difficult to fake.
12. ___ A gamble with an expected value greater than zero.
13. ___ A gamble with an expected value of zero.

a. adverse selection
b. asymmetric information
c. better-than-fair gamble
d. costly-to-fake principle
e. disappearing political discourse
f. expected value of a gamble
g. fair gamble
h. free-rider problem
i. lemons model
j. moral hazard
k. risk-averse person
l. risk-neutral person
m. statistical discrimination

Multiple-Choice Questions
Circle the letter that corresponds to the best answer. (Answers are at the end of the chapter.)

1. When collecting information about some good or service, many people first ask their friends and family members for their opinions. This is because
   A. one can trust them to tell the truth.
   B. it is usually the least costly information.
   C. it is always the best information.
   D. their credibility is better than a salesman's.
   E. their credibility is better than Consumer Reports.

2. The reason the marginal benefit of information curve is downward sloping is because
    A. some information is useless.
    B. most information is useless.
    C. information is subject to the law of diminishing marginal return.
    D. there is only so much to learn about a product.
    E. consumers prefer blissful ignorance.

3. The marginal cost curve for information is upward sloping because
    A. most information is false.
    B. consumers start with the least expensive sources and progress to more expensive sources.
    C. there is only so much to learn about a product.
    D. some information is useless.
    E. most information is misleading.

4. Tom goes to the local stereo store to learn about high end equipment. The salesperson spends an hour talking with Tom and demonstrating equipment. Tom then leaves and orders the system he liked from an Internet store and saves $250. Tom is a(n)
    A. smart shopper.
    B. jerk.
    C. free rider.
    D. example of adverse selection.
    E. example of statistical discrimination.

5. Frank is considering moving to Denver. There is a 70% chance that he will find a job that pays $1,000 more than what he currently earns and a 30% chance he will find one that pays $3,000 less. The expected value of moving to Denver is
    A. -$200.
    B. $200.
    C. $700.
    D. $900.
    E. $1,000.

6. The relevance of expected value to the search decision of the consumer is because
    A. the outcome of a particular search is certain.
    B. one may not be able to purchase the good after it is found.
    C. the outcome of a particular search is uncertain.
    D. one always knows the value of the next search.
    E. one only continues to search if the expected value is positive.

7. Phil is offered the following gamble: a 60% chance of winning $1,000 and a 40% chance of losing $1,500. This gamble is a(n)
    A. unfair gamble.
    B. fair gamble.
    C. Better-than-fair gamble.
    D. Worse-than-fair gamble.

E. almost-fair gamble.

8. Dave is risk averse while Scott is risk neutral. Both are confronted with the following gamble: win $5,000 with the probability of .65 or lose $9,000 with a probability of .35. One can predict that
   A. both will accept the gamble.
   B. only Scott will accept the gamble.
   C. only Dave will accept the gamble.
   D. neither will accept the gamble.
   E. Scott will accept the gamble and Dave might.

9. The "personals" section in the local newspaper is an attempt to
   A. increase the marginal benefit of searching for love.
   B. reduce the marginal benefit of searching for love.
   C. reduce the marginal cost of searching for love.
   D. increase the marginal cost of searching for love.
   E. help the chronically lonely.

10. In the context of search theory, the legal contract of marriage exists to
   A. fulfill religious requirements.
   B. make men and women respectable.
   C. solve the commitment problem.
   D. stifle the growth potential of women.
   E. ensure reproduction.

11. As applied to the market for used cars, the first link in the lemons model is that
   A. sellers will always overstate the condition of their cars.
   B. buyers will always overstate their reservation price.
   C. more lower quality cars will be offered for sale in the used car market.
   D. sellers will always understate the condition of their cars.
   E. buyers will always understate their reservation price.

12. The second link in the lemons model when applied to used cars is that because most used cars offered for sale are of less-than-average quality, then
   A. those with a better-than-average quality car have a greater incentive to sell.
   B. the amount of overstatement by sellers of the car's condition declines.
   C. those with a better-than-average quality car have a greater incentive not to sell.
   D. the extent of buyers' understatements of their reservation price declines.
   E. those with a better-than-average-quality car have a smaller incentive to keep their cars.

13. Using conspicuous consumption as a signal for ability produces a social inefficiency because
   A. consumption and ability are very poorly correlated.
   B. conspicuous consumption is, by definition, inefficient.
   C. a positional arms race ensues, with greater and greater amounts being spent on conspicuous consumption.
   D. earnings and ability are very poorly correlated.

E. $5,000 suits are simply unnecessary.

14. Jim and Dylan are both applying for the same job. To the employer, both seem identical
except for one feature: Jim has a college GPA of 2.75 and Dylan's is 3.5. The employer will
likely
    A. flip a coin to decide who to hire.
    B. pick Dylan because he is the better worker.
    C. pick Dylan because the employer believes a higher GPA means a better worker.
    D. ignore the difference in GPA's when deciding.
    E. not hire either.

15. The reason insurance companies, universities, and employers use statistical discrimination in
decision making is because
    A. it has not been made completely illegal to do so.
    B. imperfect information is better than no information.
    C. inaccurate information is better than perfect information.
    D. imperfect information is as good as perfect information.
    E. it favors the majority.

16. Which of the following political issues is least likely to encounter disappearing discourse?
    A. Abortion.
    B. Legalization of drugs.
    C. The death penalty.
    D. Agricultural price supports.
    E. Prayer in school.

17. In general, risk averse persons will
    A. search more than risk-neutral persons.
    B. search the same amount as risk-neutral persons.
    C. search significantly more than risk-neutral persons.
    D. search more or less than the average person.
    E. search less than risk-neutral persons.

18. When the expected value of searching increases,
    A. fewer searches occur.
    B. the number of searches does not change.
    C. more searches occur.
    D. better searches occur.
    E. the costs of searching fall.

19. Imagine a world in which landlords always fix problems quickly, tenants never damage
property, and always pay their rent in a timely fashion. In such a world,
    A. lease agreements would still exist to solve the commitment problem.
    B. lease agreements would be unnecessary.
    C. lease agreements would only serve the interests of landlords.
    D. lease agreements would only serve the interests of tenants.

E. rents would rise.

20. Tim and Larry are both thrill seekers. Tim has life insurance and Larry does not. One can predict that
A. Larry will engage in fewer life-threatening activities.
B. Tim will engage in fewer life-threatening activities.
C. Tim and Larry will have the same frequency of participation in life-threatening activities.
D. Larry will engage in more life-threatening activities.
E. Tim's life insurance has no bearing on his behavior.

Short Answer Problems
(Answers and solutions are given at the end of the chapter.)

1. Expected Value and Risk Preference
Understanding search theory requires a basic grasp of the concept of expected value and how it applies to the risk preference of individuals.

   A. Suppose Denise is offered the following gamble: she has 33% chance of winning $1,200 and 66% chance of losing $600. The expected value of the gamble is ($792/0) _____ and thus it is a (fair/better-than-fair) _____ gamble. If one does not know Denise's preference for risk, one can predict she (will not/might/will) _____ accept the gamble.
   B. Denise reveals that she is risk averse. As a result, she will (accept/reject) _____ the gamble.
   C. Daniel is presented with a gamble: he has a 25% chance of winning $2,000, a 50% chance of winning $2, and a 25% chance of losing $2,000. The expected value of the gamble is (0/$1) _____, which means it is a (fair/better-than-fair) _____ gamble. If one does not know Daniel's preference for risk, one can predict he (will not/might/will) _____ accept the gamble.

2. Optimal Search
The following question will review the technique for solving search problems. Juan is looking for an apartment in Pittsburgh. In Pittsburgh, 75% of the two-bedroom, one-bath apartments rent for $925 a month and 25% rent for $600. The marginal cost of Juan's search is $15 per apartment (i.e., the marginal cost of looking at the second apartment is $30).

   A. The marginal benefit of looking at another apartment is ($325/$81.25) _____. Juan should therefore examine at most (5/4) _____ apartments.
   B. If the marginal cost of Juan's search rises to $25 per apartment, he will look at a total of (4/3) _____ apartments.
   C. If Juan discovers the above percentages are inaccurate and only 12% of the apartments rent for $600, then the marginal benefit of an additional search is ($39/$325) _____. With a marginal search cost of $15 per apartment, Juan will look at (1/2) _____ apartments.

3. The Lemons Model

The importance of the lemons model to the market for used goods is hard to overstate. The subsequent question reviews how the model works and suggests one way to eliminate the problem. Two types of used Fender Stratocasters guitars are available for sale: those originally made in the United States and those originally made in Mexico. It is impossible for the buyer to know which is which but the seller does. The value of a used United States Stratocaster is $900, while a used Mexican Stratocaster is worth $400. The United States Stratocasters are 30% of Fender's production and the Mexican Stratocasters are 70%. No seller is forced to sell for less than the guitar's value.

A. The initial reservation price for a used Stratocaster will be ($550/$650) _____. At this offer price, the (United States/Mexican) _____-made Stratocaster will be withdrawn from the market.

B. The effect of withdrawal will be that Mexican-made Stratocasters will become a (larger/smaller) _____ fraction of the used-guitar market and will move the reservation price of buyers (up/down) _____.

C. As the reservation price changes, United States Stratocasters will (return to the used market/become even more scarce)_____. Ultimately, (most/all) _____ of the United States Stratocasters are withdrawn from the market and the reservation price of used Stratocasters is ($550/$400) _____.

D. Suppose Fender had placed a tiny code stamped inside the cavity of its guitars that identified the country of manufacture but had not explained the meaning of the number. If Fender finally announced the meanings of the codes, then the market for used Stratocasters would (be unchanged/split into two separate markets) _____, with sellers of United States Stratocasters receiving ($900/$550) _____ and sellers of Mexican Stratocasters receiving ($550/$400) _____.

IV. Economic Naturalist Application

The problem of asymmetric information is highly evident in the labor market. Even though, for most of you, graduation is still a few years away, it can prove useful to think about what you wish to signal to employers. For example, some frequently repeated advice is to leave your GPA off your resume if it is average. Analyze this advice. What signal are you sending to employers? Could their assumption be worse than the truth? Another common suggestion is for women to use their initials rather than their first names. Will this ploy succeed in fooling employers?

Answer:

V. Go to the Web: Graphing Exercises Using Interactive Graphs

Search the web for information about national health care coverage. How would a federal program of national health care solve the adverse selection problem? Would it worsen the moral hazard problem?

Answer:

To review an answer to this question, and to learn more about the use of economic theory to analyze this issue (and other microeconomic issues), please go to the Electronic Learning Session in the Student Center at the Frank/Bernanke web site: http://www.mhhe.com/economics/frankbernanke2.

VI. Self-Test Solutions

Key Terms

1. l
2. i
3. a
4. e
5. h
6. f
7. k
8. b
9. j
10. m
11. d
12. c
13. g

Multiple-Choice Questions

1. B
2. C
3. B
4. C

5. A
6. C
7. B
8. A
9. C
10. C
11. C
12. C
13. C
14. C
15. B
16. D
17. E
18. C
19. A
20. A

Short Answer Problems

1.
A. 0; fair; might
B. reject
C. $1; better-than-fair; will

2.
A. $81.25; 5
B. 3
C. $39; 2

3.
A. $550; United States
B. larger; down
C. become even more scarce; all; $400
D. split into two separate markets; $900; $400

Chapter 13
Labor Markets, Poverty, and Income Distribution

I. Pretest: What Do You Really Know?
Circle the letter that corresponds to the best answer. (Answers appear immediately after the final question).

1. The optimal number of workers for a perfectly competitive firm to hire occurs when
   A. total labor costs equal total revenues.
   B. the lowest possible wage is accepted by workers.
   C. the wage rate equals the marginal product of the last worker.
   D. the wage rate equals the value of marginal product of the last worker.
   E. the largest output is achieved.

2. The value of the marginal product curve is downward sloping because
   A. firms must lower price to sell more.
   B. at lower wages, only less-qualified workers are available.
   C. of the law of diminishing marginal product.
   D. profits decline as more workers are hired.
   E. productivity rises as more workers are hired.

3. Decisions to pursue higher education or graduate school are best thought of as _____ decisions.
   A. unwise
   B. costly
   C. consumption
   D. investment
   E. parental

4. According to the textbook, the incidence of winner-take-all labor markets is
   A. shrinking.
   B. growing and spreading into new industries.
   C. shrinking in the entertainment industry.
   D. growing only in the entertainment and sports industries.
   E. roughly constant.

5. Compensating wage differentials measure
   A. the amount a worker gains when switching employers.
   B. the positive or negative premium placed on a job's working conditions.
   C. the amount a worker gains when switching occupations.
   D. the social approval of a job.
   E. the amount a worker gains when switching industries.

6. An employer that practices an arbitrary preference for some group, e.g., males or whites, pays for his prejudice by
   A. charging a higher price.
   B. producing less.
   C. receiving lower profits.
   D. cutting costs in other areas.
   E. doing nothing; there is no cost to his discrimination.

7. Based on the data presented in the textbook, between 1945 and the early 1970s, the growth in income in the U.S. was
   A. approximately 3% for all income groups.
   B. approximately 7% for all income groups.
   C. much larger for the low-income groups.
   D. much larger for the high-income groups.
   E. negative for most of the period.

8. The Earned Income Tax Credit program operates like a
   A. tax on wages.
   B. lump sum transfer.
   C. wage subsidy.
   D. in-kind transfer.
   E. minimum wage.

9. In general, a means-tested welfare benefit will
   A. retard the incentive to work..
   B. have no effect on the incentive to work..
   C. enhance the incentive to work..
   D. ensure that only the truly needy get benefits.
   E. encourage honesty about earnings.

10. Suppose Tim gets four welfare benefits of $25 each and when he earns an extra dollar, each of the benefits is reduced by one dollar. When he earns less than $25, the implied "tax rate" on his extra dollar of earnings is
    A. 50%.
    B. 100%.
    C. 200%.
    D. 300%.
    E. 400%.

Solutions and Feedback to Pretest
For each question you answered incorrectly, we strongly recommend taking the time to review the appropriate material before continuing. In the table below, the relevant textbook pages are listed for each question as well as the pertinent Learning Objective from the following Key Point Review.

Correct Answer	Textbook Page Numbers	Learning Objective
1. D	pp. 328-30	2
2. C	pp. 326-28	1
3. D	pg. 331	3
4. B	pp. 336-37	7
5. B	pp. 333-34	5
6. C	pp. 334-36	6
7. A	pp. 337-38	8
8. C	pp. 340-46	10
9. A	pp. 340-46	10
10. E	pp. 340-46	10

II. Key Point Review

Learning Objective 1: Define the marginal product of labor and the value of the marginal product of labor.
The analysis of labor market behavior might at first seem different from the analysis of the market behavior for some consumer good. While it is true that no one really buys or sells his labor, the basic supply-and-demand framework is still well suited to the task of explanation and prediction. Consider how a firm would determine the worth of a worker. Obviously, workers are employed so that the firm can produce output to sell. **Marginal product (MP)** is the extra output the firm can produce as a result of hiring an extra worker. The number of extra units a particular worker produces is insufficient information to decide if he or she should be hired. Output price times marginal product results in the **value of marginal product (VMP)**. The benefit of hiring the worker, measured in dollars by the VMP, can be compared to the cost of hiring the worker, the wage rate. To profit maximize, a perfectly competitive firm should continue to hire workers as long as the VMP of the last worker is greater than or equal to the wage rate.

Learning Objective 2: Discuss the shape of the market demand curve for labor, the market supply curve for labor, and the labor market equilibrium.
Construction of the labor market follows a familiar pattern. The market labor demand curve results from the horizontal summation of the VMP curves for all the firms in the competitive environment. The labor supply curve for any particular industry is upward sloping. At the intersection of the market labor demand and supply curves an equilibrium is achieved. If the market is not at an equilibrium, the wage will be driven up or down as needed.

Learning Objective 3: Define human capital and the theory of human capital and describe how it affects wages.

Human capital is the combination of factors such as education, experience, training, energy, and work habits. **Human capital theory** asserts that a person's VMP is directly proportional to his stock of human capital. Occupations that require a greater stock of human capital must pay more. The decision of how much human capital to acquire becomes an investment question. One must compare the higher future earnings to the current costs of more schooling and lower earning. A present value framework is necessary because some of the costs and most if not all of the benefits are in the future.

Learning Objective 4: Define a labor union. Explain how it contributes to differences in wages.

A **labor union** is a group of workers who bargain collectively with employers for higher wages and better working conditions. The effect of a labor union is similar to that of the minimum wage. In the newly unionized labor market, wages rise and the newly unemployed workers move to the nonunion labor market, driving nonunion wages down. One might wonder how union firms could survive competing with nonunion firms. Part of the answer is that since the union labor market will have an abundance of workers looking to join, union firms can be quite selective about whom they hire. While the unadjusted wage differential between union and nonunion workers is as high as 50%, once the stock of human capital is accounted for, the differential falls to 10%. Another part of answer may be that unions succeed in improving communication between workers and management. Finally, the higher-than-anywhere-else wage of the union worker gives him or her much incentive to perform at least well enough not to lose the job.

Learning Objective 5: Define compensating wage differentials and discuss their role in wage differences.

Why do lifeguards earn a lower hourly wage rate compared to garbage collectors? The answer lies in the attractiveness of a job's working conditions. **Compensating wage differentials** are the wage differences based on the working conditions of the job. For example, jobs that are relatively free of workplace injuries pay less than similar jobs with higher workplace injury rates. And jobs with attractive work schedules (e.g., teaching) pay less than similar work done on the nightshift. Differentials can even exist for characteristics that are difficult to measure, like social approval.

Learning Objective 6: Define employer and customer discrimination and discuss their contribution to differences in wages.

Women and minorities continue to receive less pay than males and whites, even when holding human capital stocks approximately constant. Supporters of marginal productivity theory would explain this as an improper or inaccurate measure of human capital. Critics who reject the claim of competitiveness in labor markets would attribute the earnings differential to discrimination. **Employer discrimination** is the arbitrary preference by the employer for one group of workers over another. Suppose firm A hires only males for $13 per hour while firm B is willing to hire females for $11 per hour. If males and females are equally productive, then firm A is paying $2 per hour per worker for nothing but a psychological benefit, and is hence unexploited . If the output market is reasonably competitive, then new firms should be able to enter and hire females and seize firm A's sales, thus driving them to hire females or shut down. Another possibility is that discrimination emanates from the consumers of the output. **Customer discrimination** occurs when buyers are willing to pay more for a product produced by a given group even though it is of no higher quality than the quality produced by other groups.

Learning Objective 7: Define a winner-take-all labor market and explain how it contributes to wage inequality.
In some labor markets the earnings differentials have become extremely large when the stock of human capital among the workers is essentially the same. Sports and entertainment are the two most visible examples. The human capital difference between the female singer with the number one earnings and the one with the number 200 earnings is minimal at best, but the earnings differential is vast. A **winner-take-all labor market** is one in which minor differences in human capital translate into massive differences in pay. The trend to note is the spread of winner-take-all labor markets into new industries. Wall Street professionals, CEO's of major corporations, and publishing executives all now exhibit elements of winner-take-all behavior.

Learning Objective 8: Describe trends in income inequality from the 1940s to the present.
Real income growth in the United States since 1945 falls into two distinct periods. From 1945 until the early 1970s, all income groups enjoyed moderate and similar growth rates of 2 to 3 percent per year. Since the early 1970s, however, the growth rates have been anything but smooth and across-the-board. For example, from 1978 to 1998, the real incomes of those in the bottom 20% were declining and those in the ranks of the middle class were growing very slowly, less than one-half of one percent per year. The real incomes of those in the top 20 percent, however, rose by more than 40 percent over this period. Likewise, the concentration of wealth in the top quintile also intensified. The wealth holdings of the top 1% now exceed the wealth holdings of all families below the 95th percentile.

Learning Objective 9: Discuss moral notions of income distribution and the effect on work incentives.
Much has been made throughout the textbook and the study guide about the marketplace and its ability to produce efficient outcomes. In the context of income equality, the free market rewards individuals who take initiative, work hard, and are willing to gamble on risky projects or investments. However, the free market has no natural provision for redistributing income to those who try and fail or those unable to try. Of course, taking initiative and risks, working hard, and having talent is no guarantee of economic success in a free market economy. John Rawls, a moral philosopher at Harvard, has proposed the following thought experiment. Imagine a group of people deciding on how income will be distributed. The income comes from above (not the result of the people's efforts) and no one knows anything about his or her own talents or abilities. Rawls claims that the rule for income distribution would be equal amounts for all. While this solution has noble appeal, it is not a solution of the real world. Income, unfortunately, does not come from above; it is primarily the result of someone's efforts. The incentive to invest in education or develop special talents would be severely lessened if the end result was that one would get the same amount of income as someone who had not worked.

Learning Objective 10: Define and discuss the following income redistribution programs: in-kind transfers, the Personal Responsibility Act, means-tested benefits, a negative income tax, the poverty threshold, the minimum wage, earned income tax credit, and public employment for the poor.

Governments reallocate income directly to the poor in the form of cash transfers and **in-kind transfers**, where, instead of cash, the poor are given goods or services. In the United States, the most important welfare program has been Aid to Families with Dependent Children (AFDC). In-kind transfers include food stamps, public housing, and Medicaid. Current welfare programs are **means-tested**: the more income one earns, the smaller the benefit. Because of the way in which the benefits are reduced, significant disincentives to work exist. To address some of the problems with welfare, the **Personal Responsibilities Act** was passed in 1996. It transferred the responsibility for welfare administration from the federal government to the states and imposed a 5-year lifetime limit on AFDC benefits for any given recipient. Other income redistribution plans also exist. One radical proposal to completely overhaul the current welfare system was proposed by Nobel laureate Milton Friedman. The **negative income tax (NIT)** involves the government granting every citizen a cash payment each year with the payment financed by an additional tax on earned income. The work disincentives of a NIT are far smaller than under the current welfare system, primarily because the tax rate on an extra dollar is less than 100%. Unfortunately, the NIT could also cause new problems. If all other welfare programs were abolished, the cash payment would be the sole source of income for those unable to work. The **poverty threshold** is the annual income level below which a family is officially defined as being poor. The NIT's cash payment would need to be as large as this figure, which in 2001 was $18,000 for a family of four. A lavish lifestyle cannot be had for $18,000, but suppose that families began to pool their payments. As more and more families realized the possibility of pooling benefits, there would be a movement of individuals out of the labor force, which would mean the tax rate would increase, driving more workers out the labor force, etc.

The oldest and most well-known income redistribution program is the minimum wage, which is a price floor for labor. Price floors generate excess supply, which when used in the context of a labor market means unemployment. Some workers who had jobs and incomes at the original wage rate will be without a job or an income after the introduction of the minimum wage. Given the inefficiencies generated by the minimum wage, some other policy should be available that would make some better off without harming others. The **earned-income tax credit (EITC)** gives low-wage workers a tax credit on their federal income taxes. The program is essentially a wage subsidy in the form of a reduced payment to the government for taxes. The advantage of the EITC compared to the minimum wage is that it does not reduce the employment of the working poor. Another proposal is to provide the poor with public sector jobs. There is obviously no work disincentive problem with a public employment program. Drawbacks to such an employment program include siphoning workers away from the private sector and establishing the true usefulness of the work being preformed. The best solution to poverty might appears to be a combination of a NIT with a relatively small cash payment and a public employment program. While the combination of an NIT with public employment would not be inexpensive, the current system requires a large amount of tax revenues and it causes many indirect costs from the numerous inefficiencies it creates. The combined program would have far fewer inefficiency costs.

III. Self-Test

Key Terms
Match the term in the right-hand column with the appropriate definitions in the left-hand column by placing the letter of the term in the blank in front of its definition. (Answers are given at the end of the chapter.)

1. ____ The dollar value of the extra output a firm receives by employing an extra unit of labor input.

2. ____ A group of workers who bargain collectively with employers for higher wages and better working conditions.

3. ____ A view of pay determination that relates a worker's wage to his or her stock of human capital.

4. ____ When consumers are willing to pay more for a product produced by members of a favored group even if the quality of the product is no better.

5. ____ A federal law passed in 1996 that transferred responsibility for welfare programs to state governments and placed a 5-year lifetime limit on AFDC benefits.

6. ____ An income tax credit available to low-income workers.

7. ____ A benefit received in the form of a good or service rather than in the form of cash.

8. ____ The extra output a firm receives when it uses an extra unit of labor input.

9. ____ A positive or negative wage difference that reflects the attractiveness of the job's working conditions.

10. ____ An employer's arbitrary preference for one group of workers over another.

11. ____ A labor market in which small differences in human capital translate into large differences in pay.

12. ____ When a benefit's level declines as the recipient earns more income.

13. ____ The level of income below which the federal government classifies a family as poor.

14. ____ An amalgam of factors such as education, experience, intelligence, work habits, and initiative that affect a worker's marginal product.

15. ____ An income redistribution proposal where every citizen would be granted a cash payment each year financed by an additional tax on earned income.

a. compensating wage differential

b. customer discrimination

c. earned-income tax credit (EITC)

d. employer discrimination

e. human capital

f. human capital theory

g. in-kind transfer

h. labor union

i. marginal product (MP)

j. means-tested

k. negative income tax (NIT)

l. Personal Responsibility Act

m. poverty threshold

n. value of marginal product (VMP)

o. winner-take-all labor market

Multiple-Choice Questions
Circle the letter that corresponds to the best answer. (Answers are given at the end of the chapter.)

1. Lou's marginal product is 12, the firm's output price is $5, and the wage rate is $40. The firm
   A. will hire Lou.
   B. may or may not hire Lou.
   C. will not hire Lou.
   D. does not have enough information to decide.
   E. will hire Lou only if he accepts a wage of $35.

2. In a competitive labor market, it is observed that the equilibrium wage rate and employment level have both risen. One can infer that
   A. the supply of labor has increased.
   B. the demand for labor has fallen.
   C. the price firms receive for their output has declined.
   D. the supply of labor has decreased.
   E. the demand for labor has increased.

3. The decision to pursue higher education or graduate school requires that one compare the _____ to the _____.
   A. cost of the education; benefits of the education
   B. discounted cost of the education; benefits of the education
   C. cost of the education; discounted benefits of the education
   D. average salary without the education; average salary with the education
   E. discounted costs of the education; discounted benefits of the education

4. A labor union in the labor market is similar to a _____ in the output market.
   A. monopsony
   B. tax
   C. cartel
   D. perfect competitor
   E. oligopoly

5. The reason nonunion firms do not always drive union firms out of business is because
   A. markets are not competitive
   B. consumers look for the union label.
   C. union firms hire more selectively, employing workers with greater human capital.
   D. union firms cut corners in other areas.
   E. nonunion firms produce significantly lower quality goods.

6. In a winner-take-all labor market, one would expect to see
   A. wage compression.
   B. few individuals willing to enter.
   C. a smooth decline in earnings from the top earners down.
   D. a sharp increase in earnings at the top.

E. a sharp increase in earnings between the bottom and the middle.

7. The best explanation for the difference in real earnings between popular singers at the turn of the century and today is that
   A. singers today are more talented.
   B. singers today can reach a much larger audience.
   C. singers of yesteryear did not have aggressive agents.
   D. labor unions for singers were formed.
   E. the elasticity of demand for singers is much smaller today.

8. Jobs with undesirable working conditions will have a _____ compensating wage differential and jobs with desirable working conditions will have a _____ compensating wage differential.
   A. larger; smaller
   B. positive; negative
   C. negative; positive
   D. negative; negative
   E. smaller; larger

9. According to the textbook, union membership has
   A. remained constant since the 1950s.
   B. expanded into white collar professions.
   C. declined by approximately 50% since the 1950s.
   D. become common in the South.
   E. increased rapidly since the 1950s.

10. In professional baseball, some players earn over $6 million per year while the average salary is $1.2 million. The explanation for this rests with
    A. a winner-take-all labor market.
    B. the best players being nearly six times better than average players.
    C. undisciplined owners overspending on players' salaries.
    D. racial discrimination.
    E. unreasonable salary demands by players.

11. Suppose that welders working offshore oil rigs earn 25% more than welders working land-based oil rigs. The difference in earnings is best explained by
    A. differences in education.
    B. differences in training.
    C. differences in working conditions.
    D. differences in abilities.
    E. discrimination.

12. Since the mid 1970s, the pattern of income growth has been one of
    A. much larger gains for all income groups.
    B. negative rates for low-income groups and enormous gains for high-income groups.
    C. smaller growth for all groups compared to the period of 1945 to the early 1970s.

D. large gains for the middle class and stagnate growth for low- and high-income groups.

E. randomness.

13. According to Professor Rawls, if income was given to a group of people and those people had no idea of their talents, they would likely prefer an income distribution that rewarded

A. sloth.

B. high IQ.

C. artistic gifts.

D. everyone with an equal share of income.

E. innovation.

14. Unlike the minimum wage, the Earned Income Tax Credit does *not*

A. cause low wage workers to be laid off.

B. cost anything.

C. improve the status of the working poor.

D. maintain the proper incentives to work.

E. discourage welfare dependency.

15. Food stamps and Medicaid are examples of

A. cash transfers.

B. in-kind transfers.

C. welfare programs that have been eliminated.

D. programs created by the Personal Responsibility Act.

E. programs created by the New Deal.

16. Compared to the current welfare system, a negative income tax would

A. have a smaller negative effect on the incentive to work.

B. be much more costly to administer.

C. destroy the incentive to work.

D. result in increasing the number of poor.

E. increase the tendency for families to break up.

17. According to the textbook, the best possible solution to the problem of poverty would seem to be

A. a combination of a negative income tax and public employment.

B. maintaining the current system.

C. a negative income tax with the tax credit equal to the poverty threshold.

D. a massive public employment program.

E. complete elimination of all efforts to assist the poor.

18. Compared to 1975, the 20% of families with the lowest incomes in the U.S. in 1998 have

A. less purchasing power.

B. fallen to 15%.

C. more purchasing power.

D. smaller nominal incomes.

E. the same purchasing power.

19. The justification for means-tested welfare benefits is to
    A. lessen the incentive to work.
    B. ensure benefits go to the truly needy.
    C. reduce the expense of the program.
    D. lessen the incentive to choose welfare over work.
    E. make sure the poor don't profit from welfare.

20. Suppose Allen cares only about income and receives one welfare benefit of $100, and for
    each dollar he earns, the benefit is reduced by one dollar. If Allen can earn _____, he
    will choose to _____.
    A. less than $100; work
    B. $100; work
    C. $100; not work and receive the benefit
    D. more than $100; not work and receive the benefit
    E. $200; not work and receive the benefit

Short Answer Problems
(Answers and solutions are given at the end of the chapter.)

1. Perfectly Competitive Labor Markets
This question will review the calculation of marginal product, the value of the marginal product, and the condition for the profit-maximizing level of labor usage. The table refers to a perfectly competitive firm.

Labor Input	Output	Marginal Product	Value of Marginal Product
1	76		
2	129		
3	170		
4	202		
5	219		
6	221		

  A. Assuming the price of the firm's output is $2.95, fill in the missing data in the table.
  B. As more workers are hired, output rises and marginal product (rises as well/falls)
      _____. The reason is that (worker quality is falling/the law of diminishing product is
      present) _____.
  C. The value of marginal product for the third worker is ($501.50/$120.95) _____,
      which means the firm will hire him or her if the wage rate is (at most $120.95/at most
      $501.50) _____.
  D. If the market wage rate is $75, the firm will hire (5/4) _____ workers. If the wage rate
      is $50.15, the firm will hire (5/4) _____ workers.

2. Means-Tested Benefits
The issue of work incentives and welfare benefits are considered in the following question.
Stella is a welfare recipient who qualifies for two means-tested cash benefits. If she does not

earn any income, she receives $300 from each benefit. For each dollar she earns (which her employer is required to report to the welfare agency), each benefit is reduced by 85 cents until the benefit equals zero.

    A. Stella's income if she does not work is ($300/$600) _____. If she earns $100 in income her benefit will be ($430/$515) _____.

    B. If she earns $250, then her total income is ($637.50/$425) _____.

    C. The equation that describes the relationship between Stella's benefit (B), benefit reduction rate (t), and earnings is _____. Thus, rounding to the nearest dollar, when Stella earns ($353/$400) _____, her benefit will be zero.

    D. The benefit reduction rate means that her earnings are being "taxed" at a rate of ($1.70/85 cents) _____ for every dollar she makes.

    E. For Stella to even consider working, her job offer would have to pay at least ($353/$600) _____.

3. Negative Income Tax

Although not a popular suggestion for welfare reform recently, the negative income tax has enjoy much support in the past and may return in the future. Suppose the current welfare system is completely eliminated and replaced with a negative income tax. The tax credit granted to all families is $15,000 and the tax on combined family earnings is 20%.

    A. Under the above proposal, families earning $50,000 would receive a cash benefit of ($5,000/$7,000) _____. Families earning $200,000 would pay taxes of ($25,000/$20,000) _____.

    B. The breakeven level of family income for this plan is ($70,000/$75,000) _____.

    C. The equation that describes the relationship between the tax credit (C), the tax rate (t), and earnings (E) the tax credit is _____.

4. Labor Topics

Explaining the differences in the earnings of individuals requires an understanding of several different factors. Two of the factors that have calculations are reviewed below.

    A. Paula has an undergraduate degree in political science and has been working as a planner at a state agency. If she continues on her present career path, the present value of her lifetime earnings is $300,000. If she takes three years off and gets a JD degree, the present value of her lifetime earnings is $360,000. The annual cost of a JD degree is $20,000 and the interest rate is 6%. The present value of the cost of a law degree is ($60,000/$56,666) _____. Her net lifetime earnings with a law degree are therefore ($303,334/$300,000) _____ so she (should/should not) _____ attend law school.

    B. Assume that workers are of the same race and either male or female. Male and female workers possess the same stock of human capital and hence are equally productive. The male wage rate is $10 per hour and the female wage rate is $9 per hour. Two firms use 100 employees each, but one firm practices discrimination while the other firm hires only females. The female work force firm will find that (its labor costs are 10% lower/the quality of its output is lower) _____. As a result, the male work force firm will be (more/less) _____ vulnerable to economic downturns. Over time, (nothing will change/the male firms will fail or hire females) _____ and the female wage rate will (rise/fall) _____ and the male wage rate will (fall/remain unchanged) _____.

IV. Economic Naturalist Application

Find information on wages paid to college-educated workers employed by nonprofit organizations (but not local, state, or the federal government) and those employed in the private sector. Pick a particular job title like marketer or public relations and compare the respective wages. Do those who work for the nonprofits earn more, less, or the same? Relate your findings to compensating wage differentials.

Answer:

V. Go tot Web: Graphing Exercises Using Interactive Graphs

Search the Web for information on the earnings of entertainers (actors, actresses, singers) and professional golfers. Compare the top 10 earners over the last 5 years with the top 10 earners before WWII. Be sure to convert the values into purchasing power so the comparisons will be valid. Do you observe a winner-take-all market? How would you test to see if the winner-take-all structure is more or less evident today compared with the years prior to WWII? What do your data indicate about the degree of a winner-take-all structure over time?

Answer:

To review an answer to this question, and to learn more about the use of economic theory to analyze this issue (and other microeconomic issues), please go to the Electronic Learning Session in the Student Center at the Frank/Bernanke web site: http://www.mhhe.com/economics/frankbernanke2.

VI. Self -Test Solutions

Key Terms

1. n
2. h
3. f
4. b
5. l
6. c
7. g
8. i
9. a
10. d
11. o
12. j
13. m
14. e
15. k

Multiple-Choice Questions

1. A
2. E
3. E
4. C
5. C
6. D
7. B
8. B
9. C
10. A
11. C
12. B
13. D
14. A
15. B
16. A
17. A
18. A
19. B
20. C

Short Answer Problems

1.

Labor Input	Output	Marginal Product	Value of Marginal Product
1	76	76	$224.20
2	129	53	$156.35
3	170	41	$120.95
4	202	32	$94.40
5	219	17	$50.15
6	221	2	$5.90

A. See table.
B. falls; the law of diminishing product is present
C. $120.95; at most $120.95
D. 4; 5

2.
A. $600; $430
B. $425
C. Benefit = 600 – (1.7×Earnings); $353
D. $1.70
E. $600

3.
A. $5,000; $25,000
B. $75,000
C. Credit = 15,000 - 0.2×Earnings

4.
A. $56,666; $303,334; should
B. its labor costs are 10% lower; more; the male firms will fail or hire females; rise; fall

Chapter 14
The Environment, Health, and Safety

I. Pretest: What Do You Really Know?
Circle the letter that corresponds to the best answer. (Answers appear immediately after the final question).

1. Prior to World War II, most consumers in the U.S.
    A. owned insurance for catastrophic illness but self-insured against routine medical care.
    B. self-insured against catastrophic illness but owned insurance for routine medical care.
    C. had no medical insurance of any type.
    D. owned medical insurance covering both catastrophic and routine medical care.
    E. were less sick than consumers today.

2. In general, the optimal amount of medical care to receive is
    A. as much as possible.
    B. enough to get well.
    C. where the total costs of the care equals the total benefits.
    D. where the marginal costs of the care equals the marginal benefits.
    E. as much as one can afford.

3. The major characteristic of an HMO is
    A. emphasis on acute medical treatment.
    B. medical treatment provided for a fixed annual payment.
    C. freedom to see nonmember physicians.
    D. medical treatment provided on a fee-for-service basis.
    E. a lack of profit-maximization motives.

4. In contrast to first-dollar insurance coverage, the efficiency concern for HMOs is that
    A. too much medical treatment will be provided.
    B. acute treatment will be overemphasized.
    C. too little medical treatment will be provided.
    D. preventive treatment will be underemphasized.
    E. price will be too low.

5. The most efficient distribution of pollution abatement among polluters is
   A. a 10% reduction for all.
   B. a fixed percent reduction for all.
   C. for large reductions from the largest polluters.
   D. for large reductions from the smallest polluters.
   E. when the marginal cost of abatement is the same across all polluters.

6. The optimal amount of workplace safety is the amount
   A. where the total benefits equal the total costs.
   B. that results in zero injuries.
   C. that results in a 50% reduction in injuries.
   D. where the marginal benefits equal the marginal costs.
   E. that results in zero deaths.

7. The growth of medical insurance in general and first-dollar coverage specifically has reduced
   the marginal cost of treatment to the consumer. Therefore, the current level of medical
   treatment in the U.S. is
   A. greater than the efficient level.
   B. equal to the efficient level.
   C. less than the efficient level.
   D. greater than or equal to the efficient level.
   E. less than or equal to the efficient level.

8. Compared to a fixed percentage reduction regulation, a tax on pollution encourages
   A. all firms to reduce pollution by the same percent.
   B. all firms to use the same technology to reduce pollution.
   C. firms that can most cheaply reduce pollution to make sizable reductions.
   D. firms that find pollution reduction expensive to pollute even more.
   E. economic inefficiency.

9. Compared to the taxing of pollution, pollution permits offer the advantage of
   A. eliciting the largest reduction in pollution from those firms that can do so most cheaply.
   B. raising revenues for the government.
   C. allowing the public to influence the amount of pollution allowed through the purchasing of
      permits.
   D. Ensuring that all firms reduce pollution by the same percentage.
   E. Ensuring that all firms use the same pollution-reduction technology.

10. Demands for greater government regulations of workplace safety rests on the belief that
   A. labor market competition is great.
   B. firms will adopt safety devices on their own.
   C. left unregulated, firms will subject workers to unreasonable risks.
   D. workers mobility is significant.
   E. workers know which industries and firms are relatively safe and which are not.

Solutions and Feedback to Pretest

For each question you answered incorrectly, we strongly recommend taking the time to review the appropriate material before continuing. In the table below, the relevant textbook pages are listed for each question as well as the pertinent Learning Objective from the following Key Point Review.

Correct Answer	Textbook Page Numbers	Learning Objective
1. A	pg. 352	1
2. D	pp. 352-55	2
3. B	pp. 355-58	3
4. C	pp. 355-58	3
5. E	pg. 358	4
6. D	pp. 361-66	6
7. A	pp. 352-55	2
8. C	pp. 358-61	5
9. C	pp. 358-61	5
10. C	pp. 361-66	6

II. Key Point Review

Learning Objective 1: Discuss the trends in healthcare coverage and healthcare expenditures over the last century.

Over the course of the twentieth century, real healthcare expenditures per capita rose more quickly than real per capita income, meaning that the share of income devoted to healthcare has grown. Certainly, some of the increase stems from the development of new and expensive medical technologies. But the most important factor in the healthcare system driving the increase in costs is the change in the method of financing. Prior to World War II, most families had medical insurance only for catastrophic illness and paid for routine care out of their pockets. Since World War, II and particularly since the mid-1960s, insurance coverage for routine medical care is commonplace, typically provided by employers or the government. Unfortunately, the impact of the growth in coverage has lead to a tremendous increase in wasteful spending.

Learning Objective 2: Apply the Cost-Benefit Principle to the decision of healthcare purchases. Define first-dollar insurance coverage. Discuss the results about the price elasticity of demand for healthcare.

Medical care is no different from other goods and services in that the optimal allocation occurs when the marginal benefit equals the marginal cost. Prior to World War II, families paid the marginal cost of routine care. The widespread adoption of routine care insurance distorts the cost-benefit comparison. **First-dollar insurance coverage** pays for all expenses generated by the insured activity. Essentially, first-dollar coverage sets the marginal cost of medical care to the consumer at zero. The actual marginal cost is, in fact, positive. Rationally, consumers use medical care until the marginal benefit equals zero, leading to significant over-utilization and an inefficient outcome. The solution is to return some of the marginal cost of medical care to the consumer. Studies of families with medical deductibles versus first-dollar coverage show reduced use of medical care without a corresponding increase in illness or disease.

Learning Objective 3: Define HMO and explain how the incentives induce less resource waste. Explain the reasons for the growth of medically uninsured individuals.

During the 1990s, in response to the high cost of traditional medical insurance coverage, a new form of healthcare delivery developed. A **health maintenance organization (HMO)** is a group of physicians providing healthcare to individuals for a fixed annual fee. The efficiency concern switches to under-provision rather than over-provision of medical care. The profits of the HMO will be larger the fewer the number of tests and procedures performed. Regardless of the method of financing medical care, the rising cost of medical care contributes to the growing numbers of uninsured families in the United States. As medical insurance becomes more expensive, those in good health will choose not to purchase it, increasing the relative number of people with poor health. Those with poor health make extensive use of costly procedures, driving premiums up further. This effect is adverse selection first defined in Chapter 12. One solution would be to have government reimburse all individuals for healthcare coverage, effectively requiring all good health people to participate in the pool.

Learning Objective 4: Describe the efficient solution for pollution abatement and contrast it with current regulatory efforts.

Environmental protection is another important area of public policy. Once having decided to address the problem, it becomes a technical question of the most efficient way of achieving a given reduction in pollution. The answer is for the distribution of effort to be such that every polluter's marginal cost of pollution abatement is the same. Most often, environmental regulations require the same pollution abatement effort from all firms, implicitly assuming that all firms have identical marginal abatement costs.

Learning Objective 5: Analyze the effects of a pollution tax and pollution permits. List the advantages and disadvantages of the two alternatives.

The first alternative to direct regulation would be a pollution tax. The government would set the maximum amount of untaxed pollution firms could emit. For emissions above the maximum the firm would pay a tax. The tax would be an increasing function of the amount emitted above the maximum. The firm would then decide how much pollution abatement it wanted to accomplish. Firms that can easily reduce pollution would and not pay the tax while firms that can't easily reduce pollution would pay the tax. Why is this a better solution? Suppose an across-the-board 10% reduction in pollution was mandated. It is quite likely that a 10% reduction asks too little from the low-cost firms and too much from the high-cost firms. By making pollution part of the profit-maximization decision, all firms have an incentive to reduce pollution and some firms will be exceeding good at doing so. The second alternative, pollution permits, is similar to a pollution tax but has other advantages. The idea is that the government decides how much pollution is acceptable and then auctions off the rights to pollute to the firms. Without a permit, the firm cannot emit pollution. Firms that can easily reduce pollution will not bid very much for the permits, while firms that cannot easily lessen pollution will aggressively bid for the permits, driving the price up. Again, pollution is now part of the profit-maximization decision with a clear payoff to reducing the amount of pollution. Permits are better than a tax in two ways. With a tax, it is not clear how high or low to set the tax to get the desired behavior. With permits, firms are biding so the appropriate price is determined as a consequence of the auction. The other advantage is that citizens can act collectively and alter the amount of pollution allowed in their area by purchasing one or more of the permits.

Learning Objective 6: Analyze the merits of worker exploitation as an explanation of workplace injuries. Discuss the optimal amount of workplace safety. Define workers' compensation.

Another common area of public policy debate is workplace safety. The origins of the debate come from the late 1800s and early 1900s when the view of employer exploitation of workers became commonly accepted. The proponents argued that unless and until government took steps to enforce safety regulations, many workers would needlessly be injured or killed on the job. Today, throughout the industrial economies extensive rules and regulations govern workplace safety. Explaining workplace injuries as a result of employer exploitation has some serious difficulties. First, safety is an amenity on which competition can be based. If workers value safety, then an employer who refuses to adopt a safety measure that is efficient (i.e., where marginal benefits are at least as large as marginal costs), risks losing his or her workers to a firm that does provide the safety measure.

Supporters of the exploitation view argue that workers are ignorant of safety devices and thus the competitive model breaks down. But even if workers are unaware, firms have the incentive to tell them. That leaves the exploitation view with one remaining argument that firms collude and collectively agree not to provide safety to workers. However, the discussion in Chapter 10 made clear that collusive agreements cannot be expected to last very long because of the incentive to cheat. A possible alternative interpretation of safety regulation is from the perspective of a positional arms race, as described in Chapter 11. Since riskier jobs pay more and if relative income is important to workers, they may over allocate themselves to risky jobs. Safety regulations are a positional arms control agreement in this view. Finally, if society decides to maintain workplace safety regulation, more efficient ways exists than the current system of direct regulation by the Occupational Health and Safety Administration (OSHA). **Worker's compensation** is a government insurance program that provides benefits to workers injured on the job. Employers pay into the system based loosely on the injury rate at their workplaces. The effectiveness of the program could be significantly strengthened if the premiums were much more closely linked to the injury rate. Then workers' compensation would function like an injury tax and would be incorporated into the profit-maximization equation.

III. Self-Test

Key Terms
Match the term in the right-hand column with the appropriate definitions in the left-hand column by placing the letter of the term in the blank in front of its definition. (Answers are given at the end of the chapter.)

1. ____ A government insurance program providing benefits to workers injured on the job.

2. ____ When insurances pays all the expenses generated by the insured activity.

a. first-dollar insurance coverage

b. health maintenance organization (HMO)

3. ____ A group of doctors that provide health services to
individuals for a fixed annual fee.

c. workers'
compensation

Multiple-Choice Questions
Circle the letter that corresponds to the best answer. (Answers are given at the end of the chapter.)

1. According to the textbook, the percentage of gross domestic product devoted to healthcare between the years 1940 and 2000
   A. declined from 4% to 2%.
   B. increased slightly from 4% to 6%.
   C. increased sharply from 4% to 14%.
   D. increased exponentially from 4% to 40%.
   E. remained unchanged at 4%.

2. The effect of widespread insurance covering routine medical care is to
   A. reduce the marginal cost of routine medical care to the insured.
   B. reduce the marginal benefit of routine medical care to the insured.
   C. reduce the equilibrium amount of routine medical care.
   D. increase the marginal benefit of routine medical care to the insured.
   E. increase the marginal cost of routine medical care to the insured.

3. Under a first-dollar medical insurance plan, the marginal cost of treating a covered illness is
   A. positive.
   B. zero.
   C. negative.
   D. a percentage of the total cost.
   E. increasing.

4. If the marginal cost of treating an illness is zero, the optimal amount of treatment to receive is the amount
   A. where the marginal benefit is zero.
   B. that cures the illness.
   C. that the doctor recommends.
   D. where the total benefit is zero.
   E. that might cure the illness.

5. The textbook cites a study comparing a group of consumers with first-dollar coverage and a group with a $1000 deductible. The study results indicate that those with the deductible used _____ amount of medical services and had _____ health outcomes.
   A. a smaller; the same
   B. a larger; better
   C. a larger; the same
   D. a smaller; worse
   E. the same; the same

6. Adverse selection is present in medical insurance because as fewer families choose to purchase insurance, the cost of premiums will _____, ensuring that _____ families buy insurance.
   A. fall; even fewer
   B. fall; even more
   C. remain unchanged; even more
   D. rise; even fewer
   E. rise; even more

7. If the marginal costs of pollution abatement are different across firms, then regulations that require fixed percentage reductions in pollution will be
   A. inefficient.
   B. fair to all polluters.
   C. advantageous to small firms.
   D. efficient.
   E. ineffective.

8. According to the textbook, the objection to selling pollution permits - that rich firms can pollute to their hearts content – is based on the mistaken belief that firms
   A. pollute because it is cheaper to do so.
   B. are profit maximizers.
   C. enjoy polluting the environment.
   D. must be treated identically.
   E. won't reduce pollution voluntarily.

9. According to the textbook, as currently administered, the worker's compensation system
   A. produces the optimal amount of workplace safety.
   B. sets the premium too high for firms with high injury rates.
   C. sets the premium too low for firms with low injury rates.
   D. charges high-injury-rate firms too little and low-injury-rate firms too much in premiums.
   E. is abused by workers faking injuries.

10. If workers' compensation premiums accurately reflected the social costs of workplace injuries, then
    A. many firms would be forced out of business.
    B. the premium would function like a tax on injuries.
    C. injury rates would rise.
    D. firms would become less capital intensive.
    E. firms would still exploit workers.

11. Medical insurance covering routine medical care became common
    A. at the turn of the last century.
    B. in the 1920s.
    C. after the Vietnam War.
    D. during the 1980s.
    E. after World War II.

12. When Dale visits his doctor, he does not pay for either the visit or any tests his doctor may order. Dale must therefore
    A. be a member of an HMO.
    B. have a medical insurance policy with a deductible.
    C. have first-dollar medical insurance.
    D. be underutilizing medical care.
    E. be a relative of the doctor.

13. The _____ the elasticity of demand for medical care, the _____ the extent of over consumption of medical treatment.
    A. larger; smaller
    B. smaller; larger
    C. larger; larger
    D. more inelastic; larger
    E. more elastic; smaller

14. The concern that HMOs provide less than the efficient level of medical care is because
    A. of the higher costs for HMOs.
    B. doctors in HMOs are less sensitive to the needs of their patients.
    C. of government regulation.
    D. of the incentive to order fewer medical procedures and enjoy greater profits.
    E. of a lack of peer review.

15. Assume that larger firms can reduce pollution emissions more cheaply than smaller firms. A fixed percent reduction in pollution emissions would therefore
    A. penalize large and small firms equally.
    B. penalize large firms more.
    C. ensure that reduction in pollution was achieved at the lowest cost.
    D. penalize smaller firms more.
    E. ensure that for the costs expended, the largest reduction in pollution was gained.

16. The major difficulty with using a tax on pollution instead of a fixed percentage reduction regulation is
    A. nonpayment of the tax.
    B. establishing the optimal size of the tax.
    C. that the public would not accept it as a viable solution.
    D. that it only works in theory.
    E. that it would cause prices to rise.

17. Which of the following would *not* be a consequence of switching entirely from fixed percentage pollution reduction regulations to either a pollution tax or pollution permits?
    A. The total cost of achieving a given reduction in pollution would fall.
    B. The distribution of pollution reduction effort among firms would change.
    C. Government revenues would rise.
    D. The total amount of pollution emitted would, necessarily, rise.

  E. The largest reductions in pollution emissions would come from those firms best able to reduce pollution.

18. For the socially efficient workplace injury rate to be zero, it would have to be the case that
  A. the marginal benefit of reduced injuries is zero.
  B. the marginal cost of reduced injuries is zero.
  C. the marginal cost of reduced injuries is large.
  D. government increases its role in regulating workplace safety.
  E. production technology becomes more labor intensive.

19. If a 2% reduction in workplace injuries is valued at $1000 and can be achieved by having workers wear large, heavy goggles, then
  A. it would be efficient to require them if the goggles cost $1000 or less.
  B. the goggles should be required by the government.
  C. injuries will be unchanged because workers will refuse to wear them.
  D. it would be inefficient to not require them.
  E. the government should provide the goggles to those workers who can't afford them.

20. Vaccinations have a(n) _____, resulting in an inefficient equilibrium.
  A. external cost
  B. small probability of causing serious side effects
  C. nonzero marginal cost
  D. limited amount of effectiveness
  E. external benefit

Short Answer Problems
(Answers and solutions are given at the end of the chapter.)

1. Healthcare Delivery
Besides the vast improvement in medical technology over the past century, the other major development was the change in the ways of financing of people's medical expenditures. This question examines the impact of moving from a self-insured system to a medical insurance system.

Number of Doctor Visits	Marginal Benefit	Marginal Cost
1	$130	$50
2	$110	$50
3	$85	$50
4	$50	$50
5	$10	$50
6	$0	$50

  A. If consumers pay the marginal costs of doctor visits, they will see the doctor (4/6) _____ times.

   B. If consumers have first-dollar medical insurance, the marginal cost of a visit is ($50/0) _____, and they will see the doctor (5/6) _____ times.

   C. The additional visits to the doctor under first-dollar coverage are (inefficient/efficient) _____ because (the additional benefits exceed the additional costs/consumers are healthier) _____.

2. Pollution Control

Pollution is a market failure and requires some sort of corrective action. The real question is what kind of corrective action impairs the market the least and moves society as close as possible to the efficient outcome. Comparing the outcomes of different methods for correcting an externality due to pollution is the objective below. Three firms will emit 20 tons of pollution each if they adopt no pollution control device. Three different devices are available with different reductions in the amount of pollution (e.g., device B reduces pollution by 2 tons for any firm that uses it while device D achieves a 10 ton reduction). The costs to the three firms of the devices are listed in the table.

Firm	No Controls 20 tons	Device B 2 ton	Device C 4 ton	Device D 10 ton
Alpha	0	$11	$25	$80
Beta	0	$3	$7	$40
Omega	0	$5	$12	$70

   A. Based on the data, firm (Alpha/Beta/Omega) _____ can reduce pollution at the lowest costs while firm (Alpha/Beta/Omega) _____ finds reducing pollution to be rather costly.

   B. In the absence of a governmental mandate, the three firms opt for (no controls/device B) _____, and (60/54) _____ tons of pollution will be emitted.

   C. Suppose the government requires all three firms to adopt device C. The reduction in pollution will be (4/12) _____ tons and it will cost ($44/$19) _____.

   D. Suppose that instead of direct regulation, the government grants the first 10 tons of pollution for free, but emissions over 10 tons will be taxed at $6 a tons. Under such a plan, Alpha would choose to adopt (no controls/device B) _____ with a cost of ($60/$59) _____. Beta will adopt (device C/device D) _____ with a cost of ($40/$43) _____. Finally, Omega will select (no controls/device C) _____ with a cost of ($70/$48) _____.

   E. With the tax, pollution is (less than/greater than/the same) _____ compared to the direct regulation requiring device C. The evidence for supporting a pollution tax is easily seen by looking at firm Beta because it (could/could not) _____ reduce pollution even further than the level set by direct regulation.

3. Workplace Safety

Three firms can choose among three workplace safety alternatives: continue with the status quo, provide safety training, or purchase new safety equipment. The injury rates for the firms under the three alternatives as well as the costs of the alternatives are shown in the table below. The cost of treating an injury is $200.

Firm	Status Quo 7 injuries	Safety Training 6 injuries	New Safety Equipment 5 injuries
X	0	$100	$700
Y	0	$50	$600
Z	0	$200	$500

A. If the three firms take no action, then they will experience a total of (21/7) _____ workplace injuries, with a treatment cost of ($1400/$4200) _____.

B. Suppose all three firms adopt the safety training program. The program has a cost to the three firms of ($350/$250) _____. The benefit to the firms is (3 fewer injuries/a $600 savings in injury treatment) _____. Therefore, the firms (will not/will) _____ adopt the training program on their own.

C. Suppose the 3 firms don't adopt the training program because OSHA issues a direct regulation requiring all firms to install the new safety equipment. The direct regulation costs the 3 firms ($600/$1800) _____ and results in benefits of ($1200/$600) _____. The regulation is therefore (efficient/inefficient) _____.

IV. Economic Naturalist Application

The textbook notes that the provision of public security measures should be subjected to the Cost-Benefit Principle if efficient outcomes are desired. In the aftermath of 9-11, extensive resources have been allocated to the strengthening and expansion of domestic security. Were these actions taken with efficiency as a primary concern? In the week following the terrorist attack, was anyone questioning the effectiveness of the proposed security measures? If someone had questioned these efforts, and had proof that the costs would exceed the benefits, would it have mattered or was efficiency discarded in the rush to react? What does all of this mean about our political system and the notion of making efficiency the first goal of public policy?

Answer:

V. Go to the Web: Graphing Exercises Using Interactive Graphs

Search the Web for data on the workplace injury and death rate by occupation and industry. Additionally, find wage data on the same occupations and industries. Is there a positive correlation between the injury rate and the wage rate? Between the death rate and the wage rate? Does an increased probability of dying on the job increase the wage rate as much as an increased probability of being injured on the job?

Answer:

To review an answer to this question, and to learn more about the use of economic theory to analyze this issue (and other microeconomic issues), please go to the Electronic Learning Session in the Student Center at the Frank/Bernanke web site: http://www.mhhe.com/economics/frankbernanke2.

VI. Self-Test Solutions

Key Terms

1. c
2. a
3. b

Multiple-Choice Questions

1. C
2. A
3. B
4. A
5. A
6. D
7. A
8. C
9. D
10. B
11. E
12. C
13. C

14. D
15. D
16. B
17. D
18. B
19. A
20. E

Short Answer Problems

1.
A. 4
B. 0; 6
C. inefficient; the additional benefits exceed the additional costs

2.
A. Beta; Alpha
B. no controls; 60
C. 12; $44
D. device B; $59 (include the tax); device D; $40; device C; $48
E.

3.
A. 21; $4200
B. $350; a $600 savings in injury treatment; will
C. $1800; $1200; inefficient

Chapter 15
Public Goods and Tax Policy

I. Pretest: What Do You Really Know?
Circle the letter that corresponds to the best answer. (Answers appear immediately after the final question).

1. Radio is an example of a good that is
   A. only nonrival.
   B. only nonexcludable.
   C. neither nonrival nor nonexcludable.
   D. both nonrival and nonexcludable.
   E. private.

2. The best example of a pure public good is
   A. cable TV.
   B. a national park.
   C. national defense.
   D. social security.
   E. education.

3. In general,
   A. government must always provide pure public goods.
   B. government is best able to provide all public goods, pure and otherwise.
   C. government should only provide public goods when private solutions fail and the benefits exceed the costs.
   D. the benefits of public goods will necessarily be less than the costs so government must be relied upon to provide them.
   E. the lack of a profit motive means government-provided public goods will be wasteful.

4. Joe earns $10,000 in income and pays $1,000 in taxes while Jack earns $30,000 and pays $4,000 in taxes. The structure of this tax is
   A. progressive.
   B. proportional.
   C. regressive.

    D. a constant percent of income.

    E. a constant amount of income.

5. In general, if a good has zero marginal costs and a positive price, the social outcome is

    A. efficient.

    B. uncertain; it may or may not be efficient.

    C. that too much will be consumed.

    D. inefficient.

    E. that too much will be provided.

6. When an externality crosses a state boundary,

    A. the individual states can easily reach a solution to the problem.

    B. it ceases to be an externality.

    C. a prisoner's dilemma develops.

    D. a federal solution is the most appropriate one.

    E. state courts can provide adequate remedies.

7. The combination of pork barrel spending and logrolling leads to

    A. inefficiently large government spending.

    B. the largest net benefit for society.

    C. the quick termination of projects that are wasteful or irrelevant.

    D. relatively short careers for politicians.

    E. under provision of public goods.

8. The major drawback to large across-the-board cuts in government spending is

    A. it has never been tried.

    B. some programs will not be cut.

    C. some programs will be reduced to zero.

    D. it completely ignores the cost-benefit principle.

    E. taxes will not be cut.

9. According to the textbook, wealthy voters often favor a progressive tax system because

    A. the wealthy are typically liberal in their political views.

    B. their CPAs will be able to reduce their tax burden.

    C. reliance on regressive or proportional taxes results in too few or low-quality public goods.

    D. they feel guilty about their wealth.

    E. it is morally correct.

10. Beyond the provision of public goods, government exists to address

    A. the redistribution of wealth.

    B. the problem of declining moral values.

    C. limiting personal freedom.

    D. externalities and property rights.

    E. national defense.

Solutions and Feedback to PreTest
For each question you answered incorrectly we strongly recommend taking the time to review the appropriate material before continuing. In the table below, the relevant textbook pages are listed for each question as well as the pertinent Learning Objective from the following Key Point Review.

Correct Answer	Textbook Page Numbers	Learning Objective
1. D	p. 374	1
2. C	pp. 374-76	2
3. C	pp. 374-76	2
4. A	pp. 376-79	3
5. D	pp. 379-81	4
6. D	pp. 384-86	6
7. A	pp. 386-90	7
8. D	pp. 386-90	7
9. C	pp. 376-79	3
10. D	pp. 384-86	6

II. Key Point Review

Learning Objective 1: Define the characteristics of nonrival and nonexcludable as they relate to goods and services.
Government is chiefly responsible for providing goods and service that possess to some degree two unusual characteristics. When consumption of a good or service by one person does not reduce the availability to others, the item is termed a **nonrival good**. A **nonexcludable good** is one for which it is costly or difficult to prevent consumption by those who do not pay for the good.

Learning Objective 2: Define and contrast the following: public goods (including pure public goods), collective goods, pure private goods, and pure common goods.
A **public good** contains both characteristics mentioned in #1 to some degree. Radio is an excellent example of a public good. One person's reception of a station is not degraded when another person starts listening, and no one can be excluded from listening even if they refuse to patronize the firms that advertise on the station. The notions of rivalry and excludability allow for four distinct types of goods to be defined. Goods and service that are highly nonrival and nonexcludable are called **pure public goods**. Government is most likely to provide pure public goods because (1) firms cannot recover their costs and (2) if firms could demand payment, the marginal cost of an extra unit is zero so for an efficient outcome, price must be zero. If a good is nonrival and excludable, it is called a **collective good**. HBO and pay-for-view movies on cable are perfect examples since some households can be excluded but the marginal cost of another household watching is zero. Most of the goods and services consumers enjoy are both rival and excludable, which makes them **pure private goods**. Finally, a good or service that is rival but nonexcludable is a **pure common good**. The idea of a pure common good was first introduced in Chapter 11 with the tragedy of the commons. The whales in the ocean are an example of a pure

common good. Collective goods are sometimes provided by government and sometimes by private firms. Pure public goods are most often made available by government, but it is not necessarily true that government must provide all pure public goods. Private firms offer broadcast radio and television, both of which are pure public goods. Indeed, the fact that a particular good meets the two criteria means little. Government should only consider providing those public goods for which the benefits exceed the costs. And then only if no lower-cost means of provision exists.

Learning Objective 3: Define the listed terms: a head tax, a regressive tax, a proportional tax, and a progressive tax. Explain how funding public goods differs from funding private goods.

One possibility for collecting revenues from taxpayers to pay for public goods is a **head tax**: all taxpayers pay the same amount in taxes. If the public good costs $1000 and there are 10 taxpayers then everyone would pay $100. Taxation schemes are classified in one of three ways based on the relationship between taxes paid and the taxpayer's income. First, a **regressive tax** means that the percentage of income paid in taxes declines as income rises. Head taxes are regressive in nature. The second scheme, a **proportional tax**, takes the same percentage of income in taxes at all income levels. Third, a **progressive tax** takes an increasing percentage of income in taxes as income rises. The federal income tax is an example. Wealthy taxpayers accept progressive taxes to ensure a larger quantity and greater quality of public goods. Exclusive reliance on regressive or proportional tax schemes would fail to fund the public goods wealthy voters indicate are the most important: parks and recreation facilities, public safety, and clean air. Whatever scheme of taxation is adopted, the central friction between consumers and government over payment for public goods stems from the amount available for consumption. For private goods, the amount consumed is directly related to the amount spent on the item. Usually, the quality of the item can be adjusted by spending more or less. In the case of public goods, only one amount is made available to all independent of their tax bill. Yellowstone National Park is available in the same amount and condition for those who had a tax bill of $0 as for those who had a tax bill of $100,000.

Learning Objective 4: Describe the difference between the market demand curve for a private and a public good. Locate the optimal amount of a public good the government should provide.

Locating the optimal amount of a public good is identical to finding the optimal amount of a private good: where the marginal benefits of an extra unit are equal to the marginal costs. The market demand curve for public goods is constructed differently than the market demand curve for a private good. In Chapter 3, the quantity demanded at every possible price for all consumers was summed to get the market demand curve. For a public good, the reservation price of each consumer for every possible amount of the public good is summed. Visually, the private good demand curve is summed horizontally above across prices, while the public good demand curve is summed vertically across quantities. Once the demand curve has been properly constructed, the point at which the demand and supply curves intersect determines the optimal amount of the public good.

Learning Objective 5: Discuss the provision of public goods by private firms and some of the potential drawbacks.
As noted above, government is not the only source of public goods. Private organizations can and do provide some public goods. Broadcast radio and television survive by selling advertising. Cable television allows for exclusion of nonpayers so that some portion of the television market is now a collective rather than a public good. Other private organizations seek public contributions to fund their public good provision.

Learning Objective 6: Explain the role of government in the cases of externalities and property rights. Discuss local versus federal provision of public goods and indicate how best to decide the proper level of government.
The justification for the existence of government extends beyond providing public goods and collecting the revenues to pay for them. Government is also called upon to correct externalities and establish property rights. As a result, governments regulate pollution, subsidize education, maintain legal systems, and perform a host of other actions designed to fix market failures. The question of which level of government is best able to provide public goods or fix an externality is not clear cut. The major justification for the formation of the federal government was the need to provide the most important pure public good: national defense. In the U.S. Constitution, most every other power was given to the states. Over time, the power of the states relative to the federal government has declined. The appropriate level of government for a particular program should be decided on the specifics of the problem at hand.

Learning Objective 7: Define pork barrel spending, logrolling, and rent-seeking and relate them to inefficient resource allocation. Discuss proposals to cut government provision of public goods by substantial amounts.
Inefficiencies abound in all governments and in all democratic societies, the efficiencies tend to be well documented. But the sources of the inefficiencies are not due to electing incompetent, ignorant, or corrupt legislators (although this does happen), but to the economic incentives inherent in the process. **Pork barrel legislation** is any bill where the costs exceed the benefits for society as a whole, but where the benefits to a particular group are quite high relative to the increased taxes they pay. Clearly, a politician who has success in bring "pork" home to his district significantly enhances the probability of his reelection. **Logrolling** occurs when one legislator supports another's pork barrel legislation in exchange for support of his own pork barrel bills. Another source of inefficiency in the political arena occurs when individuals or firms engage in socially unproductive efforts to win a prize, know as **rent-seeking**. Typically, a government funded project is going to be located in one geographic area or another and the presence of the project means higher incomes. Different towns and cities will try to persuade the legislators to site the project with them. In the process, local taxpayers foot the bill for trips by the legislators to visit the location. Private firms can also fall victim to rent-seeking when the government gives notice of its intent to sell the rights to, say, cellular phone services. To solve the problems of government inefficiency some critics, including well-known economists, have argued the only solution is to make large, across-the-board cuts in government spending. One need only look to the educational system in California to see the problem with ignoring cost-benefit analysis when making choices.

Learning Objective 8: Define crowding out and assess the impact of taxes on the economy.
When government has insufficient revenues to cover its obligations it seeks other revenues by
borrowing from the credit market. The government borrowing puts upward pressure on interest
rates and thereby cause some private investment projects to be canceled. The private investment
canceled due to higher interest rates induced by government borrowing is called **crowding out**.
Finally, when society is trying to locate a good to tax to raise revenues for a public good that
meets the cost-benefit criteria, it should look to goods and services producing a negative
externality. By taxing negative externalities, society adds to total economic surplus in two ways.
First, the taxing of the externality improves efficiency in that market; second, the provision of
the public good also increases efficiency if it passes the cost-benefit criteria.

III. Self-Test

Key Terms
**Match the term in the right-hand column with the appropriate definitions in the left-hand
column by placing the letter of the term in the blank in front of its' definition. (Answers
are given at the end of the chapter.)**

1. ____ A good that is difficult or costly to exclude nonpayers from consuming.

a. collective good

2. ____ A tax for which the percentage of income paid out in taxes declines as income rises.

b. crowding out

3. ____ Government spending for which the marginal costs exceed the marginal benefits for the whole of society, but for the voters of the politician sponsoring the bill the marginal benefits exceed the marginal costs.

c. head tax

4. ____ The socially unproductive efforts of people or firms to win a prize.

d. logrolling

5. ____ When a good or service is to some degree both nonrival and nonexcludable.

e. nonexcludable good

6. ____ A good that is to some degree nonrival but excludable.

f. nonrival good

7. ____ A tax for which the percentage of income paid out in taxes rises as income rises.

g. pork barrel spending

8. ____ When all taxpayers pay out the same dollar amount in taxes.

h. progressive tax

9. ____ The practice of supporting someone else's pork barrel legislation in exchange for his or her support of your pork barrel legislation.

i. proportional tax

10. ___ When the government borrows money, thereby driving interest rates up and causing some private investment by firms to be cancelled.

j. public good

11. ___ When the consumption of a good by one person does not reduce the good's availability to other consumers.

k. pure common good

12. ___ A tax for which the percentage of income paid out in taxes is constant.

l. pure private good

13. ___ Goods that are to a high degree both nonrival and

m. pure public good

nonexcludable.
14. ___ A good that is both rival and excludable.   n. regressive tax
15. ___ Goods that are rival but nonexcludable.   o. rent-seeking

Multiple-Choice Questions

Circle the letter that corresponds to the best answer. (Answers are given at the end of the chapter.)

1. Which of the following items is an example of a nonrival but excludable good?
   A. Pay-per-view movies.
   B. Corn.
   C. National defense.
   D. Broadcast TV.
   E. Access to the Internet.

2. A copy of the movie *Pulp Fiction* at the video store is a _____ good; when it is shown on HBO it is a _____ good; and when it is shown on CBS it is a _____ good.
   A. private; public; pure public
   B. collective; private; public
   C. private; private; collective
   D. private; collective; public
   E. private; private; public

3. According to the textbook, collective goods tend to be
   A. provided only by the government.
   B. over consumed.
   C. provided only by private firms.
   D. provided by the government in some cases, by private firms in other cases.
   E. provided by government if the costs exceed the benefits.

4. If government needs to raise revenues to pay for a public good, the ideal tax structure would be to tax
   A. all citizens by the same amount.
   B. all citizens in proportion to their willingness to pay for the public good.
   C. all citizens by the same proportion of their income.
   D. only the citizens that use the public good.
   E. only the citizens that are willing to pay for the public good.

5. Which of the following is not a proper justification for charging the government with the responsibility for collecting revenues to finance a public good?
   A. No single individual may have a reservation price high enough to pay for the public good.
   B. Negotiation between private citizens about each person's contribution is costly.
   C. Individuals may attempt to free ride on the contributions of others.
   D. The costs of the public good exceed the benefits.
   E. The number of citizens affected may be so large as to render private negotiation impossible.

6. A sales tax applied to all consumer purchases would be considered a _____ tax because
_____.
   A. proportional; the percentage of income spend on consumption is constant as income rises.
   B. regressive; the percentage of income spent on consumption declines as income rises.
   C. regressive; the sales tax percentage is the same for all consumers.
   D. progressive; the percentage of income spent on consumption rises as income rises.
   E. progressive; the amount paid in sales tax rises with income.

7. Karl earns $25,000 while Angel earns $40,000. If they are subject to a regressive tax structure,
   A. Karl and Angel will pay the same amount in taxes.
   B. Karl will pay a larger amount in taxes.
   C. Angel will pay a larger amount in taxes.
   D. Karl will pay a larger percentage of his income in taxes.
   E. Karl and Angel will pay the same percentage of income in taxes.

8. The reason the demand curve for a public good is constructed differently than for a private good is because
   A. all consumers will have the same amount of the public good.
   B. all consumers have the same reservation price the public good.
   C. consumers can consume different amounts of the public good.
   D. the government is going to provide the good.
   E. tax revenues will be used to pay for the public good.

9. HBO shows movies without commercial interruption. This is because HBO
   A. can exclude nonpaying viewers.
   B. executives decided to differentiate themselves from other networks.
   C. shows only movies that are very inexpensive to rent.
   D. is prohibited from showing commercials.
   E. is subsidized by the government.

10. The development of pay-per-view technology
   A. converted a collective good into a private good.
   B. allows consumers to see movies that were previously unavailable for several years.
   C. converted a public good into a collective good.
   D. has made all consumers worse off.
   E. converted a private good into a public good.

11. The most appropriate level of government to provide public goods is
   A. local.
   B. state.
   C. federal.
   D. county.
   E. dependent on the specific public good in question.

12. One of the original justifications for the creation of a federal level of government was
    A. the ability to deficit spend.
    B. economies of scale in the provision of military defense.
    C. to encourage local diversity in the types of public goods provided.
    D. greater responsiveness to the will of the voters.
    E. better decision making.

13. Which of the following reasons does *not* help explain the presence of pork barrel legislation?
    A. The benefits to the voters of the district are large.
    B. The increased tax payments to voters outside of the district are small.
    C. Voters tend to reelect politicians that secure benefits for the district.
    D. The ideology of the political party in power.
    E. The increased tax payments to voters inside the district are small.

14. According to the textbook, in repeated experiments when a $20 bill is auctioned such that two top bids pay the auctioneer and then the top bid receives the $20 bill, the
    A. top bid is $1.
    B. top bid is $10.
    C. sum of the top two bids frequently exceed $50.
    D. top bid is $20.
    E. sum of the top two bids is $20.

15. Taxing a good that has a negative externality results in
    A. a gain in economic surplus from both the reduced consumption and the provision of public goods funded by tax revenue.
    B. a loss of economic surplus.
    C. a gain in economic surplus only from reduced consumption.
    D. a gain in economic surplus only from the provision of public goods funded by the tax revenue.
    E. possibly a gain or a loss in economic surplus.

16. The primary factor that limits the ability of private firms to supply public goods is
    A. the nonrival characteristic of public goods.
    B. the lack of well-defined demand.
    C. custom and tradition.
    D. the nonexcludable characteristic of public goods.
    E. diseconomies of scale.

17. To properly justify the governmental provision of a public good, it must be the case that the _____ and that _____.
    A. good is indeed a public good; is the only necessary requirement
    B. benefits exceed the costs; no lower cost provider exists
    C. voters desire the good; no new taxes will be needed
    D. benefits exceed the costs; is the only necessary requirement
    E. benefits exceed the costs; all voters value the good equally

18. Mandy pays $12,000 in taxes and earns $150,000. Moe pays $7,000 in taxes. If the tax system is proportional, then Moe's income is
    A. less than $87,500.
    B. more than $30,000.
    C. $87,500.
    D. more than $87,500.
    E. impossible to calculate.

19. The incentives for pork barrel spending are strong because the benefits to the politician's voters are _____, the extra tax paid is _____, and the chances of reelection are _____.
    A. large; small; increased
    B. large; large; decreased
    C. small; large; decreased
    D. small; small; increased
    E. large; small; decreased

20. Suppose the federal government must turn to the financial markets to borrow in order to meet its obligations. As a result,
    A. interest rates rise but no other impact occurs.
    B. interest rates fall.
    C. interest rates are unaffected.
    D. interest rates fall and greater private investment occurs.
    E. interest rates rise and private investment is reduced.

Short Answer Problems
(Answers and solutions are given at the end of the chapter.)

1. Providing Public Goods
The problem of public goods is one of many benefits, but none benefit enough individually to ensure the provision. This question demonstrates the basic features of all public good problems. The data in the table is for a water purifying device that costs $1,300. For a tax proposal to pass, a simple majority (2 voters) is needed and all voters vote.

Voter	Reservation Price	Income
Mary Ann	$200	$2,000
Joyce	$400	$7,000
Mike	$800	$8,000

    A. The social benefit of the device is ($1,400/$533.33) _____, which (does/does not) _____ exceed the cost of the device. Thus, the purchase and installation of the device (lowers/raises) _____ total economic surplus. As individuals, (Joyce/Mike/no one) _____ will find it worthwhile to purchase the device.
    B. Suppose it is proposed that government provide the device and collect taxes to pay for it. If government could establish the actual reservation price for each taxpayer, then

charging each (93%/33%) _____ of his or her reservation price would raise the correct amount of tax revenue. Under such a system, Mary Ann pays _____, Joyce _____, and Mike _____. The voters would (approve/disapprove) _____ the proposal.

C. Since government does not know the reservation price, and instead a head tax equal to one third of the cost of the device is proposed. The proposal would receive (2/1) ____ votes in favor and therefore (pass/fail) _____.

D. It is now proposed that a proportional income tax be used to fund the device with a tax rate of 7.75%. The vote would be (3/2/1) _____ for and (0/1/2) _____ against so the proposal would (pass/fail) _____.

2. Demand Curve for Public Goods

The construction of market demand for a public good is quite different from the way a market demand curve for a private good is calculated. The difference is that everyone, by definition, receives the same amount of the public good. The table below has reservation prices for several different consumers.

Quantity of the Good	Citizen A's Reservation Price	Citizen B's Reservation Price	Citizen C's Reservation Price	Citizen D's Reservation Price
40	$1	$2	$3	$4
30	$2	$3	$4	$6
20	$3	$4	$6	$8
10	$4	$6	$8	$10

A. Assume the good in the table is a private good. At a price of $4, quantity demanded will be (100/70) _____ units.

B. Assume the good in the table is a public good. The total value to society of 30 units of the good is ($10/$15) _____.

C. If the good in the table is a private good, the total value of 10 units is ($100/impossible to say) _____, while if the good is a public good, the total value of 10 units is ($28/$280) _____.

3. Rent-Seeking

When government-funded projects are announced, some practical issues have to be decided: where should the project be located, what contractors should be used, and so on. If the decisions to be made are based on factors other than lowering the cost of provision, then rent seeking is likely to develop.

The city of Hammer is going to grant an exclusive contract to provide cable TV for the next 5 years. The economic profit of the contract is thought to be $50 million. Firm 1 and firm 2 are competing for the contract. Although it is not explicitly stated as part of the decision making, the city council, city manager, and other influential citizens of Hammer do enjoy being wined and dined.

A. In the absence of lobbying efforts by either firm, the expected value of the contract is ($50/$25) _____ million.
B. If firm 1 spends $5,000 on entertaining the city officials and firm 2 spends nothing, the expected value of the contract to firm 1 is ($49,995,000/$24,997,500) _____ and to firm 2 it is ($24,997,500/0) _____.
C. If, in response to firm 1 spending $5,000, firm 2 decides to spend $100,000 on city officials to fly them to Hawaii to see a cable system that firm 2 developed there, then firm 1's expected value of the contract now is (0/$24,950,000) _____ and the expected value to firm 2 is ($24,950,000/$49,900,000) _____.
D. If both firms have spent exactly $50 million to persuade the city officials that they would be the best choice, both firms (would/would not) _____ have an incentive to cease spending on lobbying efforts.

4. Across-the-Board Tax Cuts

Surprisingly, some well-known economists have argued in favor of large, across-the-board spending cuts. The assumption being that government can never spend a taxpayer's money as well as the taxpayer can. This question examines the pitfalls of this solution to excessive or wasteful government spending.

	Marginal Benefit	Marginal Cost	Total Spending on the Public Good
Public Good A	$33	$33	$1,500
Public Good B	$12	$20	$800
Public Good C	$19	$11	$700

A. By the Cost-Benefit Principle, the data suggest that spending is too large for public good(s) (A/B/C) _____, exactly correct for (A/B/C), _____ and too little for (A/B/C) _____.

B. A proposal to cut spending by 10% for all public goods would (improve/reduce) _____ total economic surplus because the amounts of public goods (A&C/B&C) _____ provided would move away from the efficient level.

C. The proper proposal for changing government spending would be to increase spending on (A/B/C) _____, reduce spending on (A/B/C) _____, or leave spending unchanged for (A/B/C) _____.

IV. Economic Naturalist Application

One of the basic points about public goods to bear in mind during debates about the inefficiency of government programs is that government is providing goods and services the private sector either will not or cannot provide. Never is when a private firm will provide police protection for a city (a private firm might contract with a city to provide police but that is not the same as providing it without a guarantee of payment by the city). In the case of recreational parks, the private sector does offer alternatives to state and national parks but you better like cartoon characters if you go to the ones in Florida. Evaluate the often-repeated claim that government should be "run like a business." Does the statement contradict itself? Explain how one can use the organizational and motivational features of a firm to provide goods and services that firms decided were impossible to provide or offered poor profit prospects.
Answer:

V. Go to the Web: Graphing Exercises Using Interactive Graphs

The Presidential elections of 2004 will likely include at least one candidate advocating the elimination of the current income tax system, which was designed to be progressive with a strictly proportional income tax. Search the Web for estimates of the proportion necessary to raise the revenues generated by the current system. Is it larger than you expected? One of the arguments presented by supporters is the current tax system is "too complicated." Is "too complicated" a necessary feature of a progressive tax scheme? Is "very straightforward an inalterable feature of a proportional tax scheme?
Answer:

To review an answer to this question, and to learn more about the use of economic theory to analyze this issue (and other microeconomic issues), please go to the Electronic Learning Session in the Student Center at the Frank/Bernanke web site: http://www.mhhe.com/economics/frankbernanke2.

VI. Self-Test Solutions

Key Terms

1. e
2. n
3. g
4. o
5. j
6. a
7. h
8. c
9. d
10. b
11. f
12. i
13. m
14. l
15. k

Multiple-Choice Questions

1. A
2. D
3. D
4. B
5. D
6. B
7. D
8. A
9. A
10. C
11. E
12. B
13. D
14. C
15. A
16. D
17. B
18. C
19. A
20. E

Short Answer Problems

1.
A. $1,400; does; raises; no one
B. 93% (= $1,300/$1,400); $186; $372; $744; approve
C. 1; fail
D. 2: 1: pass

2.
A. 100
B. $15
C. $100; $280

3.
A. $25
B. $49,995,000; 0
C. 0; $49,900,000
D. would not

4.
A. B; A; C
B. reduce; A & C
C. C; B; A

Chapter 16
International Trade and Trade Policy

I. Pretest: What Do You Really Know?

Circle the letter that corresponds to the best answer. (Answers appear immediately after the final question).

1. An open economy is one that
    A. relies on a market system to allocate scarce resources.
    B. relies on central planning to allocate scarce resources.
    C. has a flexible exchange rate.
    D. trades with other countries.
    E. does not trade with other countries.

2. Autarky is a situation in which a country is
    A. economically self-sufficient.
    B. an open economy.
    C. producing a combination of goods and services inside the production possibility curve.
    D. producing a combination of goods and services outside the production possibility curve.
    E. consuming a combination of goods and services outside the production possibility curve.

3. The consumption possibilities for a(n) _____ economy are equal to production possibilities, while the consumption possibilities for a(n) _____ economy are usually greater than (and never less than) production possibilities.
    A. open; closed
    B. closed; open
    C. market; centrally planned
    D. centrally planned; market
    E. micro; macro

4. The price at which a good or service is traded on international markets is called the _____ price.
    A. supply
    B. demand
    C. relative
    D. world
    E. production

5. If the world price is less than the domestic price of a commodity in a closed economy, when that economy begins to trade, the economy will _____ the commodity.
    A. stop consuming
    B. stop producing
    C. be self-sufficient in
    D. become a net importer of
    E. become a net exporter of

6. Consumers of imported goods are _____ as a result of trade and producers of exported goods are _____ as a result of trade.
    A. winners; losers
    B. winners; winners
    C. losers; winners
    D. losers; losers
    E. unaffected; unaffected

7. Protectionism is the view that free trade
    A. must be restricted to ensure maximum possible consumption.
    B. must be protected against any legal barriers to imports or exports.
    C. is injurious and should be restricted.
    D. is efficient and an application of the equilibrium principle.
    E. protects both consumers and producers from inefficiency.

8. A quota is
    A. a legal limit on the quantity of a good that may be imported.
    B. a legal limit on the price of a good that may be imported.
    C. a tax imposed on an imported good.
    D. a tax imposed on an exported good.
    E. a menu cost.

9. A tax imposed on an imported good is called a
    A. tariff.
    B. quota.
    C. protection tax.
    D. capital inflow.
    E. capital outflow.

10. Restriction of free trade is
    A. efficient.
    B. inefficient.
    C. an application of the equilibrium principle.
    D. an application of the principle of comparative advantage.
    E. a way to increase overall production.

Solutions and Feedback to Pretest
For each question you incorrectly answered, we strongly recommend taking the time to review the appropriate material before continuing. In the table below, the relevant textbook pages are listed for each question as well as the pertinent Learning Objective from the following Key Point Review.

Correct Answer	Textbook Page Numbers	Learning Objective
1. D	p. 445	1
2. A	p. 449	2
3. B	pp. 449 - 54	2
4. D	P. 455	3
5. D	p. 455	3
6. B	p. 457	3
7. C	pp. 458 - 60	4
8. A	pp. 460 - 63	4
9. A	p. 458	4
10. B	p. 463	5

II. Key Point Review
This chapter addresses the topic of international trade and its effects on the broader economy. It begins with a review of comparative advantage and the benefits of trade, and is followed by a discussion of the reasons for opposition to trade and an analysis of the effects of trade restrictions.

Learning Objective 1: Define a closed economy and an open economy. If needed, review the production possibilities curve developed in Chapter 2.
Chapter 16 assumes a reasonable understanding of the fundamentals of the production possibilities curve developed in Chapter 2. Since the production possibilities model is the starting point for international trade, a review of Chapter 2 is recommended. A **closed economy** means an economy that does not participate in international trade. An economy that does participate in international trade is called an **open economy**.

Learning Objective 2: Define consumption possibilities and autarky. Describe the effect of opening an economy up to free trade.
An economy's **consumption possibilities** are the combinations of goods and services that the economy's population might feasibly consume. Recall that a production possibilities curve shows the maximum amount of one good that can be produced at every possible level of production of the other good. In a closed economy, the consumption possibilities are identical to the production possibilities: the amounts produced domestically represent the amounts that can be consumed. **Autarky** exists when a country is economically self-sufficient, i.e., it is a closed economy. When an economy is opened to international trade, the consumption possibilities nearly always expand (consumption possibilities can never contract due to switching to an open economy).

Learning Objective 3: Define world price. Show the effects when the domestic price exceeds the world price. Repeat the exercise when the world price exceeds the domestic price. Identify the winners and losers in both circumstances.

While it is nearly always true that the consumption possibilities expand with the opening of an economy to international trade, which improves the choices available to the economy as a whole, some individual markets will be made worse off. The **world price** of any good is simply the price at which it trades in international markets. Depending on a country's comparative advantage, the world price can be greater than or less than the domestic price. Suppose that the domestic price exceeds the world price. Once the domestic market is opened to international trade, the world price becomes the actual price, i.e., the domestic price is irrelevant. Domestic quantity supplied declines and domestic quantity demanded increases. The difference between domestic quantity demanded and domestic quantity supplied at the world price is accommodated by the international market: the difference is equal to the amount imported. Alternatively, if the world price is greater than the domestic price, the world price still becomes the actual price. As a result, domestic quantity supplied rises and domestic quantity demanded falls. The difference between domestic quantity supplied and quantity demanded is again taken care of by the international market: the difference is equal to the amount exported.

> **Note:** When the domestic market is opened to international trade and the domestic price differs from the world price, a shortage or surplus will temporarily exist. For example, if the domestic price is greater than the world price and the domestic market is opened to international trade, the domestic price will be an above-equilibrium price and will result in a surplus until the domestic price falls to the equilibrium (world) price level.

Identifying the winners and losers as an economy moves to openness depends on whether the individual market is a net importer or net exporter. In the case where the domestic price exceeds the world price—when the country is a net importer—domestic consumers are better off and domestic producer are worse off. The consumers are better off because the price is lower and the quantity greater in the open economy. Domestic producers are worse off because price is lower and their share of the domestic market is now less than 100 percent. When the country is a net exporter of the good—the world price is greater than the domestic price—the outcome is reversed. Domestic consumers are the losers now because the price is higher and the domestically available quantity is smaller. Domestic producers are winners because price is higher and production is larger.

Learning Objective 4: Define protectionism, tariff, and quota. Describe the effects of a tariff and classify the winners and losers. Repeat the process for a quota.

The political view that asserts that free trade is harmful to the domestic economy and should therefore be restricted is known as **protectionism**. Protectionism can be implemented in two ways. A **tariff** is a tax imposed on imported goods. A **quota** is a legal limit on the quantity of a good that can be imported. A tariff serves to raise the world price in the domestic market. Predictably, the higher price results in a greater quantity supplied from the domestic producers and a smaller quantity demanded by domestic consumers. The overall amount of imports falls.

The tariff raises revenues for the government, equal to the tariff times the post-tariff level of imports. The clear winners from a tariff are domestic producers who sell more at a higher price and the government which claims a new source of revenues. Domestic consumers are the obvious losers for now they consume less and pay a higher price. A quota sets an absolute amount that can be imported. This drives the domestic price above its free trade level (the world price). In fact, it drives the domestic price up to the point where the distance between the domestic quantity demanded and the domestic quantity supplied equals the amount allowed by the quota. The winners and losers under a quota mirror those under a tariff. Domestic producers sell more at a higher price and domestic consumer purchase less at a higher price. However, government is not collecting any revenues when it imposes a quota.

Learning Objective 5: Discuss the economic inefficiency induced by blocking free trade. Analyze alternative solutions to tariffs and quotas.
Barriers to free trade cause the total size of the economic pie to be smaller, so tariffs and quotas violate the Efficiency Principle. Why would a government adopt policies that reduce economic efficiency? Because even though total economic activity rises, every individual does not benefit from free trade. In particular, domestic producers are always losers when free trade is allowed and the world price is below the domestic price. It is far easier for the domestic producers of a particular good to organize and attempt to influence the political process than it is for the domestic consumers of the particular good. The Efficiency Principle suggests that the size of the economic pie is larger with free trade than either with a closed economy or with an economy practicing protectionism. The justification for using the Efficiency Principle as the guiding rule is clear for free trade. The extra economic pie generated by free trade could be used to assist those injured by the free trade, i.e., the domestic producers. The form of the assistance depends on the affected industry, but it would commonly include longer unemployment benefits and/or retraining programs.

III. Self-Test

Key Terms
Match the term in the right-hand column with the appropriate definitions in the left-hand column by placing the letter of the term in the blank in front of its definition. (Answers are given at the end of the chapter.)

1. ____ A legal restriction on the amount of an imported good allowed into a country.
2. ____ An economy that participates in international trade.
3. ____ An economy that is economically self-sufficient.
4. ____ A view that free trade is harmful and should be restricted.
5. ____ A tax placed on imported goods.
6. ____ An economy that does not participate in international trade.
7. ____ The combinations of goods and services an economy might feasibly consume.
8. ____ The price at which a good trades for in the international market.

a. autarky
b. closed economy
c. consumption possibilities
d. open economy
e. protectionism
f. quota
g. tariff
h. world price

242

Chapter 16

Multiple-Choice Questions
Circle the letter that corresponds to the best answer. (Answers are given at the end of the chapter.)

1. To maximize its gains from trade, a nation should
   A. maximize net exports (or its trade surplus).
   B. export products in which it has a comparative advantage.
   C. export as many products as possible by subsidizing domestic producers that could not otherwise compete with foreign producers.
   D. create jobs by subsidizing industries that employ the large numbers of workers.
   E. subsidize the purchase of imports in order to achieve the highest level of total consumption.

2. If Sierra Leone has a comparative advantage in the production of coffee, and its previously closed economy is opened to trade coffee for imported steel, Sierra Leone's
   A. steel industry will benefit at the expense of its steel consumers.
   B. steel industry will benefit at the expense of its coffee industry.
   C. steel consumers will benefit, as will its steel producers.
   D. coffee producers will benefit and as will its coffee drinkers.
   E. steel consumers and coffee producers will benefit.

3. If quotas are imposed on French clothing imported into the United States
   A. both French and American consumers are penalized when they buy clothing.
   B. both French and American producers of clothing are penalized.
   C. American producers and consumers of clothing are penalized.
   D. American clothing producers benefit but American consumers of clothing are penalized.
   E. French producers and consumers of clothing benefit.

4. Protectionist policies are implemented by governments because
   A. they benefit domestic consumers
   B. they benefit politically powerful groups.
   C. they are efficient and, therefore, increase the total economic pie.
   D. it is unfair for domestic workers and producers to have to compete with the low wages and costs in poor countries.
   E. it is the most effective way to protect the global environment.

5. A country will benefit the most from trade if it
   A. has a closed economy to protect its producers from low-cost, inferior goods produced in low-income countries.
   B. exports to the rest of the world while maintaining protectionist policies on imports into its economy.
   C. has an open economy and subsidizes its less-competitive producers.
   D. has an open economy and produces those goods in which it has the lowest opportunity cost and exchanges them for other goods.
   E. has an open economy and produces those goods in which it has the highest opportunity cost and exchanges them for other goods.

International Trade and Trade Policy 243

6. The voluntary export restraints (VERs) on the importation of Japanese automobiles into the United States benefited
   A. Japanese and American automotive producers.
   B. Japanese and American automotive consumers.
   C. American automotive producers and consumers.
   D. Japanese automotive producers and consumers.
   E. Japanese automotive producers and American automotive consumers.

7. Compared to a quota, a tariff on shoe imports
   A. avoids an increase in the price of domestic shoes.
   B. does not harm foreign shoe producers, whereas a quota does.
   C. does not harm domestic shoe producers, whereas a quota does.
   D. does not harm foreign shoe consumers, whereas a quota does.
   E. generates revenue for the government, whereas a quota does not.

8. In all likelihood, the U.S. government chose to negotiate quotas (VERs) on the importation of Japanese automobiles during the early 1980s rather than imposing tariffs because
   A. quotas generated tax revenues for the government that tariffs would not have created.
   B. quotas are less harmful to domestic consumers than are tariffs.
   C. they reduced the probability of retaliation by the Japanese government.
   D. the Japanese auto producers wanted to raise the price of their cars.
   E. they had less adverse effects on capital outflows from the United States to Japan.

9. Autarky is a situation created by
   A. a trade deficit.
   B. a trade surplus.
   C. protectionist policies.
   D. an open economy.
   E. a closed economy.

10. Quotas and tariffs are similar in that both
    A. generate revenues for the government that imposes them.
    B. increase the prices of goods and services in domestic markets.
    C. increase the revenues of the firms importing the goods and services.
    D. harm domestic and foreign producers.
    E. harm domestic and foreign consumers.

11. If a small, open economy can produce twice as much wheat as corn using the same resources and the world price of corn equals the world price of wheat, then to maximize consumption possibilities, this economy will produce _____ and trade.
    A. only wheat.
    B. only corn.
    C. equal quantities of corn and wheat.
    D. twice as much corn as wheat.
    E. half as much wheat as corn.

12. The demand for soybeans in a country is given by $D = 5 - 0.2P$, where P is the price of a bushel of soybeans. Supply by domestic producers is given by $S = 1 + 0.8P$. Both demand (D) and supply (S) of soybeans are measured in millions of bushels. If the world price of soybeans equals 5 and this economy is open to trade, then this country will
   A. export 1 million bushels of soybeans.
   B. export 2 million bushels of soybeans.
   C. neither import nor export soybeans.
   D. import 1 million bushels of soybeans.
   E. import 2 million bushels of soybeans.

13. The demand for DVD players in a country is given by $D = 300 - 0.2P$, where P is the price of a DVD player. Supply by domestic producers is given by $S = 100 + 0.8P$. The world price of a DVD player equals 100 and this economy is open to trade. If a quota of 50 units is placed on DVD player imports, the quantity of DVD players demanded domestically will change from ____ with trade but no quota, to ____ with trade and a quota.
   A. 260; 270
   B. 260; 280
   C. 280; 270
   D. 280; 260
   E. 270; 260

14. The demand for DVD players in a country is given by $D = 300 - 0.2P$, where P is the price of a DVD player. Supply by domestic producers is given by $S = 100 + 0.8P$. The world price of a DVD player equals 100 and this economy is open to trade. If a tariff of 50 per unit is placed on DVD player imports, the quantity of DVD players produced domestically will change from ____ with trade but no tariff, to ____ with trade and a tariff.
   A. 180; 220
   B. 180; 260
   C. 260; 220
   D. 260; 180
   E. 260; 180

15. An economy has two workers, Paula and Peter. Each day of work Paula can produce 300 bushels of pea or 100 pots, and Peter can produce 200 bushels of peas or 100 pots. Paula and Peter work 200 days per year. The world price is 2.5 bushels of peas for one pot. If this economy is closed to trade, the maximum possible consumption will be ____ pots, compared to ____ pots if this economy is open to trade.
   A. 20,000; 40,000
   B. 40,000; 20,000
   C. 40,000; 44,000
   D. 44,000; 20,000
   E. 44,000; 40,000

16. A more efficient alternative to restricting trade is
    A. to compensate the winners.
    B. to compensate the losers.
    C. autarky.
    D. to repeal the law of comparative advantage.
    E. a system of voluntary export restraints.

17. The difference between the world price and the domestic price of a good goes to _____ when a tariff is imposed on the good and to _____ when a quota limits the importation of the good.
    A. the government; private individuals or firms
    B. the government; the government
    C. the government; the market
    D. private individuals or firms; the government
    E. private individuals or firms; private individuals or firms

18. A quota on a good _____ the domestic price of the good, _____ domestic production of the good, and _____ domestic consumption of the good.
    A. increases; increases; increases
    B. increases; increases; decreases
    C. increases; decreases; decreases
    D. decreases; decreases; decreases
    E. decreases; increases; increases

19. If a tariff is placed on a good, domestic producers of the good are ____, domestic consumers of the good are _____, and the government is a _____.
    A. winners; winners; winner
    B. winners; winners; loser
    C. winners; losers; winner
    D. losers; losers; winner
    E. losers; winners; winner

20. The workings of the free market ensure that goods will be produced where the opportunity cost is the _____ and traded to countries that _____ have a comparative advantage in the good.
    A. highest; do
    B. highest; do not
    C. highest; may or may not
    D. lowest; do
    E. lowest; do not

Short Answer Problems
(Answers and solutions are given at the end of the chapter.)

1. Production Possibilities in a Three-Person Economy
In this problem you will draw a production possibilities curve for a three-person economy, reviewing the implications of the principle of comparative advantage for production.

Assume the country of Islandia has only 3 workers, Maria, Tom and Patty, each of whom works 50 weeks per year. Maria can produce 100 shirts or she can catch 10 pounds of fish per week. Tom can produce 50 shirts or catch 20 pounds of fish per week. Patty can produce 200 shirts or catch 40 pounds of fish per week

A. Maria's opportunity cost of producing 1 pound of fish per week is _____ shirts, Tom's opportunity cost of producing 1 pound of fish per week is _____ shirts, and Patty's opportunity cost of producing 1 pound of fish per week is _____ shirts.

B. Maria's opportunity cost of producing 1 shirt per week is _____ pounds of fish, Tom's opportunity cost of producing 1 shirt per week is _____ pounds of fish, and Patty's opportunity cost of producing 1 shirt per week is _____ pounds of fish.

C. Based on their respective opportunity costs, if Islandia were to allocate resources to the production of shirts, _____ would be the first worker to begin producing shirts, _____ would be the second worker to begin producing shirts, and _____ would be the third worker to begin producing shirts

D. On the graph below construct the annual production possibilities curve for Islandia, identify the location of the "kinks" in the curve (label them A and B), and label each section of the curve to indicate who is producing the shirts.

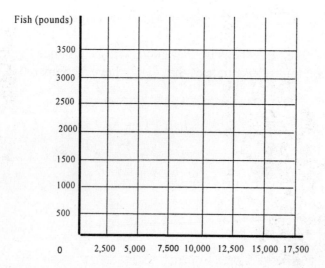

E. To produce 1 to 5,000 shirts, the opportunity cost of producing shirts in Islandia is _____ pounds of fish. To produce 5,001 to 15,000 shirts the opportunity cost of producing shirts in Islandia is _____ pounds of fish. To produce 15,001 to 17,500 shirts the opportunity cost of producing shirts in Islandia is _____ pounds of fish.

F. Thus, as Islandia allocates more resources to the production of shirts, the opportunity cost of producing shirts (increases / decreases / remains constant) _____ . This reflects the core principle of _____ .

G. As a result of the above core principle, the shape of Islandia's production possibilities curve is _____ .

2. Consumption Possibilities with and without International Trade

This problem will help you better understand the gains that a country can achieve by opening its economy to international trade. You will determine the opportunity cost of producing goods, draw a consumption possibilities curve, and calculate the gains from trade.

Assume the country of Nordica has two workers, Ian and Michelle. Ian can produce 1,500 bicycles per year or 1,500 articles of clothing. Michelle can produce 1,500 bicycles or 750 articles of clothing per year.

A. Ian's opportunity cost of producing 1 bicycle is _____ articles of clothing, and Michelle's opportunity cost of producing 1 bicycle is _____ articles of clothing.

B. Michelle's opportunity cost of producing 1 article of clothing is _____ bicycles, and Ian's opportunity cost of producing 1 article of clothing is _____ bicycles.

C. If Nordica has a closed economy and Ian only produces articles of clothing and Michelle only produces bicycles, identify the point of Nordica's production (label it A) on the graph below.

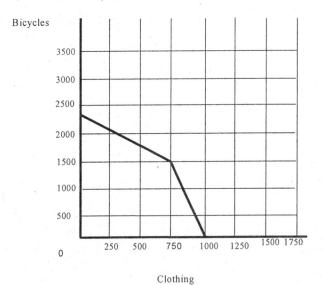

D. Assume the world prices are such that 2 bicycles can be traded for 1 article of clothing. If Nordica opens its economy to world trade, on the above graph draw its consumption possibilities curve such that it just touches (i.e., is tangent to) Nordica's production possibilities curve at point A.

E. If Nordica chose to trade 250 of the 750 articles of clothing it is producing on the world markets, it could obtain _____ bicycles.

F. On the graph above, locate the point on Nordica's consumption possibilities curve (label it B) that would represent the number of bicycles and articles of clothing it could consume after it traded 250 articles of its clothing. After the trade, the consumption possibilities curve indicates that Nordica can consume _____ articles of clothing and_____ bicycles.

G. Had Nordica remained a closed economy, it could produce 500 articles of clothing and _____ bicycles.

H. By comparison to a closed economy, opening its economy to world trade resulted in Nordica gaining _____ bicycles.

3. Closed versus Open Economy

In this problem you will analyze the economic impact of a closed and an open economy using the supply and demand model. The following graph shows the domestic supply and demand for wool in Upperlandia.

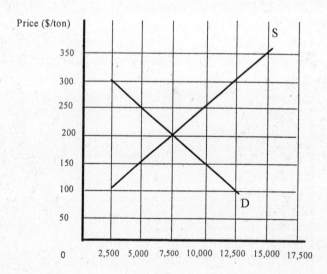

A. If Upperlandia has a closed economy, the equilibrium price of wool would equal $_____ per ton and Upperlandia would produce _____ tons of wool.

B. Assume the world price of wool is $150 per ton. On the graph above, draw a curve representing the world price of wool (label it P_w).

C. Given the domestic supply of and demand for wool and the world price of wool, if Upperlandia opened its economy to trade it would produce _____ tons of wool, consume _____ tons of wool, import _____ tons of wool, and the domestic price of wool would fall to $ _____ per ton.

D. As a result of opening the Upperlandian economy to trade, the trade winners would be (domestic wool producers / foreign wool producers / domestic consumers / foreign consumers) _____ and (domestic wool producers / foreign wool producers / domestic consumers / foreign consumers) _____ , while the trade losers would be (domestic wool producers / foreign wool producers / domestic consumers / foreign consumers) _____ and (domestic wool producers / foreign wool producers / domestic consumers / foreign consumers) _____ .

E. Assume the domestic wool producers convinced the Upperlandia government to impose a quota of 1,000 tons of imported wool. On the graph above, draw the curve that would reflect the effect of the quota on the Upperlandia wool market (label it $P_w + Q$).

F. As a result of the quota, the price of wool in Upperlandia would rise to $_____, domestic consumption would equal _____ tons of wool, and domestic production would rise to _____ tons of wool. Wool imports would decline to _____ tons of wool.

4. Trade Protectionism

In this problem you will analyze the economic impact of tariffs and quotas using the supply and demand model. Assume the demand for cellular phones by the consumers of Surica is given by Demand = 320 – 0.6(price of cellular phones) and the supply by domestic Surica producers is given by Supply = 200 + 0.6(price of cellular phones).

A. Assuming that Surica is a closed economy, the equilibrium price for cellular phones in the domestic Surica market would be $_____, and the equilibrium quantity would equal _____ .

B. If the Surica economy is opened to trade and the world price of cellular phones is $75, the consumption of cellular phones in Surica would equal _____, domestic production of cellular phones would equal _____, and Surica would import _____ cellular phones.

C. Assume that, at the request of Surica cellular phone producers, the Surica government imposes a tariff of $20 per cellular phone. After the imposition of the tariff, Surica consumption of cellular phones would equal _____, domestic production would equal _____ cellular phones, and Surica would import _____ cellular phones.

D. The tariff raised the price of cellular phones by $_____ and reduced imports by _____.

E. The Surica government would receive $_____ from the tariff.

IV. Economic Naturalist Application

In March, 2002 President Bush authorized tariffs on a large variety of imported steel products after the U.S. International Trade Commission concluded that foreign countries were dumping steel in the U.S. Identify the (political) cost to President Bush had he decided to not to interfere with free trade. Would the same pressure exist if he was in his second term rather than his first? Now identify the cost to President Bush for having imposed tariffs. Hint: consider Western European countries with steel industries similar in inefficiency to the U.S. firms. Finally, given that the Republican Party strongly identifies itself with the principles of free trade and the desire to reduce the presence of government in the economy, do you think voters (particularly supporters) will place much negative weight on the President claiming to support free markets and then taking an action as incongruent as imposing tariffs?
Answer:

V. Go to the Web: Graphing Exercises Using Interactive Graphs

Is Increased Economic Globalization Always a Good Thing?

The economic benefits of increasing internationalization are well known: increased consumption possibilities and the promise of higher material standards of living. Indeed, this was the economic argument that helped to promote passage of the North American Free Trade Agreement in the 1990s, as well as other multicountry trade agreements that reduce trade barriers. However, in recent years there have been mounting concerns about global capitalism as protestors, mostly from developed nations, have drawn attention to their cause by disrupting international economic meetings. Based on supply and demand analysis of trade, discuss which groups would be most likely to protest free trade and why.
Answer:

To learn more about the use of economic theory to analyze this issue (and other microeconomic issues), please go to the Electronic Learning Session in the Student Center at the Frank/Bernanke web site: http://www.mhhe.com/economics/frankbernanke2.

VI. Self-Test Solutions

Key Terms

1. f
2. d
3. a
4. e
5. g
6. b
7. c
8. h

Multiple-Choice Questions

1. B
2. E
3. D
4. B
5. D
6. A
7. E
8. C
9. E
10. C
11. A
12. A
13. C
14. A
15. C
16. B
17. A
18. B
19. C
20. E

Short Answer Problems

1.
A. 10 (= 100/10); 25; 5
B. .1 (= 10/100); .4; 2
C. Maria, Patty, Tom

D.

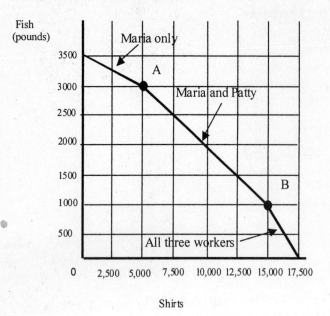

Shirts

E. 1 (Maria has a comparative advantage in producing shirts and she can produce a maximum of 5,000 per year. Because she would be the first worker to produce shirts, Islandia's opportunity cost would equal her opportunity cost); 2; 4
F. increases; increasing opportunity cost
G. bowed outward

2.
A. 1 (= 1500/1500); 1/2
B. 2 (1500/750); 1
C.

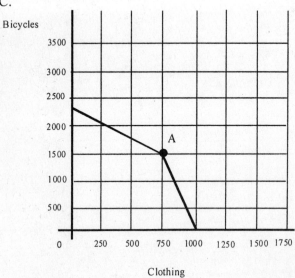

Clothing

D.

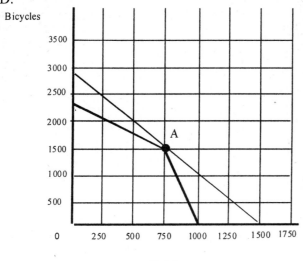

E. 500 (The world price is 2 bicycles = 1 article of clothing. Thus, 250 x 2 = 500)

F.

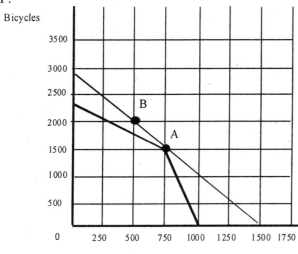

; 500; 2000

G. 1,750

H. 250 (= 2,000 – 1,750)

3.

A. $200; 7,500

B.

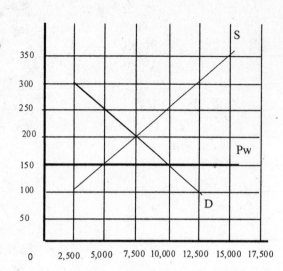

C. 5,000 (at the world price of $150 per ton of wool, the quantity supplied is 5,000); 10,000 (at the world price of $150, the quantity supplied is 10,000); 5,000 (10,000 – 5,000)

D. domestic consumers; foreign wool producers; domestic wool producers; foreign consumers

E.

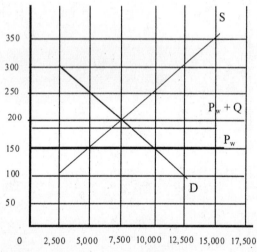

F. $190; 7,000; 8,000; 1,000

4.

A. $100 (320 – 0.6p = 200 + 0.6p, or 120 = 1.2p. Thus, 120/1.2 = p); 260 (320 – 0.6 x 100, or 320 – 100)

B. 275 (D = 320 – 0.6 x 75, or 320 – 45); 245 (S = 200 + 0.6 x 74, or 200 + 45); 30 (275 – 245)

C. 266 (D = 320 – 0.6 x 95, or 320 – 54); 254 (S = 200 + 0.6 x 95, or 200 + 54); 12 (266 – 254)

D. $20; 18 (30 – 12)

E. $240 (20 x 12)

8 chapters
70 questions

Ch. 3 Supply & Demand
  8 questions
  Shifts vs. movements
  Normal + Inferior Goods

Ch. 4 Elasticity
  7 questions

Ch. 6 + 8 Cost & Perf. Comp.

14 questions

Ch. 9 Monopoly

7 questions
Find output & price

34 questions new stuff

Externalities